SCOTTISH
AERODROMES
OF THE FIRST WORLD WAR

SCOTTISH
AERODROMES
OF THE FIRST WORLD WAR

MALCOLM FIFE

TEMPUS

'For the Forgotten Flyers.'

Front cover: A Bristol Scout D of the Royal Flying Corps at Raplow Aerodrome, Stirling, in 1916.

Back Cover: A field at Falleninch Farm on the west side of Stirling Castle was developed into a training aerodrome for 43 and 63 Squadrons before they deployed in France. B.E.2s and Avro 504s are parked beside the farmhouse. (From a painting by Dugald Cameron, licensor www.scran.ac.uk)

First published 2007

Tempus Publishing Limited
The Mill, Brimscombe Port,
Stroud, Gloucestershire, GL5 2QG
www.tempus-publishing.com

© Malcolm Fife, 2007

British Library Cataloguing in Publication Data.
A catalogue record for this book is available from the British Library.

ISBN 978 0 7524 4272 3

Typesetting and origination by Tempus Publishing Limited
Printed in Great Britain

CONTENTS

PREFACE

While Scotland's role in the aerial conflict of the Second World War has been the subject of numerous books and articles in the press, its contribution to the First World War has mostly gone unnoticed.

Some of the earliest trials in Britain with powered aircraft were undertaken near Blair Atholl in the Scottish Highlands, four or five years after the Wright brothers had made their first flight in 1903. By 1912, the Royal Navy had established a seaplane station at Rosyth. The following year saw one of the first military aerodromes in Britain being created near Montrose. It was the base for No.2 Squadron of the Royal Flying Corps (RFC) in the period immediately before the War. This squadron undertook many exercises with other army units. The lessons learned here were put into practise when the squadron was deployed to France at the outbreak of the conflict. It had the distinction of being one of the first RFC squadrons to go into action. At this time there were many military commanders who regarded aircraft as little more than a novelty. The War Office had expressed concern 'that they would frighten the horses'!

For the first couple of years of the First World War, RFC aircraft were basically confined to the role of providing reconnaissance for the soldiers on the ground. Even by 1916 there were only a few hundred military pilots in the British armed services. From this point onwards, however, there was an exponential growth in the numbers of aircraft deployed in the front line. They also began to be used in more diverse roles including bombing enemy troops and their supporting infrastructure. Single-seat fighters were built in increasing quantities in an effort to establish supremacy in the skies. The rapid expansion in the number of military aircraft resulted in an insatiable demand for new aircrew. Training aerodromes were built across the length and breadth of Britain. In Scotland, Montrose Aerodrome which had once housed No.2 Squadron, now trained pilots. There was some doubt about the suitability of the Scottish climate for this role as the fragile training machines could not fly in strong winds. Eventually it was decided that conditions here were no worse than some other parts of Britain. Montrose trained numerous pilots not only from Britain but from many of the Commonwealth countries as well. When the USA entered the war, many Americans received tuition here in the skills of aircraft repair and maintenance before being posted to France.

Another training aerodrome was opened in 1916 at Turnhouse, near Edinburgh. In 1917, it was decided to concentrate flying instruction at a number of larger aerodromes known as Training Depot Stations. This lead to the building of several new aerodromes in Scotland, at Leuchars, Edzell, Crail and Gullane. Compared to the earlier aerodromes which had grown up in a haphazard manner these were large well-planned affairs with their buildings laid out in a well-ordered fashion. Most of them had a relatively short life as they were still under construction when the war ended. Scotland also played a major role in the advanced training of pilots. It was found that pilots who had graduated from the flying schools were ill-equipped

An airship flying over East Fortune Aerodrome, 1918. The picture is from a colour painting by John Lavery, R.A. R.S.A, who was an official war artist. (Courtesy of the Imperial War Museum, IWM Art.1276)

to deal with the hazards of operational flying at the Front. Many new pilots were to last a few weeks before being shot down. In an attempt to remedy this, a small number of aerial fighting schools were formed to give the new aircrew a taste of combat conditions. The course was only around a week in duration, but was found to be of great value in reducing the number of casualties amongst the new airmen. Ayr Aerodrome hosted one of the aerial fighting schools which was later transferred to Turnberry Aerodrome to cater for its expansion. Several of the instructors were well-known 'aces' who had been withdrawn from operational squadrons so they could disseminate their experiences to the trainee pilots. Many American pilots also passed through Turnberry before going on to serve on the front line. In addition to Ayr and Turnberry, there were plans to build a third training facility in Ayrshire. This was to be a sophisticated gunnery range with moving targets located on the banks of Loch Doon. There was also to be a major aerodrome, along with a base for seaplanes. While many of the aerodromes were built on a very limited budget this scheme had huge sums of money spent on it with the total cost reputed to run into millions of pounds. Despite the huge financial outlay, doubts were expressed about the project and its construction was eventually abandoned in early 1918.

The First World War not only saw the aircraft being used as a major instrument of war; the submarine was introduced into a major conflict situation too. The Royal Navy employed a large number of flying machines in the form of both seaplanes and non-rigid airships to counter this underwater menace. Dundee Seaplane Station had the distinction of mounting operational patrols for almost the entire duration of the war. Few other bases in Britain could lay claim to this distinction. As the years drew on, the threat to ships from German submarines rapidly increased. Passage through the English Channel for them was eventually blocked by submarine nets stretching across its waters. Therefore if they intended to attack shipping in the Atlantic they had to navigate round the northern coast of Scotland. The Royal Navy built a number of seaplane stations in the Orkney Islands in an effort to intercept the enemy submarines as they passed through these waters. The First World War also saw the airship being used in a military role for the first time. They had the advantage of being able to remain in the air for many hours at a time and their slow airspeed made them suitable for searching for hostile submarines. Airship Stations were established at Luce Bay, East Fortune, Longside and

A Bristol M.1 of No.1 Fighting School flying over the coast near Turnberry Aerodrome. (From a colour painting by Dugald Cameron)

briefly at Caldale in the Orkney Islands to patrol the sea lanes off Scotland. Unlike the German Zeppelin, the Royal Navy used much smaller non-rigid airships which virtually consisted of a large bag containing hydrogen gas under which the crew cars were suspended. Despite being vulnerable to strong winds, which accounted for three fatal crashes in the seas off Scotland, these craft flew large numbers of successful missions escorting convoys. Huge structures were built to them as they were equally vulnerable to adverse weather conditions on the ground as in the air. This was also true for aircraft which were made out of wood and fabric and could not be left outdoors for long in the Scottish climate before deteriorating. The sheds to house the rigid airships were among the biggest structures to have been ever built in Scotland. The Royal Navy had hoped to obtain a large fleet of rigid airships but by the end of 1918 only a very small number had been delivered. Their German equivalent, the Zeppelin, put in a brief appearance over Scotland in 1916. These craft would dwarf even the largest airliner in service in the twenty-first century and could undertake missions lasting several days, a feat no modern flying machine could manage. The Zeppelin's main claim to fame was the bombing of Edinburgh on one occasion. In response to this threat, a network of Home Defence squadrons was formed to defend the east coast of Southern England to as far north as Edinburgh. Numerous small landing grounds were created in south-east Scotland which the Home Defence aircraft could use in an emergency. While many were situated on the coast, others were located upon upland areas on the edge of the Lammermuirs, such as at Gifford. Many of them were hardly used and fell into disuse at the end of the war. With the re-vamping of Britain's air defence and improved aircraft performance, the Zeppelins found it too hazardous to venture over the country and the raids faded away.

By the end of the First World War, the Royal Navy led the world in shipborne aircraft with the operating of the first flat-top aircraft carrier. Numerous other warships could launch land planes from the tops of their gun turrets. Much of the pioneering work on flying aircraft from warships was carried out at Scapa Flow within the Orkney Islands. The early experiments involved launching seaplanes from ramps and this later progressed to aircraft with wheeled undercarriages. One of the main catalysts for the development of British shipborne aviation was the fear of the German Zeppelin. The Admirals of the Grand Fleet believed that this flying machine gave the enemy a great advantage in being able to monitor their movements in the North Sea. Seaplanes, with their sluggish performance, could not intercept the high flying Zeppelins so various methods of launching landplanes from warships were devised. This in turn led to the evolution of the aircraft carrier. Another significant development in naval aviation was the advent of the torpedo carrying aircraft. The first operational squadron flying Sopwith Cuckoos practised launching their torpedoes in Belhaven Bay near Dunbar.

To support the operations of the RNAS, several aerodromes were established around the Firth of Forth, including East Fortune and Donibristle. Turnhouse was also used by shipborne aircraft. To operate and maintain the aircraft and airships required the skills of many trades, some traditional and others only recently established. Carpenters and sailmakers could easily be trained to repair aircraft which were made out of wood and fabric. Modern professions provided meteorologists, photographers and wireless operators, which were all essential functions in the new field of military aviation. Another new invention, namely motor transport, was employed extensively in support of flying activities. Lorries were used to recover crashed aircraft or transport unserviceable machines between aerodromes. Personnel were transported in the station staff car or in the motorcycles and side cars.

With the rapid expansion of both the RNAS and the RFC in the latter part of the First World War there was a huge demand for new aircraft. Many First World War machines only lasted a few months before they were destroyed in action or had to be withdrawn from service as they became unserviceable. Numerous factories throughout Britain were adapted to manufacturing aircraft. This could be achieved relatively easily due to their unsophisticated structure. In Scotland, the aircraft industry was concentrated in and around Glasgow. Many Clyde shipbuilders converted part of their premises for the production of aircraft. They produced well proven designs although the firm of Beardmore built some prototypes, most of which never progressed to volume production. When the war ended the orders for new aircraft dried up and most of the premises closed or reverted to their previous function. The decline in military flying in Scotland was equally dramatic as its rise, with most of the airship stations and aerodromes closing a few months after the end of the hostilities. Only a small number of military aerodromes survived the cull. Appropriately they specialised in providing support for aircraft based on Royal Navy carriers. When the Second World War broke out, Scotland again became the centre of shipborne aviation. Naval aerodromes were built on the shores of Scapa Flow and flying boats were based in large numbers around the coast of Scotland. Large numbers of aircraft carriers operated from the Firth of Clyde. The airships, however, did not return and had disappeared for good. Other First World War aerodromes such as Montrose and Turnberry were again used to train pilots. Some of those who had flown in the First World War re-enlisted to serve in the RAF.

By the early twenty-first century, few physical remains of the First World War aerodromes survive in Scotland. Unfortunately all the large airship sheds were demolished in the 1920s and 1930s. Although several aerodromes were brought back into use in the Second World War, the original buildings were usually demolished and replaced by modern structures. Other aerodromes such as Moorpark at Renfrew and Donibristle in Fife have succumbed to urban development. Not only have most of the traces of the early air stations entirely disappeared, but so have many of the official records. Little documentation exists for the Aerial Fighting School located at Ayr and Turnberry with much of its history having been lost to time. Fortunately, some pilots who passed through them, wrote about their experiences e and they give a brief but incomplete glimpse into the histories of the aerodromes.

In the following text the word 'aerodrome' has been used in preference to 'airfield'. The latter term was not widely used in Britain until the Second World War when it was adopted from the Americans. Also the term 'aircraft shed' has been used to describe the structure for housing for aircraft. The word 'hangar' was not used in the First World War with the exception of portable canvas structures.

CHAPTER ONE

PRELUDE TO WAR

'What a dream it was, what a nightmare it has become.' Orville Wright penned these words in 1917 as he observed how powered flying machines had become an instrument of war. Referring to his invention of the powered aircraft which first took to the air in 1903, 'We thought that we were introducing into the world an invention which would make further wars practically impossible.' Orville Wright realised from the beginning that aeroplanes would have a military role in the form of aerial reconnaissance. The troop movements of hostile powers could be monitored from the air, hence surprise attacks would no longer be possible and the threat of armed conflict reduced.

The order for the world's first military aircraft was placed by the US Army in 1908 with the Wright brothers. They specified that it should carry two persons, at a speed of at least 40mph and a range of 125 miles. While undergoing trials it crashed, seriously injuring Orville Wright and killing its passenger. A replacement machine was delivered the following year but afterwards interest in military aviation in the USA waned. Other countries stepped in to take up the gauntlet, particularly France and Germany. In Britain, the Army Balloon Factory at Farnborough gave financial backing to S.F. Cody and Lt J.W. Dunne to develop their own designs of powered aircraft.

Some of the first trials of military aircraft in Britain were undertaken at Blair Atholl in the heart of the Scottish Highlands. Lt J.W. Dunne had been interested in making an aircraft possessing automatic stability. The Balloon Factory commissioned him to develop his ideas. They first took the form of gliders and later powered aircraft, all distinguished by having swept wings. On completion, these machines were taken to Scotland where they could be tested in secrecy. A Dunne D.1a biplane glider was tested at Blair Atholl between July and October during 1907. For take-off the machine rested on a trolley. Col. Capper achieved a number of short flights from downhill launches but the glider was eventually damaged. It was repaired and two engines were added to the airframe. A track of wooden planks were laid for it to take off. On its first attempt to become airborne the aircraft veered off course and was damaged. After this set back Lt J.W. Dunne and his party decided to leave Blair Atholl before the arrival of winter.

However, they returned the following year. The Dunne D.3 glider was assembled between 2 and 19 September. Lt L.D. Gibbs then test flew it over the next month. The longest flight achieved was only 157ft. A second machine, the Dunne D.4 biplane also arrived here towards the end of 1908. It was a biplane with swept wings sitting on a four-wheel undercarriage. Flying trials were carried out between 15 November and 4 December but it only managed to become airborne for short distances from a level take-off. The maximum distance it covered was 120ft. The paper the *People's Journal* in August 1913 ran an article on Lt J.W. Dunne's exploits in this part of the country:

It was long ago as in 1906 that Lt Dunne conducted his experiments at Glen Tilt. Few events in the recent history of flight have been so interesting as the success of this automatic stability aeroplane. The machine is probably the oldest in design in the United Kingdom and has survived practically unchanged from an experimental model which was issued as early as 1906, that is to say, two years before any power driven aeroplanes were in use on the Continent. In that year mysterious accounts appeared of secret experiments with an aeroplane on the Duke of Atholl's estate at Glen Tilt. The most elaborated precautions were taken to prevent unauthorised people from seeing what was done. The Royal Engineers who assisted in the experiment were taken to the flying ground by night and many of them had no idea exactly in what part of the country they were. The precautions taken were so great that the aeroplane was painted so that anyone seeing it from a distance would assume that it was the ordinary type of gliding machine instead of being constructed in the V shape which is the basis of Lt Dunne's theory. The peculiar design of the machine consisted in the attempt to acquire automatic stability by making the wings bend backwards from the central point at which the engine and the pilot's seat is placed, so that the wings by lying well behind the centre of the machine, took the place of the tail in the ordinary aeroplane.

Alarmed at the sums of money being spent on such projects, some £2,500, the military withdrew funding to both S.F. Cody and Lt W. Dunne. Both of them went on to develop their own designs with the help of private finance. The War Office lost interest in aircraft development, concentrating on balloons until late 1910. The following year Sir William Nicholson, Chief of the Imperial General Staff wrote that 'aviation is a useless and expensive fad advocated by a few individuals whose ideas are unworthy of attention'.

   With both France and Germany investing large sums in their aircraft industries, concern was expressed by some circles of the British government that the country was being left behind in this field. In February 1911, an army order was issued which created the Air Battalion of the Royal Engineers. The following year this was replaced by the RFC. It consisted of a Naval Wing, a Military Wing and a Central Flying school which was to train pilots for both wings. The aircraft were based solely in the south of England. The initial proposals for the RFC Naval Wing were modest, with just eight landplanes planned, plus the possible purchase of fourteen seaplanes. Contemporary documents often refer to seaplanes as hydroplanes. It was the politician Winston Churchill, then in charge of the Admiralty and a proponent of naval aviation, that first suggested that such machines be called seaplanes. In November 1912 a letter to the Admiral Commanding Coast Guard and Reserves outlined plans for new air stations:

I am to inform you that their Lordships have approved the gradual establishment of a regular chain of stations for naval aircraft along the coasts of the United Kingdom within easy flight of each other. These stations will serve as starting points and bases for naval aircraft working with the squadrons and flotillas at sea. The positions of the aircraft stations will be in the vicinity of the following places:

Hydro-Aeroplane Stations (only those in Scotland listed)
Rosyth
Aberdeen
Cromarty
Scapa Flow
Clyde Space
Airship Stations

The first steps in this plan were taken with the construction of a seaplane station at Port Laing (sometimes referred to as Carlingnose), North Queensferry and a short distance to the east of Rosyth. Three aircraft sheds had been erected by October 1912 with two Short biplanes and

Montrose Broomfield Aerodrome in early 1914. A B.E.2a, No.328, of 2 Squadron, RFC is flying over the recently erected hangars with two Maurice Farman Longhorns, Nos 214 and 215, on the ground being prepared for flight.(Fleet Air Arm Museum – Bruce/Leslie Collection)

one Maurice Farm biplane based here. It was the first military air station in Scotland. This event had not gone unnoticed by the press and the *Dunfermline Journal* published a feature on it. It has been quoted at some length as it gives a revealing insight into the plans for naval aviation in the vicinity of the Firth of Forth:

> The creation of an aviation base at Port Laing marks an important era in the aerial defence of the Forth. In due course, not only will at least four hydroplanes be constantly maintained here but a fleet of aeroplanes as well. The station will be under the joint control of the naval and military authorities, and its cost of construction and maintenance will be borne jointly by the two services in proportions yet to be agreed upon. It is intended that in future rather a large staff shall be maintained here and some use will be made of the centre as a training ground for recruits to the Royal Flying Corps and for training those naval officers who decide to take up this wing of the service in future. So, soon as the Rosyth station is in completed working order the machines maintained there will be constantly employed in testing their paces in the Firth of Forth with various expeditions seawards. The true value of a hydroplane of the Farman pattern – that which has arrived at North Queensferry – is but very imperfectly realised at the moment while its potential worth to the fleet can only be guessed at. The destroyers now told off to protect the Firth of Forth will be able to adopt a much wider radius of action and to remain at sea for longer periods than was previously the case, since the aircraft to be maintained at Rosyth will be available for scouting purposes every day and will be able to make prolonged excursions out to sea.
>
> A definite range of coast will be assigned to the new centre and this will probably be from Scapa Flow in the North to the Tyne in the south. The principal duty of the aeroplanes and hydroplanes maintained at Rosyth, however, will be to patrol the shores of the North Sea and to report any untoward happenings there to the shore authorities and likewise to any warships that might be in the vicinity. It is also proposed that at least one dirigible balloon shall in the near future be stationed at Rosyth. Though rather overshadowed at the moment

by the aeroplane and hydroplane, the dirigible balloon is still regarded as having a very distinct future before it for both military and naval purposes.

The hydroplanes now to be stationed near Rosyth will in due course be called upon to work in close co-operation with the submarines that will shortly be based permanently in the Firth of Forth. It has been proved conclusively during the past few months that much useful work can be carried out by this joint effort, the hydroplane skirmishing high in the air to ascertain as precisely as may be the movements of a hostile fleet and then returning to where its assisting submarines are lurking and conveying the information to them in order that they may strike home.

Despite the optimistic outlook for the seaplane station at Rosyth depicted in the above article the station had closed by early 1914 and its aircraft moved to Dundee. The planned seaplane stations at Aberdeen and on the Clyde never materialised even at the height of the First World War. One of the main causes for this was the restricted funds available to develop a Naval Air Arm.

In May 1913, the cruiser *Hermes* was commissioned for special duties attached to the Air Service as parent ship of the Aeroplane and Airship Section of the Naval Wing of the RFC. It had been adapted to carry three seaplanes. The first flight of a British aircraft from a ship had taken place on 10 January 1912 when a modified Short S38 became airborne from a wooden trackway constructed on the battleship HMS *Africa*. HMS *Hermes* was at the centre of a major naval exercise held on the east coast in the summer of 1913. It was part of Red Force, which was to sail to any location as ordered by its commander and carry out scouting patrols with its aircraft. The opposition was Blue Force, whose task was to locate HMS *Hermes* and its seaplanes as they sailed up the coast. In conjunction with these manoeuvres two temporary seaplane stations were established, one at Leven on the northern shore of the Firth of Forth and the other, Cromarty, as part of Blue Force. Their aircraft were late in being delivered due to a strike by dockers at Hull and Leith. By the end of July 1913, Leven had three seaplanes on strength: Short Seaplane No.42, Maurice Farman Seaplane No.71 and Borel Seaplane No.86. On 26 July 1913, Short Seaplane was airborne for thirty-one minutes patrolling the mouth of the Firth of Forth. It developed engine trouble and the mechanics worked all night stripping and re-assembling it. The following day it was on patrol again flying over May Island. No sign of Red force was detected. The Maurice Farman Longhorn S7 suffered an accident while flying across the Forth on 25 August 1913. Although the exercises with HMS *Hermes* ended by the autumn, the camp at Leven took on a semi-permanent appearance and remained in use until early 1914. Short Seaplane No.42 was still operating from here then. On one occasion it attempted to take off with a wireless set but was unable to become airborne. There was some discussion about whether to make Leven a permanent seaplane base but it was decided against. Therefore, all the assets were concentrated at Dundee Seaplane Station by the beginning of the First World War.

Another short-lived seaplane station was established at Cromarty at the entrance to the Cromarty Firth. On 4 July 1913 a Bessonneau hangar arrived here after being towed on a lighter from Sheerness. It was set up near the Coastguard station on an area of land where local fishermen dried their nets. Thirty officers and men had arrived the previous month to begin work on the new base. They were housed at the YMCA naval buildings in an old factory. The first two aircraft were delivered by sea to Invergordon aboard the tanker SS *Burma* which also brought 2,000 tons of oil for the storage tanks. The machines were then loaded aboard railway wagons and transported to Dingwall. The final leg of their journey to Cromarty was undertaken on a lorry. Many of the naval personnel had no previous experience of working with aircraft and some difficultly was encountered in assembling them. Three French mechanics assisted with preparing the Maurice Farman No.117 for flight. By the end of July, a Sopwith Seaplane No.59 and Borel Seaplane No.85 were also ready for operation. As part of Blue Force a patrol was organised three times a day, at 9 a.m., 11.45 a.m. and 4 p.m.,

HMS *Hermes* on exercise at Scapa Flow, Orkney Islands, in 1913. It has been converted to carry floatplanes, or hydroplanes as they are referred to in the original caption. One is on the bows and the other on the stern of the warship. Two small arrows point to their location. (The Orkney Library and Archive)

In the summer of 1913, a temporary base for seaplanes was established on the seashore at Leven, Fife. Royal Navy personnel and a couple of civilians along with a dog have positioned themselves in front of a Borel monoplane fitted with floats. Single-winged aircraft at this point in time were a rarity with biplanes reigning supreme in the skies. (Fleet Air Arm Museum – Bruce/Leslie Collection)

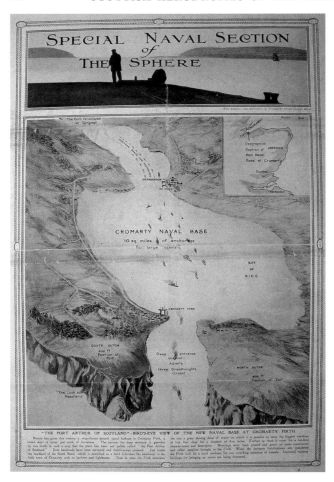

Left: A contemporary bird's-eye view in the April 1913 edition of *The Sphere* illustrating the recently established Royal Navy base in the Cromarty Firth. Although sheltered bodies of water such as this were ideal for operating seaplanes, rather surprisingly, no flying-boat station of any consequence was established on its shore during the First World War. Possibly this was due to the fact it was rather distant from the main centres of activity in the North Sea. (Dunfermline Carnegie Library, Local History Collection)

Below: Sopwith HT seaplane, No. 59, taxies in the sheltered waters of the Cromarty Firth. The Royal Navy established a short lived seaplane station at this important naval anchorage in 1913. This seaplane was the second machine to arrive here. It was caught by a gust of wind on a turn and dived into the water at the beginning of September 1913. The damaged machine was later towed to the shore and repaired. (Fleet Air Arm Museum – Bruce/Leslie Collection)

Wight 1914 Navyplane Pusher Seaplane, No.129, taxiing out for take-off in the Moray Firth from its base at Fort George. The engine is situated at the rear of the seaplane pointing backwards. Such machines were given the name 'Pusher'. When the engine was mounted at the front of the aircraft facing forward they were placed in the 'Tractor category'. The photograph was probably taken in late 1914. (Fleet Air Arm Museum – Bruce/Leslie Collection)

between Cromarty, Nairn, Lossiemouth and Tarbet Ness, the distance being about 60 miles. The pilot had orders to note the movements of any ships and submarines coming within this area and as far beyond as he could see. The patrols commenced on Thursday 24 July at 9 a.m. Nothing was seen on patrol on this day or the next. On 26 July the patrol sighted submarine D.3 off Lossiemouth. The pilot reported its presence to other warships in the area using an Aldis lamp. It was subsequently put 'out of action' by torpedo boats. Like Leven, the seaplane station at Cromarty remained in business once the summer exercises had ceased. The exercises and experiments with radio and bomb sights continued until October 1913. During this month one of the biggest naval manoeuvres ever held in peacetime took place in the vicinity of the Cromarty Firth. A huge armada of over 370 vessels participated. Winston Churchill, First Sea Lord of the Admiralty, journeyed north to witness the event. He was very interested in the role aircraft could play in future naval operations and while there insisted in being taken up on two occasions for a flight in a seaplane. Admiral Jellicoe was also thrilled with his trip in the Borel aircraft. While many of his colleagues wished to move the main base of the Grand Fleet north to Scapa Flow in the Orkney Islands, Winston Churchill favoured the Cromarty Firth as it was closer to the German Naval Bases. The Royal Navy would be able to react more quickly to contain any attempted break out from them.

It was decided to establish a permanent seaplane station in the vicinity of Invergordon naval base. Cromarty was deemed too exposed for this role and a number of other sites were assessed including Balintrail, Ferrytown and Nigg. They were all rejected and Fort George at the entrance to the inner Moray Firth was eventually selected. It had more sheltered waters as well as being home to a large military garrison. In the final months of 1913, the aircraft and stores were moved from Cromarty to their new home. The Bessonneau hangar was dismantled and transferred by tug to Fort George. Fields at Ardesier and at the Carse of Delnies were also inspected with the intention of establishing an aerodrome in the vicinity of Fort George but nothing came of this plan. The seaplane station was established in the shadow of the huge stone walls of the 18th century Hanovarian fortifications. It, however, had a brief existence like the other bases. Borel Seaplane No.85 was based here when war broke out. Later in the year, Wight 1914 Navyplane Pusher Seaplane was delivered on 12 October. Just over a week later it was damaged when it landed in a heavy swell. The machine was repaired, but in April 1915 was completely wrecked and lost in rough sea during a strong gale. It appears that the seaplane base was abandoned shortly after this date and operations transferred elsewhere. The newly formed Army Wing of the Royal Flying Corps also decided to break out of its confines in southern England and set up an aerodrome in Scotland. A memo written in February 1913 discloses the following information on the deployment:

> An important phase in the development of the aerial land forces was reached yesterday with the departure of a detachment of army aeroplanes from Farnborough, en route for Montrose, the new station of the Royal Flying Corps in Forfarshire. According to the system evolved for the establishment of bases at various centres in the United Kingdom, pilots of both the naval and military services are now being trained at the new Central Flying School at Upavon. As regards the military pilots, when their flying course is completed the graduates pass on to one of the squadrons of the Military Wing, the Headquarters of which is at Farnborough, and their technical education is completed during service with these units, where they become skilled in flying machines and in the application of their craft to military purposes. In the normal course each new unit which is termed a squadron will first be formed and receive its initial training at Farnborough, after which it will in due course be transferred to one of the new stations selected. The present move to Scotland is being carried out under this system, Montrose being the first station to be formed away from Head Quarters, with the exception of Larkhill where a detachment of the Royal Flying Corps has been stationed over since the Corps was constituted in May last. The Squadron selected to carry out this first move is one of the first two of the Aeroplane Squadrons originally formed. It is designated the No.2 Squadron, Royal Flying Corps, No.1 Squadron being an Airship Squadron and No.3 being the one at Larkhill.
>
> Notwithstanding the changeable weather, it is hoped by arranging for various halting places en route to ensure the successful completion of the journey and to gain the valuable cross country experience which will be afforded in accomplishing the transfer of the machines to their new station by the mode for travel for which these are designed. It is a journey to be attempted by first class pilots only since the variations of weather conditions to be expected in so long a journey at this time of year make it difficult to accomplish except in numerous stages.

Montrose was intended to be the first of twelve planned aerodromes to be spread across Great Britain. Winston Churchill had influenced this choice of site for the aerodrome in Scotland. From Montrose, aircraft could defend both Rosyth and Cromarty naval air stations. This would not be the case if Scapa Flow became the main naval base, a move which Winston Churchill opposed.

The initial five aircraft to set off for Montrose were three Maurice Farmans, Nos 207, 215 and 266 along with two B.E.2s, Nos 216 and 217. The first aircraft arrived at its destination on 26 February 1913 but missed the landing ground and touched down at Sunnyside Royal Hospital. The first aerodrome at Montrose was located at Upper Dysart Farm some three miles to the south of the centre of town. Earlier the same month an advanced party had arrived and erected portable canvas tents to house the aircraft. Thus, the first military aerodrome in Scotland had come into being. Its personnel numbered around 130, many of whom were housed in an Army barracks in the town. 'Some of the rooms are somewhat small and gloomy,' was part of an appraisal from Maj. James Burke, the commander of the men, and who was far from satisfied with the choice of location. It was unsuitable for practising take-offs and landings, so a temporary encampment was set up on the beach at St Andrews in Fife. Tents were

Dysart Aerodrome, Montrose, 1913. An early version of the B.E.2, No.218, It is sited in front of the canvas hangars. (From a colour painting by Dugald Cameron)

erected on the Bruce Embankment to house the biplanes and the local residents turned out in large numbers to watch the flying. Another attraction of this site was that there were several garages in the immediate vicinity that could supply petrol for the aircraft. From the outset, No.2 Squadron had negotiated with a number of farmers and landowners in the vicinity of Montrose to use part of their properties as emergency landing grounds. The locations included Muirhouses at Kirriemuir, 'could approach very low from all sides as country is open and has very few trees' and Edzell, 'used for grazing, warning therefore asked for'.

Another disadvantage of the location was that their were very few troops based in this part of Scotland with which No.2 Squadron could exercise with. The Commanding Officer of the RFC in his report of 6 August 1913 to the War Office recommended that Montrose be retained as an aerodrome. Points in its favour included the fact that there were not many spectators in this part of the country as well as the climate:

> With good weather the mental attitude towards flying can be got forwards a step, by inducing the idea and spirit that it can be done as a part of regular training and finally that the effort required to fly a modern machine in a 20 mile wind is small. Without a doubt the climate of Montrose is extraordinarily good. A glance at the weekly reports and the hours of flying will show that while flying has been done daily and for long distances across country in this neighbourhood, little flying other than instructional has been done before breakfast and practically none after luncheon. The housing of machines is very much affected by the climate and it is only in a dry place, Montrose, that it would have been possible to keep machines in portable sheds for the length of time we have without their having very seriously deteriorated.
>
> Sea fog we have experienced but as it comes with an east wind and this is not the prevailing wind, it is of little importance, but what is of importance is the absence here of that fog, mist or drizzling rain, which so often ruins an ideal flying day elsewhere. The bracing

vigorous nature of the air increases the desire for outdoor exercise and consequently tends for fitness and absence of nerves and irritability. Certainly, it is safe to say that as far as climate is concerned, Montrose is a particularly good aviation station and the question of climate deserves serious consideration.

When No.2 Squadron was stationed at Montrose it flew in all weathers, frequently when the wind was faster than the machines. More than once 'tortoise races' on Maurice Farmans were organised, where the winner was the machine that was blown back fastest over a given course!

No.2 Squadron's aircraft participated in numerous military exercises during 1913. During April of that year a 'war' took place in Scotland with hostile forces, 'the Reds', landing troops on the coast and occupying Montrose, Forfar, Brechin and Arbroath. The defending forces, 'the Blues', were mobilised at Perth to repel the invaders. The paper, *The People's Journal*, ran a feature on these manoeuvres:

> The Red or hostile force which was represented by a company of the 5th Black Watch with portions of other branches of the service took up their position in the vicinity of Abertyne, Perthshire where they came into touch with the scouts of the Red. It would appear that the days for hidden feints and strategical movements on the part of opposing commanders are relegated to the past. While the forces were manoeuvring for positions in the neighbourhood of Rossie Priory, overheard far up in the air sailed an aeroplane from the Blues. Round and round it circled while the powerful binoculars of one of its occupants searched out the disposition of the defending force. When the exact position of the Reds was satisfactorily located the aeroplane rose to a tremendous height and rapidly fled back to the Blue invaders with its secrets. On the way, as disclosed in the report it dropped a few bombs on five submarines lying in Dundee Harbour.
>
> Owing to the part the aeroplanes were taking in the manoeuvres great interest was manifested throughout the districts. The local trains were crowded during the afternoon. Thousands of persons congregated at Elliot, the Headquarters of the Blues, where they waited the appearance of two aeroplanes from Dysart, near Montrose. These were discerned in the course of the evening. One of them alighted, much to the pleasure of the spectators and afterwards proceeded southward.
>
> In the Abertyne district where the Reds were advancing to the attack, there were also large crowds of sightseers, all deeply interested in the new style of warfare. Every point of vantage in Dundee was black with the crowds gazing skyward and in the course of the evening there was great excitement as the aeroplanes circled overhead. At eight o'clock the bugles sang truce, the victory being awarded to the defenders.

The following month the press reported that extensive aerial manoeuvres would shortly take place in Perthshire. In conjunction with this it was reported that some of the eleven sheds at Montrose aerodrome were to be dismantled and re-erected in the vicinity of Perth. 'Reconnaissance flights in Perthshire have been a long time in view. Two months ago requests were made by the commander at Montrose for temporary use of fields as landing places in different parts of the county'. The paper also reported, 'As the purpose of the scheme is to see how "the land lies" the airmen and their aeroplanes will be stationed at Perth for a considerable period. There will likely be two, if not three aeroplanes utilised for the manoeuvres'.

Later that year No.2 Squadron took part in a number of more ambitious exercises. On 7 August aircraft set off for exercises in Ireland via Stranraer. This was the first time a formation of military aircraft had flown across the Irish Sea. Only six machines completed the journey to the final destination at Rathbane Camp, near Limerick. The opposing armies were located in a small area and it was difficult to employ the aircraft to their full advantage in the reconnaissance role. The small stone-walled fields that characterized the area created problems for the aircraft taking off

The NAVAL BASE at ROSYTH : *The Flying Station on the Forth*

"THE SPHERE" 14ᵗʰ APRIL 1913

Port Laing (Carlingnose) Seaplane Station in early 1913. The seaplane sheds were built by Cowleson & Co. of Glasgow in the Autumn of the previous year. The Structures sit at the top of the beach, a short distance from the Forth Rail Bridge. (Dunfermline Carnegie Library, Local History Collection)

and landing. At least one machine, No.273, became so sodden with moisture that it had to make the final part of its return journey by ship and rail.

Maj. J. Burke had also been busy that summer looking for alternative sites for an aerodrome. At the end of July he wrote to the Officer Commanding the Military Wing of the RFC that he had discovered a splendid location at Broomfield on the northern edge of Montrose. Most of the area was grass and was owned by the town council:

> The surroundings are very good and if wished a pilot could get height without leaving the aerodrome and short straights could be carried out. If the new aerodrome could be got, I think it would be quite worthwhile abandoning without getting anything in return as the saving in tyres, petrol and oil by being close to the barracks would probably equal the rent of the existing aerodrome.

A further point in favour of Broomfield was that a railway line ran close to the edge of the site. In those days this factor was a major consideration when evaluating a new site for an aerodrome.

In Glasgow, three wooden buildings were being prepared in kit form to be assembled at Dysart. These were versions of what were known as Indian Army Sheds and were to replace the canvas hangars. Maj. J.Burke had his request to move to Broomfield with No.2 Squadron approved. The new aircraft sheds were re-directed to the new location and work on erecting them had commenced by the winter of 1913. With the onset of winter Maj. Burke was keen to transfer his aircraft to Broomfield which was more sheltered than their current base at Dysart. On 1 January 1914, the aircraft of No.2 Squadron made the short flight to their new home but many of the buildings were not yet ready for occupation. This lead to a dispute between the Royal Engineers who were work still working on the structures and the RFC. The Commanding Officer of the RFC wrote in response to the complaint:

> I much regret if the occupation of the sheds at Broomfield Aerodrome took place irregularly. I should explain, however, that the matter was very urgent, as the tent sheds in which the

MONTROSE AERODROME A TRIAL SPIN

The newly completed Montrose Broomfield Aerodrome, *c.*1914, with its pattern side-opening aeroplane sheds. These buildings still stand in 2006 and are among the oldest surviving aerodrome buildings in Britain. (Angus Council Cultural Services)

aeroplanes were housed were liable to blow down at any moment and had for several weeks only been kept by strenuous exertions. In view of the delicate nature as well as the great cost of aeroplanes, the early transfer for the machines to permanent sheds was most important.

No.2 Squadron only benefited from their newly created facilities for a relatively short time. On 11 May ten B.E.2s commenced their journey south to Netheravon, Wiltshire for exercises with the other operational units of the RFC. Several were involved in accidents en route, one of which claimed the lives of two of its crew. The remaining aircraft and pilots did not return to Broomfield Aerodrome at Montrose until 18 July. War was declared the following month and the Squadron flew south again, their destination this time being France. The ground crews and equipment were transported by a convoy of lorries to Glasgow where they embarked for the continent. Between 13 and 15 August, No.2 Squadron with its B.E.2s, No.3 Squadron from Netheravon composed of Bleriots and Henry Farmans, No.4 Squadron from Netheravon with B.E.2s and No.5 Squadron, from South Farnborough, with Henry Farmans, Avros, and B.E.8s all descended on northern France. Meanwhile, back at Montrose the airfield was virtually abandoned and was little used for flying until August the following year.

CHAPTER TWO

SEAPLANE STATIONS

As mentioned previously, several seaplane stations were established around the coast of Scotland prior to the outbreak of hostilities in 1914. They included Cromarty and Rosyth (Port Laing) which seemed obvious choices as they were major anchorages for Royal Navy warships. Hence it may appear somewhat surprising that Dundee became the main operational seaplane station on the Scottish mainland for the duration of the First World War. In the early twentieth century, the Firth of Tay was home to the seventh submarine flotilla which had twelve vessels. In the years leading up to the First World War there were plans to make it into one of the most important naval bases of the East Coast with a force of twenty destroyers to be based there.

At the end of January 1914, plans were well advanced to move Maurice Farman Longhorn Seaplane No.71 and Borel Monoplane No.86 from their base at Port Laing (North Queensferry) to Dundee. Not only were its aircraft on the move, at least one of the sheds of the seaplane station at Port Laing was dismantled and erected at Dundee. One reason for the transfer of the entire station was attributed to the expiry of the lease on 28 February 1914. Seaplanes had also operated from Port Seton on the opposite side of the Firth of Forth around this time. There were, however, no sheds or any other facilities for them here. An order to the CO of Port Laing informed him that, 'You are therefore to take immediate steps to move all machines, stores, etc. to Dundee. Machines as far as possible should be dismantled and packed in travelling cases.' The site chosen at Dundee lay on the north bank of the Firth of Tay and at the eastern extremity of the docks. The growth of the city had yet to engulf the area immediately behind the seaplane station which in the early twentieth century were still open fields.

A memo written on 26 March 1914 entitled *Notes and Suggestions For the Air Stations at Dundee and Leven* gives a good insight into the development of the new seaplane station:

1. In the event of the three 100hp. Short seaplanes being retained for use at the Dundee Station, they would be housed in the three corrugated sheds which are erected there.
2. The remaining machines would be housed in the Bessonneau tents until the proposed large shed is built.
3. It would be inadvisable to attempt to get these machines to the Dundee base until the temporary pier is built. This I am informed can be built by the 15th April, if the order to proceed with it is given.
4. Until this pier is built, I suggest that the ground at Leven be retained and the machines be kept there until they can be flown round, as repeated reassembling of machines is not a good thing for their efficiency.
5. The ground at Dundee is at present without any fencing round it. I have applied to the S.C.E. Rosyth some weeks ago for this to be done and also that the latrines and petrol stores should be proceeded with at once but up to the present nothing has resulted from

my application. There are no latrines of any sort near the sheds and a temporary fence is urgently needed and should be proceeded with at once.

6. The ground is not very suitable for a land machine and when more buildings than at present are erected it will be quite impossible to land there. I submit that one of the Bessonneau tents be erected at St Andrews where a plot of ground can be obtained temporarily at very low prices. This tent could be used for housing seaplanes as well as land machines. The beach at St Andrews is an ideal one for either land or sea work in a westerly wind which is the prevailing wind in this part.

7. The three sheds at Dundee should be levelled and floored with cement slabs. The floor of these sheds is at present 18in below the level of the ground outside and no attempt has been made to level it.

8. These improvements i.e. levelling fencing, and construction of latrines and petrol stores, can be best carried out while the personnel and machines are at Leven and I submit that the necessary orders to commence them be given at once.

The seaplane station at Leven on Largo Bay had initially been set up for naval exercises in the summer of the previous year but seems that it had become a semi-permanent fixture by 1914. The extensive area of flat sands at St Andrews attracted the military planners as well. 'This place is extremely good for land machines for which Dundee is totally unsuited as the beach runs north and south and the sea is quite calm during the prevailing westerly winds'. The commanding officer at Dundee wished to erect a spare Bessonneau tent on the seashore at St Andrews and base two of his seaplanes there. It appears nothing came of this suggestion and no permanent base was established at this location. A landing ground, however, was created at Barry in the early years of the war, some eight miles to the east of Dundee Seaplane Station for use by RNAS landplanes.

By May 1914, there were six aircraft at Dundee but Maj. R. Gordon, its commander, was not happy with the situation. Maj. R. Gordon complained to his seniors that he did not have enough personnel to keep his machines in proper order. There were three sheds at the station but no permission and no authorisation had yet been given to commence work on the permanent buildings planned for the site. Security was poor as there was no perimeter fence to stop intruders from entering the site. The Naval staff at Dundee were at this time not concerned with an attack by Germans but by British citizens, namely the suffragettes. A policeman had apprehended four women entering the Bessonneau tent late one night. On 5 June Royal Marines were sent to guard the seaplane station.

As war grew closer, the facilities at Dundee were still in a dire state. In July, Maj. R. Gordon made further complaints about the station under his command. They included the fact that the temporary slipway for launching the seaplanes was a sloping plankway, some 20ft wide. It was not covered by the water for two hours each side of low water. Also, Seaplanes could not be launched from it in strong winds. During the same month the Military and the Naval Wings of the RFC were divided and the Admiralty established the Royal Naval Air Service (RNAS). When war was declared in August, they had their aircraft dispersed at eleven locations on mainland Britain. In Scotland most of their assets were centred on the seaplane station at Dundee. They amounted to a meagre three aircraft consisting of a Short Seaplane S41 No.42, Maurice Farman Seaplane No.71 and Borel Seaplane No.86. No war duties had been assigned and the base was then operating on a care and maintenance basis. This all changed when HMS *Finder* was sunk off May Island and Dundee was placed on an operational footing for the first time. Four Short seaplanes were sent from Clacton and a further three seaplanes, along with their pilots, arrived from Killingholme. By the autumn operation patrols were being flown from Dundee but not without incident. On 29 September, a Short Admiralty 74 seaplane failed to return from a North Sea patrol. Its crew of two, Flt Lt Vernon and Flt Lt Ash, both perished.

A detachment of seaplanes were also based at Granton Harbour, Edinburgh. During December the number of aircraft stationed here varied between one and three Short

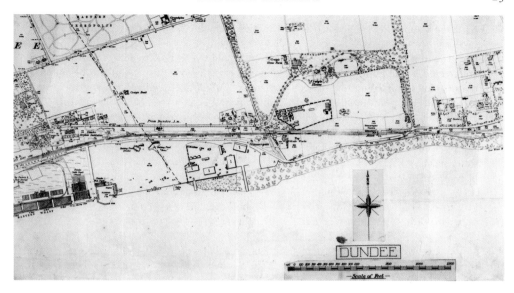

Dundee Seaplane Station, 1918, which was located on the Firth of Tay on the eastern edge of the docks. The site can be distinguished by the two slipways extending out into the water. There were four large seaplane sheds including two measuring 200ft by 100ft extending across a site of twelve acres. The main Dundee to Aberdeen railway line skirts the edge of the station. On its northern side is a second site of a further twelve acres which contained huts providing accommodation for the station's personnel. Some, however, were billeted in private buildings. In the latter part of the twentieth century, Dundee's Docks have been extended eastwards incorporating the former seaplane site, which was also sometimes known as Stannergate. (The National Archives)

Granton Harbour, near Edinburgh, had a permanent detachment of seaplanes in late 1914. Even when this ceased, it was used from time to time by them. This Wight 840 Seaplane, No.1400, is on a delivery flight from Beardmore's to Dundee Seaplane station in September 1915. During the following year, this seaplane was wrecked off Dundee but both crew members were rescued. (Fleet Air Arm Museum – Bruce/Leslie Collection)

Admiralty 74 Type Seaplanes and Short Tractor Biplanes. A report dated 6 December stated that a Short Tractor Seaplane flew a patrol out to the Bass Rock, May Island and Largo Bay. There was 'nothing to report'. However, it suffered engine problems when it landed back at Granton. Three of the other seaplanes were either being repaired or dismantled at Dundee. Usually, only one or two machines were available for patrols each day. The missions were usually 1–1½ hours' duration. Strong winds and poor weather prevented flying on several days in December. At the end of December 1914, Short Tractor seaplane was order to patrol an area off Dunbar to look for a German cruiser that had earlier been reported off Flamborough Head the previous night. Nothing was seen. On returning back to Dundee the seaplane's float was damaged by ice in the Firth of Tay. Back on land the station had a number of other problems to contend with. Many of the personnel had been housed in a gymnasium and the local orphanage but were required to vacate this in early December. New accommodation was about to be completed on the base, but a number of ratings had to sleep in the guard house. Also the commanding officer requested that a cook and ships steward be posted to the seaplane station. The personnel had to make their own arrangements for meals!

1915 saw the arrival of a number of new seaplane types. In April an Avro Tractor seaplane was delivered but failed its acceptance test. It could barely take off from the Firth of Tay. Flt Lt C. Draper did, however, manage to fly it under the Tay Rail Bridge. He often used to amuse himself by flying seaplanes backwards and forwards under the numerous spans of this structure Capt. Graham Donald was of the opinion that he was:

Undoubtedly the world's finest pilot. He used to fly quite regularly through the Tay Bridge, which is not like the Forth Bridge. The Tay Bridge was built on stone pillars quite reasonably far apart. He used to fly through quite gaily. One day he challenged me to follow him through. So I followed just a comfortable distance behind. As he went through, it struck me that it wasn't enough for me anyway. So I may as well admit it here and now, I funked it at the last moment. I was on the old short biplane and I just pulled her up and went over the bridge, not right through.

Flt Lt C. Draper also landed an aircraft on the golf course at St Andrews, perhaps the only pilot to ever do so, much to the dismay of the Royal & Ancient Golf Club.

In May, Sopwith Admiralty 860 seaplanes, No.929 and No.930 were assembled at Dundee Seaplane Station. They were little better than the Avro but did manage to carry out a number of anti-submarine patrols. On 7 August, one of them made a forced landing in the sea. While being towed back to Dundee the plane overturned and was nearly totally submerged. It was a complete write-off. When A.H. Sandwell was posted from the RNAS flying school at Eastbourne to Dundee in July 1915, there were only five aircraft: two Sopwiths with the then new and more or less untried 225hp. Sunbeam engines, two Avros with 150hp. engines of the same make and an early Short tractor, No.78 with a 160 (twin 80) Gnome rotary engine. He only received an hour's instruction in an Avro seaplane which was unable to become airborne from the Firth of Tay if there were two persons on board. After that A.H. Sandwell taught himself how to fly seaplanes. He recalled that operational patrols were often only flown with one person on board as the machines could not become airborne with the addition weight of the observer. With a shortage of this category of crewman, an engineer or even a carpenter were sometimes substituted. The pilot had little time to look for submarines or other activity as he spent most of his time trying to keep his machine airborne. It was later learned that German Naval intelligence rated the danger from British seaplanes off this part of the Scottish coast as very low!

According to A.H. Sandwell:

The nightmare of all seaplane pilots was the forced landing from engine trouble many miles from shore. We had a special signal for this eventuallity. You had to land into whatever kind of sea there happened to be at the moment. Even the North Sea can produce a pretty good lop at times especially off Peterhead, which was in the Dundee patrol area. First of all, one had to make a dead stick landing on a surface with corrugations and moveable ones at that often measuring 15ft from trough to crest, and sometimes more. If that was safely accomplished: and it was in a surprisingly large number of cases–there was still plenty to do. You could not climb out and walk to the nearest telephone to ask for a service car with mechanics. The wireless didn't function from the surface and pigeons were not introduced until the summer of 1916, so there was no hope of communicating with the base. Unless your observer had managed to send out the code-call just mentioned before you landed, you figured that they might send out to look for you, if it hadn't become dark in the meantime, when you became overdue. Even if he had sent it, unless it had been acknowledged you knew not whether it had been received or not. So the first job was to find out what the matter with the engine and if it could be remedied. If it could and was and you managed to get into the air again, you were lucky indeed.

The situation was not helped by the fact that the Achilles heel of the British aircraft industry was the production of aircraft engines. Prior to the war, magnetos for the engines were supplied by Germany. Britain had to establish its own industry and unfortunately, those that were used to power some types of seaplane engines were liable to failure. By the end of the war around forty-four different types of aero engine were in use by British aircraft and many of them were unreliable. The Dragonfly engine had a life of about 2½ hours before it malfunctioned.

It should also be remembered that aircrew had no lifejackets or parachutes at this time. On a more positive note, they could always cling to the wreckage of their seaplane which was made of wood and had several floats providing some buoyancy. The nightmare became a reality for A.H. Sandwell when he had to make a forced landing in August 1915 close to the Bell Rock Lighthouse. A fishing boat initially took his partially submerged seaplane in tow. A few hours later, a destroyer arrived on the scene and took over the tow, returning the pilot and his machine to Dundee late at night. During that month, the station had three seaplanes flying on a regular basis. They were a Short Tractor Seaplane No.78 which flew a total of 490 miles, Avro 510 Tractor Seaplane No.134 clocked up only 40 miles and Sopwith Admiralty 860 No.929, with a total of 250 miles. At that time, Dundee seaplane base also had four aircraft on strength which were based at Montrose Aerodrome.

The construction of the seaplane base seems to have been completed by this time. Grahame Donald, a pilot who was posted here from Calshot, gave a favourable initial impression that the station was very well laid out:

A real permanent station, fine concrete slipways, permanent corrugated iron sheds for the seaplanes, quite decent little mess and good quarters for the men. As things went it was a very well laid out station.

The thing was very well laid out in that the sheds and the slipway were placed properly, close to one another without having to push the seaplanes round corners and this way and the other way to get them onto the slipway. At Dundee the big doors would open very quickly. And each seaplane sat on its trolley with its wheels straight out the shed onto the head of the slipway and the slope of the slipway had now been worked out with the other earlier seaplane stations. It was just about right and she didn't run away and take charge. Got your engine running, warmed up, crew trundled you, still on the trolley, right down the slipway, seaplane floats off the trolley, you open up your engine and away you go–on the surface of the water. So the launch was quite quick. Not unlike getting a lifeboat away. But as I say, after you'd got taxi-ing on the surface of the water it wasn't always such a happy event getting off the water.

In the closing months ten Wight Admiralty 840 Seaplanes were delivered from Beardmore. Some only had brief careers here. The bombs of No.1409 exploded while taxying, totally wrecking the machine on 21 December 1915. Its crew of two, Lt D. Iron and 2nd-Lt G. Gilmore were posted as missing.

The final months saw the delivery of another new type arrive at Dundee in the form of a Sopwith Baby. These went on to serve aboard seaplane carriers including HMS *Engadine* with the station serving as the shore base for them. In February 1916 there were five Wight 840 Seaplanes on operational strength. Contemporary records record only one patrol flown during the month. Of the sixteen flying hours flown in total by the five machines most were practise flights which included bomb dropping. Bad weather prevented flying for about a week in the middle of the month. The following month the number of Wight 840 Seaplanes had increased to seven but again most of the flying amounted to little more than practise flights. At the end of the month several patrols were flown over the Firth of Forth.

In April 1916 there were only three trained pilots at Dundee including the Commanding Officer from HMS *Engadine*. A telegram was sent requesting that additional pilots should be posted here. In the summer new machines arrived by rail including three Short 827 Type Seaplanes and the first two of many Short 184 Seaplanes. During May, a number of submarine patrols were flown. One Seaplane left for Inchkeith for submarine spotting exercise. This island in the Firth of Forth appears to have received visits from seaplanes from time-to-time throughout the war years. At the end of the 1916 the following seaplanes were in active use:

Short Admiralty 827 Seaplane	8256
Short Admiralty 827 Seaplane	8257
Short Admiralty 827 Seaplane	8645
Short Admiralty 827 Seaplane	8647
Short Admiralty 184 Seaplane	9053
Short Admiralty 184 Seaplane	9071
Short Admiralty 184 Seaplane	9072
Short Admiralty 184 Seaplane	9087

Between them they managed to notch up 2,400 miles flying during December within thirty-four hours' flying. Most were again practise flights with one patrol flown between South Shields and Dundee.

During 1917 further Sopwith Babys arrived at Dundee, some by rail. This year also saw the deployment of some new types, including a Fairey Hamble Baby and a Short 320 seaplane. On the debit side, orders were given on 3 February to transfer six Short 184 Seaplanes to Malta. These were to be replaced with other machines when available. Even in 1917 the number of patrols flown per month was very low. For example, in March only three were flown out of a total of thirty one flights. The remainder included twelve practise flights, four bomb dropping flights, three solo practise flights and one hydrophone exercise flight. At that time there was concern at the increasing enemy submarine activity at the mouth of the Firth of Forth. It was intended to deliver two small 'America' flying boats equipped by hydrophones in an effort to counter this problem. On 13 July 1917, a Short 184 Seaplane N1133, actually dropped a 100lb bomb on a U-boat some sixty miles north-east of the Bell Rock lighthouse. Shortly after the seaplane suffered from engine failure and made a forced landing in the sea. The machine sank while under tow but the two crew were saved.

A new Short 184 was delivered on 16 June 1917 making the final part of its journey by rail after having to make a forced landing at Berwick-Upon-Tweed. Several other machines suffered mishaps during the course of the year. N1135 experienced engine failure and had to land in the mouth of the Firth of Forth Its crew were picked up by the armed trawler *Strathearn* but the Short 184 Seaplane was a write off. Another aircraft was totally wrecked when it crashed into the pier at Dundee Fish Dock. Fortunately its crew escaped with minor injuries. A more serious accident occurred on 8 November when Short 184 Seaplane N1661

The surface of the Firth of Tay looks none too calm in this picture but it has not deterred this Short 184 floatplane from taking off. The picture was taken in late October 1917, a time of year when strong winds can be expected. The luck of this machine based at Dundee Stannergate Seaplane Station ran out the following year when it made a forced landing on the sea and sank. (Fleet Air Arm Museum – Bruce/Leslie Collection)

caught fire and crashed in the sea in flames, fifteen miles north east of St Abbs Head. Flt Sub-Lt E. Andrews and AAMI G. Bickle both perished in the accident. On the day before Christmas there was another tragic event. FLS F. Cressman, a Canadian, and AM2 G. Shearer took off in Short 184 Seaplane, N1638 accompanied by a second aircraft. When they left Dundee the weather conditions were good for flying. Some twelve miles south-east of Fifeness, FLS F. Cressman's machine developed engine trouble and had to put down in the sea some twelve miles south-east of Fifeness. The second seaplane sent out a distress message on their behalf and went to search for help. By the time they returned to the site of their colleagues' downed machine, the sea had become cloaked in fog and the seaplane was forced to head for home. Help, however, was on the way in the form of numerous naval vessels including destroyers and mine-sweepers. Shortly after the light had faded the sea was lashed by gale force winds and the search had to be abandoned. Since 1916, seaplanes had carried passenger pigeons to summon rescue if they had to land in the sea. Around midday, on Christmas Day, one such bird turned up at Dundee bearing the following message, 'Still right side up but expected to turn over at any moment. If help doesn't come soon I'm afraid we're for it, but we're making a good fight. Cheerio, Cressman'. It was written at 3.00 a.m. A couple of days later a communication arrived at Dundee stating that a fishing boat had found what they thought to be the remains of a seaplane.

In the autumn of 1917 A.H. Sandwell returned for a second tour of duty to Dundee Seaplane Station. 'Here I spent the happiest six months, followed by an only slightly less happy half year of my whole war service with the cheeriest mess-mates it was ever my fortune to meet.' He was second in seniority to the CO, Sqn-Cdr Victor Wilberforce.

We introduced night flying on numerous occasions for the sheer joy of it, to the delight of youngsters, the confusion of the local searchlight batteries who lacked practise and the terror of the inhabitants who thought they were being raided. The expenditure of Very's lights and parachute flares was terrific on these occasions.

Dundee-based Seaplane Type 74, No.79, being pushed out into the Firth of Tay for launch. It was delivered by rail on 22 September 1914. This example also operated from Granton Harbour on the Firth of Forth in November 1914. On New Year's Day, 1915, it suffered engine failure and had to make a forced landing in heavy seas off Fifeness. The seaplane broke up but its crew of two were rescued. (Fleet Air Arm Museum – Bruce/Leslie Collection)

The area of the North Sea patrolled by seaplanes from Dundee Seaplane Station was extended and in 1918 numerous patrols were flown, unlike in previous years. No enemy submarines were sunk, but not a single ship was lost to enemy action in the area under their jurisdiction. The station also had well equipped workshops which serviced aircraft for other bases and seaplane carrying ships.

New machines arrived in the form of Curtiss H.16 'Large America' flying boats. One example, N4066 dropped two bombs on an enemy submarine, some twenty-five miles east of Montrose on 3 June 1918. Three months later this type was involved in the most serious flying accident of the war to befall Dundee Seaplane Station. Curtiss H.16, N4070, returning from a convoy patrol, hit a ship's mast on the Firth of Tay and burst into flames on 21 September 1918. Three of its crew were killed, Capt. A. Holland, 2nd AM F. Wilson and 2nd AM E. Marriott. The only survivor, 2nd-Lt F. Atkins, was injured. Another attack was made against an enemy submarine on 26 July 1918 by Short 184 Seaplane, N1831. The visibility was good and the sea calm:

> Both pilot and observer sighted the very distinct wake of a periscope about 100 yards on their starboard side steering south-west at an apparently high speed. The seaplane immediately did a steep right turn gaining height and dropped two 100lb bombs from a height of about 70ft. Both bombs landed practically together close to and just astern of the periscope. An attempt was made to warn a trawler and large steamship which were about one mile and a mile and a half respectively south-west by west of the position but it was not considered that her signals were understood. The seaplane proceeded about six miles south and communicated with HMS *Vidette* by aldis lamp. The seaplane searched the area with this destroyer but nothing further was sighted.

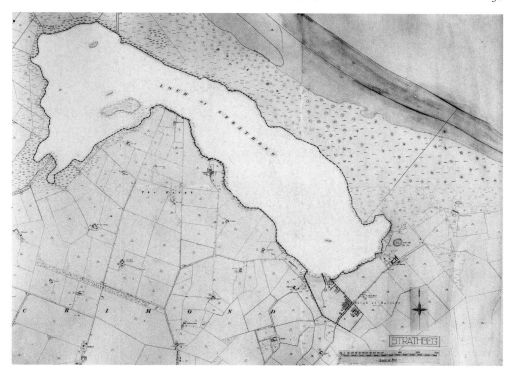

Strathbeg Loch Seaplane Station, 1918, located in Aberdeenshire, inland from Rattray Head. The loch is the largest body of water in north-east Scotland, but is very shallow and separated from the sea by a narrow band of sand dunes. The station occupied twenty-eight acres at the southern end of the loch and was around a mile from the sea. There was only one seaplane shed here, measuring 70ft by 70ft along with a slipway. A pier was especially constructed for the base with its own light railway. Other facilities included a wireless hut and mast, ammunition store and offices. The sixty personnel were housed in huts. Almost all traces of the station have vanished over the succeeding years. A large naval air station was built on land immediately to the south of the Strathbeg Loch towards the end of the Second World War. (The National Archives)

The following day another seaplane from Dundee observed a patch of oil in approximately the same position and bombed it. Nothing further was seen. The seaplane then communicated with airship NS7 and asked her to drop a bomb on the same patch. This was carried out but it was thought the bomb did not explode. Throughout the summer Short 184 Seaplanes and the Curtiss H16 'Large America' flew several patrols on most days. The latter sometimes covered up to 400 miles in their missions. In a memo to senior RAF officers who now controlled all military aircraft, the C-in-C at Rosyth wrote:

> …to bring to your notice the excellent work carried out by Dundee Air station. This station has carried out continuous patrol work, very often in exceedingly bad weather and I am informed by the convoy officer on these escorted convoys on occasions when the visibility has been very poor, is deserving of the very highest praise. I am advised that on no occasion have Dundee Seaplanes been known to miss a convoy through errors in navigation.

By October 1918, the seaplane station's function was given as Station for 249 Squadron Headquarters and No.401 Float Seaplane Flight for Anti-submarine Patrol duties and for No.257 Squadron Headquarters and Nos.318 and 319 (Felixstowe F.2A) Seaplane Flights for Reconnaissance duties. These squadrons are under the control of the C-in-C, Rosyth for Operations. In addition there was an Acceptance Depot for seaplanes. Finally, there was a training flight with Felixstowe F.2a seaplanes. The total strength is given as twelve Float Seaplanes and six Felixstowe F.2a Boat seaplanes. The base had 353 personnel, including a number of women employed on domestic duties.

When the war ended, operations were rapidly wound down. In August 1920, the site was ready to be handed over to the Board of Trade by the Air Ministry although flying had long ceased there. The seaplane station, however, received a new lease of life when it was brought back into use in the Second World War by the Fleet Air Arm. Walrus and Vought Kingfishers now took off and landed on the waters of the Firth of Tay.

Although Dundee was by far and away the most important seaplane station on the Scottish mainland, several other minor ones were established towards the end of the War. Buchan, the most easterly part of Scotland was an obvious choice for operations as this land mass is thrust out into the North Sea. Many convoys past close to its coast. Although there was a lack of large inlets and sheltered bays on the north-east coast, there was a large body of water in the form of Strathbeg Loch which lay within half a mile of the sea. As early as 1913, Lt Cdr Longmore from Cromarty RNAS Station had thought it suitable for seaplanes but had some misgivings about disturbing the local wild flowers. In the meantime seaplanes from Dundee as well as airships patrolled this area. With increased submarine activity off British waters coupled with the availability of new seaplanes it was decided to build a base on the southern edge of the loch in 1917.

It was intended to base large flying boats here. In conjunction with this Curtiss H.12 'Large America' flying boat, No.8688 flew north to Dundee in October 1917 for trials on Strathbeg Loch. Official approval was given to base this type here. This dune loch, however, sometimes had a depth of only 3 or 4ft. When such conditions prevailed it was intended to base two flying boats at Peterhead which lay a short distance to the south. Maintenance of the aircraft would also be carried out here.

By early 1918, construction of the seaplane station was underway. There were ambitious plans to base eighteen 'Large America' flying boats here from July 1918 onwards. Doubts were expressed about this plan and one senior officer wrote 'Strathbeg is doomed; hopelessly small. Unsuitable for 'Large Americas'. Don't send Shorts in lieu of Americas for these are useless here. In arranging priorities we put Strathbeg very low on the list'. In the summer, an occasional Short 184 Seaplane from Dundee would touch down on the loch to be refuelled. The autumn saw a more permanent presence of these seaplanes here. A.H. Sandwell stated that he spent 'a couple of dismal months up there'. Its role in October 1918 was as a 'station for 400 Float Seaplane Flight of 249 Squadron (H.Q. at Dundee) for Anti-submarine Patrol and duties carried out in co-operation with Units of the Grand Fleet. This Flight is under the control of the C-in-C, Rosyth for Operations'. There were only sixty-two personnel based here. After a brief spell of use the station closed in March 1919. The Loch was never used as a base for seaplanes again but towards the end of the Second World War, Crimond aerodrome for the Fleet Air Arm was constructed on the edge of Strathbeg Loch. The Seaplane Repair Base at Peterhead was a small scale affair as well. In October 1918 it had seventy-seven personnel on strength but it too had closed by 1919. Like its sister-station at Strathbeg it has disappeared, leaving hardly a trace. It was situated at the southern edge of Peterhead Bay. Towards the end of the twentieth century its site was occupied by a quay to serve the North Sea oil industry.

A number of other harbours on the north-east coast saw temporary deployments of seaplanes during the First World War. For example, Wight 840 Seaplane No.837 and Short 184 Seaplane No.185 operated from the harbours at Banff and McDuff on mine spotting duties in August 1915. Two years later another Short 184 Seaplane operated from Fraserburgh Harbour.

At the opposite end of Scotland, the Firth of Forth saw seaplanes operate from Granton Harbour on an irregular basis in 1915. On the northern shore, Hawkcraig Point,

Short 184 floatplane, No.9077, operating from Fraserburgh Harbour. It is being lifted out the water by one of the dock cranes, with a group of curious civilians standing nearby. Note that one of the aircraft's crew is standing on the front of one of its floats, probably to assist the crane driver in guiding it into position. (Fleet Air Arm Museum – Bruce/Leslie Collection)

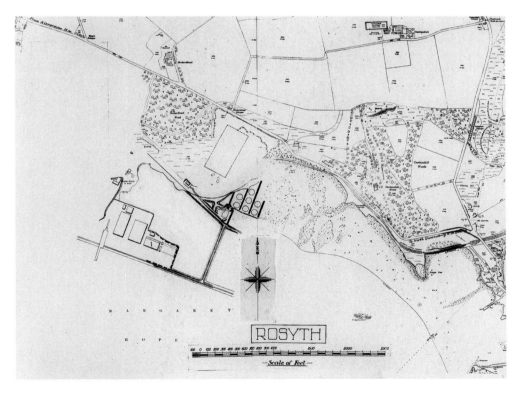

Rosyth Seaplane Station, 1918, was located inside Rosyth Naval Base. It consisted of two seaplane sheds, each 200ft by 100ft, but one was used as a store. The site closed in 1918, being replaced by Donibristle Aerodrome in its role of servicing naval aircraft. (The National Archives)

Aberdour, which had served as a seaplane station in 1913 continued to be used by seaplanes including Sopwith Babys and Short 184 Seaplanes. A seaplane station was created at the Royal Navy Base at Rosyth in 1917. A report by the Grand Fleet Committee on Air Requirements, 3 February of that year, made the following comments:

> In the part, training has undoubtedly suffered for want of spare seaplanes. The aircraft which should be kept tuned up for immediate active service have had to be used for constant training. This defect is being put right at Scapa where there will be exercising seaplanes as soon as the 'Campania' returns. At Rosyth, however, the situation is not so satisfactory and it is desirable that a place to stow, fly and repair at least six machines should be provided as soon as possible. Some measure of this kind we understand to be in contemplation but if the efficiency of the seaplane carriers is to improve it is highly desirable that there should be as little delay as possible.

By the end of 1917 a seaplane station and slipway had been established on a quayside inside Rosyth slipway. It served as a shore base for seaplanes carried by Royal Navy ships. Around the same time, aircraft were rapidly displacing seaplanes on board ships because of their higher speeds and overall superior performance. It would have been more appropriate to build an aerodrome than a seaplane base at Rosyth as by 1918 large numbers of Sopwith Pups and Camels were passing through the base. There was surprisingly never an official landing ground here but the playing fields appear to have been utilised when the need arose. At the end of 1918 plans were afoot to close this facility and transfer all work to the newly completed Donibristle Aerodrome. At Inverkeithing Bay a crane was erected to haul seaplanes out the water and transport them here on a purpose built railway for servicing.

The little-known Hawkcraig Seaplane Station, c.1917/1918, Aberdour, Fife, viewed from the waters of the Firth of Forth. (Fleet Air Arm Museum)

Short Seaplane 184, N1650, at Hawkcraig, c.1918, ready for launch down what appears to be a very steep slipway down to the water. It is housed in nothing more than a large tent. This aircraft was built by the Phoenix Dynamo Manufacturing Co. It was still at Hawkcraig in January 1919. (Fleet Air Arm Museum)

SEAPLANE STATIONS IN THE ORKNEY AND SHETLANDS ISLANDS

From the moment war was declared, the Royal Navy had a major task in defending its own bases. The activities of enemy submarines so worried the Admiralty that seaplane bases were established at Scapa Flow and Thurso on the representations of no less that the C-in-C of the Home Fleet on 13 August 1914. A Short S.38 Biplane was delivered to Thurso by rail but had left by the end of August. By the end of the year this base had been merged with Scapa Flow and abandoned. The traditional bases of the Royal Navy had been located on the south coast of England to combat France, Spain and the Netherlands. The new threat from a recently united Germany resulted in the Royal Navy establishing new bases at Rosyth, Invergordon and Scapa Flow to counter the German threat. The latter consisted a large area of sheltered water on the southern edge of the Orkney Islands which could accommodate large numbers of ships.

In contrast to most other long-established bases there were almost no shore facilities to cater for the 100-odd ships of the Royal Navy anchored here in August 1914. Seaplane patrols commenced from here in the same month. At the beginning of September, the commanding officer of the seaplane base wrote:

> I have now here five seaplanes and four pilots including myself. Require if possible, I may have two more seaplane pilots sent here. I consider the scouting work carried out by seaplanes here to be important.

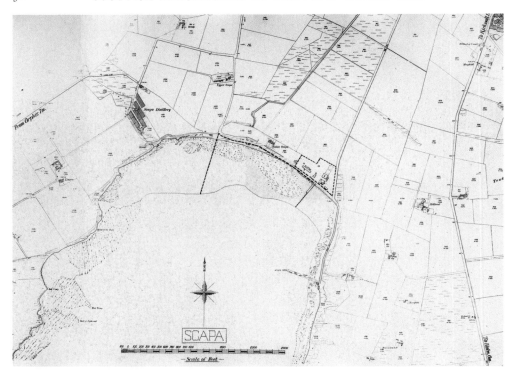

Scapa Seaplane Station, 1918, was located on the Orkney mainland at the head of Scapa Bay. Kirkwall was two miles to the north with a population of 3,800. The station was fairly small, only being six acres in size. 'The sea is immediately to the south separated from the station by a public road. The foreshore is a sandy beach. The water is sheltered and affords good mooring facilities.'

The facilities at Scapa Flow Seaplane Station were somewhat limited, even at the end of the war. There were two seaplane sheds, each 69ft by 69ft and two canvas Bessonneaux hangars. In addition, there were an engineers, carpenters, tinsmiths and smiths workshops. Also on the site was a wireless telegraphy installation and hut. There were just two huts and a separate officers' quarters for the personnel working here. The landscape has change little since the seaplane station relinquished the site. The road on the seashore which separated it from the seashore still skirts round the head of Scapa Bay to this day. (The National Archives)

In the same letter he also requested a four-seater car and a two-ton lorry. A report on 16 September 1914 records that Seaplane 97 (Henry Farman Pusher Seaplane) took off a 5.30 a.m. and flew up the east side of the Orkney Islands. Later in the day at 5 p.m., Seaplane 156 (Henry Farman F.22H Pusher Seaplane) flew a patrol up the east coast of the Orkney Islands as far as Sanday Sand and back over the inland harbours. Visibility was around thirty miles. Other seaplanes based at Scapa Flow on that date included two Short Admiralty Type seaplanes and one Sopwith Bat Boat Pusher Amphibian flying boat. The latter machine was damaged while taxiing at the end of September. The remaining seaplanes continued to fly two or three patrols each day over the waters surrounding the Orkney Islands. With the onset of winter, the strong winds precluded flying on numerous days. The seaplane base was initially a ramshackle collection of buildings. It was built at Nether Scapa at the head of Scapa Bay on the Orkney mainland. Temporary structures were erected to house the three seaplanes and two aircraft that had been allocated here. In early September there was one Bassonneaux hangar and two Piggott tents. The latter were considered to be useless for the weather experienced by the Orkney Islands and they were replaced by a further two Bessonneaux hangars. The base was exposed to the full force of the south-westerly winds

Scapa Flow Seaplane Station, Orkney Islands. The two sheds or hangars in the foreground along with the other buildings have been camouflaged and blend in well with the surrounding terrain. The slipway for the seaplanes and floatplanes on the left side of the picture has been exposed by the low tide. (The Orkney Library and Archive)

and it was not long before disaster struck. One of the hangars collapsed in a gale damaging several aircraft. One of only two Sopwith Boat Pusher Amphibian Flying boats to serve with the RNAS was destroyed in this manner on 21 November 1914. It was decided to relocate the base to a less exposed position but a new seaplane station did not commence construction until 1916. This was located at Houton Bay, to the west.

In the meantime anti-submarine patrols were flown from Scapa Flow. The seaplane carrier HMS *Campania* came into service in 1915 and carried six seaplanes. When not at sea the machines were repaired and serviced at the shore base. The seaplane station at Scapa Flow was also responsible for assembling newly delivered aircraft. They included a number of Wright 840 seaplanes delivered on board a collier. The machines were then deployed on HMS *Campania*. Other types that arrived in the course of the year included Short 184 Seaplanes and a Sopwith Schneider Seaplane, No. 3707. A number of Short 827 Seaplanes were also delivered by sea, some of them by a puffer. One example of the type was lost, No. 823, when it exploded while firing at a balloon.

In a letter from the Royal Navy Headquarters dated 22 September 1917, to the Admiral Commanding Orkneys and Shetlands, details plans of how they intended to strengthen the RNAS presence here:

…relative to the future of the Air Service in the Orkney Islands, I am to acquaint you that approval has been given for the establishment of Seaplanes of the 'Large America' type in the Orkney Islands to be increased to 18 and that a further increase to a total of 36 machines is contemplated.

Short Seaplane Type 827, No.823, in the water at Scapa Flow in the Orkney Islands. This machine saw service on board the seaplane carrier HMS *Campania* from April 1915 onwards. It suffered a number of mishaps including striking wreckage while taking off on 11 June 1915, damaging one of its floats. Three months later it suffered an explosion while firing at a balloon. By the end of the year it was in store at Scapa Flow seaplane station but it returned to service the following year. (Fleet Air Arm Museum Bruce/Leslie Collection)

1. These seaplanes are to be used to carry out intensive anti-submarine patrols in the summer months of next year. Similar provision is made at Peterhead and in the Shetlands.
2. It is anticipated that the station at Houton will meet requirements as regards maintenance and repair of the machines based in the Orkney Islands but that Stenness Loch will have to be used for working so large a number.
3. Considerable expansion will be required and it is realised that a certain amount of new construction etc. will be necessary.
4. The greatest importance is attached to an efficient patrol being developed by the Spring of 1918, and the station will require to be expanded so as to be capable of coping with the work contemplated. It is probable that a large increase in the Kite Balloon establishment will be required.

The America flying boats required large sheds and slipways and could not be accommodated at the original Scapa Flow Seaplane Station. While construction began in earnest in 1917 at Houton Bay, to prepare for the influx of the large flying boats, the origins of a base appear to date back as early as 1916. During that year huts were being built on the site and a concrete slipway was laid to handle Shorts seaplanes. By the end of the year large numbers of RNAS personnel had arrived and were accommodated in cabins. At the start of 1918 numerous Sopwith Baby and Campania Seaplanes could be seen on the slipway here.

As the year progressed the large flying boats began to arrive here. Among them were a small number of Curtiss H.16 'Large America' flying boats accompanied by greater quantities of Felixstowe F.2 and F.3 flying boats They immediately began flying anti-submarine patrols in the seas surrounding the Orkney Islands. Submarine nets had been strung across the English Channel between England and France hence any U-boat heading for the Atlantic had to travel round the north coast of Scotland. Often they would surface near Fair Isle to check their compasses which in those days were not gyroscopic.

Houton Bay and the seaplane station at its head. The complex is dominated by a large maintenance shed. There are several small sheds or hangars to the right of it. There are also two large slipways leading down to the sea for the seaplanes. (The Orkney Library and Archive)

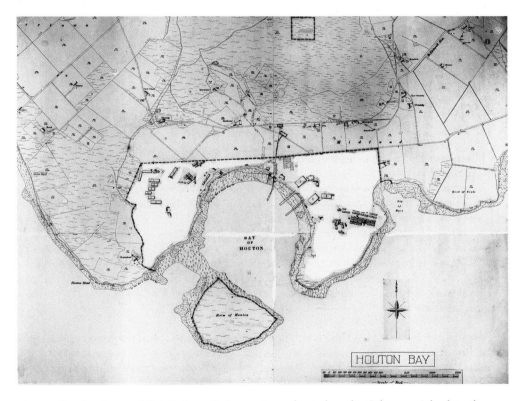

Houton Bay Seaplane and Kite Balloon Station, 1918, was located on the Orkney mainland on the north-west shore of Scapa Flow. The complex sprawled across some 188 acres including a small island. There were three seaplane sheds, two 200ft by 100ft and the other 180ft by 60ft. There was an engineers' workshop along with a carpenter, tinsmith and blacksmith. Houton Bay station also had a meteorological hut, engine store, and test house. Unusually, there was a butcher's and tailor's shop for the personnel based on the station. There were thirty-eight officers and 312 other ranks deployed at the seaplane station. The kite balloon base had a further forty-nine officers and 215 other ranks in the autumn of 1918. At that time, building work was still in progress and was not due to be completed until March 1919. Although the seaplane base has long since vanished the landscape in which it was located has seen little change. (The National Archives)

A Short 184 sits between a large complex of hangars at Houton Bay Seaplane Station in the Orkney Islands. Note the large size of its floats which would do little for its aerodynamics. Fleet Air Arm Museum. (Bruce/Leslie Collection)

The patrols mounted by the new flying boats could last as long as four or five hours and sometimes extended as far as Cape Wrath. Loch Erribol was a favourite hiding place for the enemy. On most flights the aircrew never caught sight of a submarine. There were, however, a few notable exceptions. Capt. H. Kendall dropped two 230lb bombs on a U-Boat on 7 July 1918 while flying Felixstowe F.3 Flying boat N4230. The same machine was involved in a second attack on 20 July. A typical patrol was described by pilot T. Crouther-Gordon, DFC flying Felixstowe F.3 Flying boat N4403. Leaving Houton at 9.25 a.m. on 7 September 1918, they flew to their designated search area in very poor visibility. All that was seen were some battle cruisers and destroyers. A report was received that a U-boat had been seen some sixty miles away near Fair Island. Upon arriving a second radio message was received stating that the U-boat had submerged eighteen miles away The weather conditions were still deteriorating and the commanding officer ordered Crouther-Gordon and his crew back to base as gale force winds were forecast. The Felixstowe flying-boat crew plotted a course back to Houton first flying north to Foula and then west to Noup Head landing back at base in choppy seas. T. Crouther-Gordon's commanding officer none the less thought that it had been a successful patrol.

Despite the delivery of the new flying boats, older types such as the Short 184 Seaplane remained in service at Houton Bay. One such example, N2652 dropped 100lb and 230lb bombs on a U-boat on 31 August. On 14 September despite the fact there were twenty-five flying boats at the base, only one was in suitable condition for operation duties! There were more machines than the service crews could keep in an airworthy condition. To look after the floats and hulls required the skill of highly trained craftsmen and there was a great shortage here. Additional staff had to be sought from Fairlie on the Firth of Clyde. The aircraft engines also required much attention and often took as long as two or three weeks to repair. Flying accidents added to the toll of available flying boats.

Felixstowe F.3, N4404 was wrecked while taking off when it struck an unseen object in the water. More seriously in September, a Felixstowe F.3 crashed in the Fair Island Channel but two crew members were rescued. Such was the state of the serviceability of the flying boat fleet that two Shorts Seaplanes had to be called on to go to their rescue.

Houton Bay Seaplane Station, 1918. The dominant feature is the seaplane sheds. This view has been taken from the north side looking south towards Scapa Flow where several large warships can be seen at anchor. (Orkney Library and Archive)

In the autumn of 1918, there were 350 personnel at Houton Bay Seaplane Station. The number of flying boats allocated to it on paper was six Floatplanes and eighteen Felixstowe F.3 flying boats. The function of the base was given as a station for No.430 Float Seaplane Flight and No.306 and No.307 Flights with Felixstowe F.3 Seaplanes for anti-submarine patrol and long reconnaissance duties. These flights were under the control of the Vice-Admiral, Orkneys and Shetlands for operations. There was also an 'F' training flight equipped again with Felixstowe F.3 Seaplanes. They were only stationed there temporarily until accommodation at Calshot became available. It was intended that two Squadrons of 'Large America' seaplanes would be based here as would the main Stores and Repair Depot for the Orkney Islands. The end of the war put paid to these plans. The closing months of 1918 saw a drift away of both men and machines. Houton Bay seaplanes, however, monitored the arrival of the surrendered German fleet at Scapa Flow.

Another seaplane station was established at Stenness Loch in 1918, some five miles to the north. Flights 309, 310 and 311 equipped with Felixstowe flying boats operated from this enclosed body of water for a brief period. The official number of machines allocated here was eighteen, but it is probable that this total was never achieved. They were engaged in anti-submarine patrol duties and operations with the Grand Fleet. There were some 200 personnel based at Stenness Loch, some of whom were housed in the Standing Stones hotel and the less fortunate in eleven huts. Flying had commenced in May 1918 but it was found that Stenness Loch, an inlet of the sea and the largest brackish lagoon in Britain, was too shallow and too exposed for seaplane operations. In the autumn all operations were transferred to Houton Bay. The Standing Stones hotel, however, was retained as the headquarters for flying operations in the Orkney Islands now under RAF control.

An advanced base for seaplanes was established at Pierowall on the island of Westray, some thirty miles to the north of Scapa Flow. Sopwith Babys were operating from here in the summer of 1917. By having a base here it would cut down the flying time to the Fair Island Channel and any U-boat negotiating the waters there. A year later, two Felixstowe F.3 flying boats were based

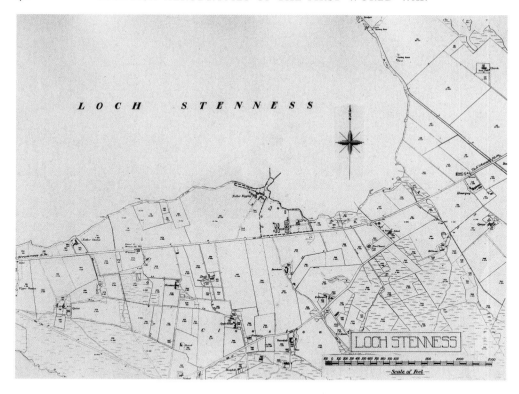

Stenness Loch Seaplane Station, 1918, in the Orkney Islands and located a short distance north of Scapa Flow. The loch has the distinction of being the largest brackish lagoon in Britain, linked to the sea by a narrow channel. The seaplane station occupied twelve acres on the southern shore of it. There were few facilities to cater for the seaplanes as there were no aircraft sheds or workshops of any form, other than a garage for the vehicles. The main road from Kirkwall to Stromness ran past the southern edge of the base. (The National Archives)

The first aircraft to be based in the Shetland Islands were the seaplanes and floatplanes at Catfirth naval air station. In this picture a Porte Baby sites on the slipway. Both its wing tips have been damaged by a gale in 1918. (Shetland Museum Photographic Archive)

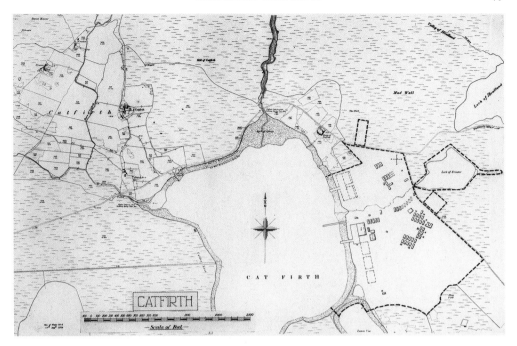

Catfirth Seaplane Station, 1918, located to the north of Lerwick in the Shetland Islands. This was Britain's most northerly permanent seaplane station in the First World War. The soil is peat on clay and the surroundings are bare and hilly. The water is sheltered and affords fair mooring facilities. For a seaplane station it was extensive in size, covering ninety acres compared with the dozen or so occupied by other similar bases. There was, however, only one large seaplane shed along with two slipways. Other technical buildings included a workshop, engine-testing shed and winch house. In addition, the seaplane station also possessed a wireless telegraphy hut, a directional finding station, a meteorological hut and a pigeon loft. These birds were carried on seaplanes to deliver messages should the crew be unable to use their wireless. The sizeable number of personnel, some 445 in total, were housed in numerous huts. In September 1918, much of the site was still under construction with it scheduled to be completed by the end of that year. It was intended that seaplanes would not operated from Catfirth seaplane station in the winter months, due to the adverse weather conditions experienced by this part of the world during that time of the year. (The National Archives)

here. N4411 piloted by Capt. P. Brend dropped a bomb on a U-boat on 29 August. It appears that the facility was only used infrequently.

In the last year of the war a seaplane station was also established on the Shetland Islands. Its purpose was to provide a means of patrolling the Fair Island Channel from its northern edge while seaplanes from the Orkney Islands covered the southern part. The site chosen was at the head of the Catfirth to the north of Lerwick. The first seaplane to arrive was a Porte Baby flying boat. It had rather a misleading name having a wingspan of a 124ft, larger than the Felixstowe F.3. In summer 1918, a large crowd gathered on the shore to watch its arrival, which is said to have been the first time an aircraft had visited the Shetland Islands. A second Porte Baby flying boat was also delivered to Catfirth. These machines had a 150ft wire aerial with a weight on the end which was wound down when the aircraft was in flight. It was reputed that while low flying, the end of one dangling aerial went through the roof of a thatched cottage near the seaplane station. The Porte Babys were reinforced by a small number of Felixstowe F.3 flying boats. Two examples of the latter type were responsible for flying the seventeen patrols mounted from Catfirth between 16 July to 16 August 1918. A small number of these

A group photograph of personnel at Catfirth Seaplane Station. They are wearing duffel coats and some are sitting on an upturned boat. (Shetland Museum Photographic Archive)

were flown eastwards to the Skerries but the rest were to be sent to the Fair Island Channel. There were plans to establish another seaplane station at Baltasound but the war came to an end before any work was started. Most of the personnel departed from Catfirth in the winter months. The radio direction-finding station continued to operate until the spring of 1919, but that was then shut down bringing the brief life of Catfirth Seaplane Station to an end. The site was sold shortly afterwards and some of the concrete huts were converted into houses. Little trace, however, now remains of the base.

By the early 1920s all the military seaplane stations and aerodromes that had guarded some of the most treacherous seas in the world had been abandoned. Germany no longer posed a threat and the limited number of RAF aircraft were mainly deployed to police the British Empire. When hostilities broke out again the skies over the Orkney Islands and Shetlands witnessed the return of large numbers of naval aircraft. This time, however, most were based on newly built aerodromes around Scapa Flow. The Shetland Islands also saw the return of flying boats which were based at Sullom Voe, as the former First World War base at Catfirth was deemed unsuitable for the new types of seaplanes now in service.

CHAPTER THREE

AIRSHIP STATIONS

In 1911, Naval Rigid Airship No. 1 was completed at Barrow-in-Furness by Vickers. For several years, the Admiralty had watched the development of the German Zeppelins with great concern. Popular science-fiction novels of the day also had done much to fuel the public fears of attacks from the air. In response to this perceived threat, Britain had embarked on her own programme to build large airships. The first of these was the Naval Rigid Airship No. 1 which was a based on German designs.

On 24 September 1911 this airship, rather unfortunately given the unofficial name Mayfly, was hauled out of its shed in preparation for its flight trials. Unfortunately, somebody forgot to untie the ropes holding her nose which resulted in the entire airship splitting into two sections. This was to have a profound effect on the development of rigid airships in Britain and it would be many years before another example would be built in the country.

Prior to this disaster, a number of non-rigid airships had been flown by the military. They were much smaller in size than the rigid airships which had a skeleton frame over which the canvas was stretched to hold the hydrogen gas. Sometimes known as blimps or gas-bags the non-rigid examples just consisted of an envelope of gas which took shape once inflated like a balloon. Underneath the envelope, a control car was suspended which house the crew and the engines to propel it forward.

For a while after the Mayfly fiasco the Admiralty ceased working on any form of airships. Developments in Germany caused them to reconsider their attitude and a couple of foreign airships were purchased for evaluation. At the beginning of 1914 all military airships came under the control of the Royal Navy and on 1 July, the RNAS was established. When war finally broke out they had a total of seven airships on strength. Much of the early experimentation had been carried out at Farnborough and it was one of the few aerodromes with sheds large enough to house the non-rigid airships. There were only three other aerodromes with facilities to operate airships, all located in the south of England.

With several astounding successes achieved in the opening months of the war by German submarines, countering their activities was given urgent attention. Although aircraft were now entering service that were capable of patrolling the seas, the Admiralty decided to develop the non-rigid airship for this task as well. The latter had the advantage of having a much longer endurance time, as well as being able to loiter over a particular stretch of water.

The Royal Navy put out to tender the requirement for a non-rigid airship that would have an operational speed of between 40–50mph, carry a crew of two and 160lb of bombs, be equipped with a wireless transmitter and could remain airborne for eight hours. Neither firms that bid for the contract produced a machine that met the required specifications. A meeting was held at Farnborough and it was the men of the RNAS that came up with a design which was based on the earlier Willows airship to which the fuselage of a B.E.2 aircraft was attached to act as the control car for its crew. The new class of airship known as the Submarine Scout

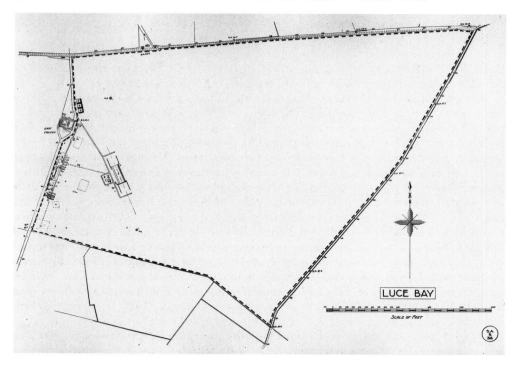

Luce Bay Airship Station, 1918, was located in the south-west corner of Scotland, near Stranraer. It was built on low-lying ground near an extensive area of sand dunes at the head of Luce Bay. The airship station occupied 444 acres of land although only six of them were utilised by buildings, the most significant of which is the airship shed shown on the left side of the plan. To support the operation of the non-rigid airships there was a silicol plant house and a gasholder with a capacity of 10,000cu.ft. There was also an engine testing house, a dope shop, and an armourer's workshop. The residential quarters were situated on the western edge of the station. They included an NCOs' mess and recreation room block and a second similar facility for the other ranks. The camp also possessed a sick-bay along with an isolation hut. There were two wells to supply water for the station. One was used for domestic use and the other provided water for the silicol gas plant. For most of its life the station only operated non-rigid airships, but in 1918 a small number of aircraft arrived to assist them in the task of coastal patrols. They were housed in Bessonneaux hangars located in the north-west corner of the site. At the beginning of the twenty-first century the former airship station site was part of West Freugh airfield. The eastern edge of the airship station was defined by a minor road which is now the B7084. On its opposite side were the dunes and the sea. (The National Archives)

or Sea Scout entered service only weeks after work had commenced on the project. These machines would have the task of patrolling the sea lanes over the next two years.

Until 1915 there had been no facilities for airships in Scotland. All this was about to change when a series of bases were established on the west coast of Britain from which the Irish Sea would be patrolled. A communication from the Director Air Department, dated 20 July 1915 states:

> With reference to the approval to establish airship patrols in the North Channel and Irish Sea a shed has now been completed at Luce Bay and an airship of the SS type has been send there and others will follow. A small portable shed has been approved at Larne for emergency use of these ships and this will be erected shortly. The shed approved for Anglesey is also completed and a portable shed will eventually be erected on the Irish Coast opposite. An SS type ship

will be sent to Anglesey in the near future. Submitted to inform the SNO's concerned and to place those ships under their orders for submarine patrol.

Luce Bay was Scotland's first airship station located 4½ miles south-east to the town of Stranraer on low lying ground close to the seashore. The area was sheltered by rising ground to the west and the hills of Galloway to the north. To the south lay the sheltered expanse of water in the form of Luce Bay from which the station took its name. By June the shed to house the airships was nearing completion. It was just over 300ft in length, 70ft wide, 50ft high and constructed out of corrugated iron. The cost was £8,900 but the large wind breaks at either end of it required a further expenditure of £4,200. The station covered some 444 acres, most of it being open ground. The accommodation was situated at its edge and was organised along naval lines with a small parade ground enclosed by whitewashed stones. The huts for the personnel each had their own washing facilities and a bathroom instead of the communal washhouse which was found at many other military bases. Unlike the other major airship stations in Scotland, which all went on to have two or three sheds, Luce Bay continued to operate with just the one shed for the entire length of the war. The base was commissioned on 15 July 1915. Its first SS airship arrived at the beginning of August. Originally it was intended to fly it to its new home, but the decision was taken to deliver it by rail to Dunragit station. The final section of the journey entailed transporting it down several miles of rural roads. Unlike most other aerodromes and airship stations Luce Bay base did not have its own railhead. A second airship arrived in a similar manner but the third was flown in.

On 23 August 1915, SS-17 airship made the first operational flight from Luce Bay. The station was responsible for monitoring activity in the North Channel, the shortest crossing between Britain and Ireland. Vital military supplies were often ferried across the narrow expanse of water. In addition, numerous cargo ships sailing up the west coast had to pass through these waters. This made it a favourite hunting ground for enemy submarines. During the early days of the war the Germans did not have enough submarines to seriously affect the transport of goods by sea. When they attacked their prey, it was often done so on the surface with the ship being sunk by the gun on the deck of the vessel. With submarines frequently operating in such a manner, it increased the chances of them being spotted by an airship patrol. For much of the time, however, the airships remained stuck firmly on the ground. Strong winds made their operation very hazardous. Even man handling them out of their shed in such conditions could result in them colliding with the edge of the structure and damaging their envelope. When the Submarine Scout airships managed to get off the ground, they often were only involved in practise flights. The engines were also unreliable on these early airships with their cylinder heads often cracking. By 17 October, SS-17 and SS-23 airships had made no fewer than twenty-three forced landings. The last operational patrol took place as early as 4 November 1915. Bad weather precluded patrols over much of the winter. The airship shed was guarded by sentries and later a motor launch was employed to patrol the near by seashore. There were concerns that Luce Bay Station's close proximity to the coast made it a viable target for a raid from enemy submarines.

The records of flying for week ending 12 February 1916 illustrates how few flights were undertaken in periods of inclement weather:

Sunday	No Flying	West Wind: 25-40mph
Monday	No Flying	West Wind: 30-45mph
Tuesday	No Flying	West Wind: 30-45mph
Wednesday	No Flying	North North West Wind: 25mph-45mph
Thursday	SS-17	Five flights round Aerodrome for bomb dropping practise
Total time in air: 61 mins		
	SS-20	Three flights round Aerodrome for bomb dropping practice.
Total time in air: 1hr 23 mins		

An aerial view of Luce Bay Airship Station in 1917 from airship, SS20. The single large airship shed is visible in the bottom right corner. Large windbreaks shelter the approaches to the hangar doors on both ends of the building. While most airship sheds were built to face the prevailing wind, the shed at Luce Bay was constructed on a north-west-south-east-axis. Next to the airship shed is a gasometer for storing the hydrogen gas. On the left of the picture are the accommodation blocks for the personnel plus a few tents. (© The Trustees of the National Museums of Scotland)

| Friday | No Flying | North West Wind: 23-35mph |
| Saturday | No Flying | South West Wind: 30-40mph |

SS-17, SS-20 and SS-23 airships were all available for patrol. SS-33 airship was awaiting the arrival of its envelope which had been doped.

In March 1916, an improved version of the Submarine Scout arrived in the form of SS-38. It had a Maurice Farman car instead of the standard B.E.2 fuselage. On 17 May there was a report of a submarine in the area but the airship sent to investigate saw no suspicious activity. For the rest of the year, a handful of patrols were flown each month accompanied by a larger number of practise flights which included bomb dropping.

The German Admiralty declared a policy of unrestricted warfare for their submarines on 2 February 1917. From this date onwards until the end of the war there was an escalation of hostile activity in the waters patrolled by the Luce Bay airships. With their operations so dependent on the prevailing winds, airship stations began to establish sub-stations where their machines could be housed should the conditions deteriorate and were unable to return to their home base. A portable airship shed was erected on the opposite side of the North Channel at Bentra, near Whitehead in Northern Ireland. Luce Bay airships often escorted the ferry, *Princess Maud*, which left Stranraer early in the morning for Larne in Northern Ireland. By the time it reached its destination the prevailing wind had often risen in strength and made the airship's return to Luce Bay difficult. Therefore, it would often moor at Bentra and return home in the evening when the strength of the wind had dropped. The first airship to have made use of this facility was SS-20 on 5 June. By the end of the war additional sub-stations had been established at Ramsey, Isle of Man, Machrihanish on the Mull of Kintyre and at Ballyliffen on Doagh Island off the coast of Ireland.

Luce Bay Airship Station, 17 June 1917 from the north-west. The large airship shed stands in a expanse of open ground with no trees or other obstacles to hinder the landing and take-off of airships. West Freugh Aerodrome was constructed on the site in the Second World War and the farm buildings visible in the foreground were demolished as a danger to flying. (Fleet Air Arm Museum)

The German submarines not only torpedoed allied ships but laid mines as well. On 5 May, SS-23 airship observed a mine exploding in the sea off Turnberry. Later in the day, another airship discovered lifebelts and buoys in the sea off Northern Ireland. They had come from a small cargo ship, the *Lodes*, which had struck a mine. The summer of 1917 saw the arrival of a new type of airship in the form of the Sea Scout. It was powered by the Rolls Royce 75hp Hawk engine, designed specifically to power non-rigid airships instead of an aircraft engine which were unsuitable for slow flight. The control car could carry three men and was watertight so it could land in the sea. The first new airship to arrive was the SSZ-11 and by the end of the year, Luce Bay had its full complement of four machines. The station now boasted its own silicol gas-plant to inflate their envelopes and no longer had to rely on a supply of gas cylinders. The new airships enabled the intensity of patrols in the North Channel to be stepped up at a time when German submarines were becoming increasingly active. During October, a collier was sunk by the gunfire from a submarine on the surface of the sea, killing its crew of twelve. As in the previous year, the onset of winter restricted flying activities. A report written by the station commander on 24 December states that:

> The weather during the past month has been chiefly noticeable for the long spell during which flying was quite impossible. From 24 November 1917 to 5 December 1917 a matter of twelve days, it was quite impossible to get the ships out of the shed with the exception of Saturday, 1 December 1917 when a short flight of ten minutes duration was made to test weather conditions. The average wind speed throughout the month has been over 28mph and altogether the weather has been most undesirable as far as airship flying is concerned. Probably the most noticeable feature in flying throughout the past month is the intense cold experienced by the crews of zero ships in this locality. The surrounding mountains are 2,000ft high and are entirely snow-capped which makes the prevalent winds bitterly cold.

Submarine Scout Zero class airship S.S.Z.20 is preparing for another mission from its base at Luce Bay in 1918. This type of machine had a purpose-built car for its crew unlike that on many of the earlier types of airships which was adopted from an aircraft fuselage. Its car had the added advantage in that it was shaped like a boat, so the airship could land on water. (Fleet Air Arm Museum – Bruce/Leslie Collection)

The report also refers to the fact that one of the airships suffered total engine failure due to mechanical causes on 20 December 1917, the first such incident to occur in over a year:

> Flt-Lt W.E.C. Parry, RN left the Aerodrome in SSZ-13 at 9.00 a.m. and proceeded on patrol. When about three miles distant from the air station his engines commenced to run badly. He therefore decided to turn back and land. He reached the aerodrome but the engine stopped when he was about 150ft up and the ship drifted slowly to the west. All attempts to start up on Remy gear proved quite useless. The pilot used the top gas valve and brought the ship down in a field about a mile away from the aerodrome. The lower deck was cleared with all despatch and by doubling across country, it was possible to get a landing party on the guys and around the car before she touched the deck. No damage was done to the airship. The report also mentions that bomb dropping was undertaken by all the pilots. Wireless operators had also practised aerial gunnery. Several birds have been shot down in the air.

The final year of the war got off to a poor start. There were numerous torpedo attacks on shipping in the North Channel. Fortunately, in most cases the torpedoes missed their target and when they scored a hit, the ship managed to limp to the safety of a near by port. On 8 February 1918, a small cargo ship actually managed to outrun an enemy submarine on the surface which was intent on its destruction. In March the airships managed to fly sixty-five operational flights. SSZ-11 airship dropped live bombs on what he thought was a submarine lurking off the Irish Coast. These were the first bombs to be dropped in anger by an airship based at Luce Bay. Despite a patch of oil appearing on the surface the enemy craft appeared to escape. Submarine attacks on shipping continued for the remainder of the year right up to the end of the war, despite the fact that that frequent patrols were mounted. Many covered distances of between 100-200 miles and were up to eight hours in duration. Some of the flights ranged as far as the island of Islay. Not all the patrols passed off without incident. On 15 July, SSZ-12 collided with the flag staff on the West Pier at Stranraer. The airship suffered damage both to its envelope and control car but was back in the air soon after. A second more serious accident occurred on 30 August, when SSZ-13 airship was destroyed. Owing to engine failure, a forced landing had to be made at Castle Head Point. Owing to the grapnel failing to hold permanently, this attempt proved unsuccessful inasmuch as when,

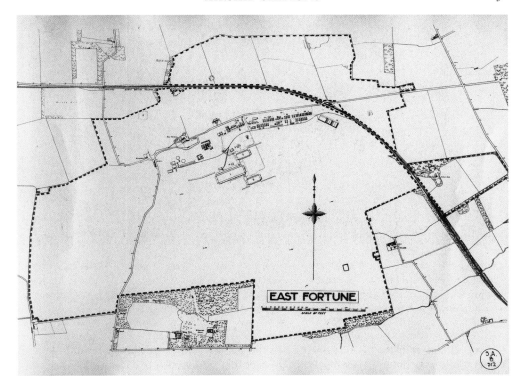

EAST FORTUNE

East Fortune Airship Station and Aerodrome 1918, was situated north-east of Haddington in East Lothian. This combined base was 1,330 acres in size, by far the most extensive military site in Scotland devoted to military flying. Only seventy acres, however, were occupied by buildings. Farming and the grazing of animals would have continued at the margins of the station as in the years prior to the war. There are four areas where the landing is very good, total area about 400 acres, otherwise the surface is undulating with a general slope to the west and south-west. Much of the area of this aerodrome where not specially prepared for flying is under cultivation. From 1917 onwards the station was dominated by one single structure namely the shed for non-rigid airships. It was flanked on either side by two smaller non-rigid airship sheds. A complex of buildings and structures were employed in the production of hydrogen gas to inflate the airships. They included a silicol gas plant, water tower, purifier house, compressor house and gas holders. The station also had its own electric light and power station. Other technical buildings housed a blacksmiths' shop, a welder's shop, annealing shop and dope store. The complex was located close to the main Edinburgh to London railway which was immediately to the north. A number of sidings extended as far as the airship sheds. The aircraft based here were housed in three aeroplane sheds, one 200ft long and 100ft wide, with annexes. The other two were 120ft by 100ft in size and also had annexes. In addition there were eight canvas Bessonneaux hangars, each 66ft by 66ft. There was a large number of buildings to house the numerous personnel based here. The camp in fact had separate quarters for the hydrogen staff as well as for the anti-aircraft crews. There was a WRAFs' mess and quarters. The facilities for those living here included washing, drying and bed airing rooms, a meat store for the officers and another one for the other ranks. The camp even had its own telephone exchange. In October 1918, work was still progressing on the aeroplane sheds. After the end of the war, the domestic site became a hospital. It continued in this role until 2004, when it closed. Many of the original corrugated buildings dating from the First World War still survived here in 2006. (The National Archives)

12ft from the ground, the grapnel temporary caught, causing the ship to swing violently round and down. This threw the crew out. At the time the crew were in standing position ready to take the first bump. The three men survived, but the airship landed in the sea and was then smashed to pieces on the rocky seashore. One of the seven code books was not recovered initially caused great concern to the senior officers at Luce Bay. A major search for it was mounted without success. It was eventually found on the seashore by a member of the public who handed it in.

In the autumn of 1918, there were 250 personnel at the station including a number of women employed on household duties. Although the site covered some 444 acres only six were occupied by buildings including the airship shed. When peace was declared, flying ceased shortly afterwards. A meteorological station continued to operate on the site. Weather forecasting had been a very important aspect of airship operations and all stations had their own meteorologists. Balloons were launched at frequent intervals to measure the direction and strength of the wind. Observations continued to be made at night using 'Chinese Lanterns', consisting of a candle suspended underneath a balloon. Details of wind strength, air pressure, temperature, cloud cover and rainfall were then transmitted from Luce Bay and other air stations the length and breath of Britain to the Met. Office in London. This enabled detailed weather forecasts to be drawn up and issued to airmen. By the end of December 1920, Luce Bay had even relinquished this role. The airship shed was put up for sale and subsequently demolished.

In the Second World War, the site was incorporated into West Freugh airfield. It continued to operate in a military role with aircraft testing bombs and weapons in near by Luce Bay into the early years of the twenty-first century.

The next airship stations to be established after Luce Bay were East Fortune and Longside. Their function was to protect shipping on the East Coast of Scotland. In September 1915, the Director of Naval Air Services gave approval for an aerodrome to be opened at East Fortune near North Berwick. It was situated close to the mouth of the Firth of Forth and it was decided around the same time that it would be ideal for airship operations. Two Coastal Type sheds, 320ft in length and 120ft in height were erected to house the non-rigid airships. Such structures were of vital importance, because an airship left outside was vulnerable to the wind and would soon be dismembered by the elements. East Fortune Airship Station was officially commissioned on 23 August 1916. The first two Coastal Type airships, C.15 and C.16 were delivered here around the same time. The latter machine was lost a few days later on 28 August when both its engines failed and it put down in the sea off Coldingham Bay. It was totally wrecked but its crew all survived. The Coastal airships were based on a French design and had a longer range than the Submarine Scout type which were the only non-rigid type in operation when Luce Bay Station opened for operations the previous year. When fully loaded, the Coastal Type airship could carry nearly half a ton of bombs for a duration of ten to twelve hours. Its maximum speed was 45–47mph and, if necessary, could remain airborne for twenty hours. The control car had accommodation for a crew of four, the coxswain occupied the front cockpit, with the pilot sitting behind him, followed by the wireless operator, with the engineer at the very back situated close to the rear engine. In common with many other British airships and aircraft, the Coastals were plagued by frequent engine problems. Their magnetos often failed and the engineers became skilled at changing them while on patrol.

By the end of 1916, East Fortune had the following machines on strength; C.15, C.20, C.24 and C.25. In the preceding months they had carried out a small number of patrols many only of two or three hours duration but some lasting up to seven hours. A number of trials flights were also carried out, including a trial involving the airship towing a practise target for the based aircraft. Admiral Sir David Beatty had a requirement for a long range reconnaissance aircraft for the Grand Fleet. It was thought that the Coastal class airship may be able to fulfil this role especially if it could have its range extended by towing it behind a naval vessel or refuelling at sea.

The demise of Coastal Airship C.16 at Coldingham Bay, near Eyemouth, Berwickshire, on 28 August 1916. A large crowd has gathered on the beach to view the partially deflated envelope of the airship. When both engines stopped over the sea due to magneto failure, C.16 based at East Fortune made a free balloon descent with the craft coming down in the sea at Coldingham Bay. Although this Coastal Airship was totally wrecked, all of the crew survived. (Fleet Air Arm Museum)

On 30 September 1916, the airship C.20 undertook the first trials in this direction exercising with the Battle Cruiser Fleet. The following year a more ambitious experiment took place on 3 May, when the airship C.15 was towed behind HMS *Phaeton* for over 2½ hours. The tow rope was then shortened to 100ft and 35 gallons of fuel were hoisted up to the captive machine.

On 16 July 1917, East Fortune was instructed to dispatch all its available airships to join the Battle Cruiser Force. Airships C.15, C.24 and C.25 took off in strong winds to rendezvous with the ships in the Firth of Forth. The joint force then headed north up the East Coast. Two of the airships then broke away from the fleet and set course for home. The third Coastal airship, C.15, remained with the naval force. Some seventy-five miles off Peterhead, it dropped a rope down on to the deck of HMS *Phaeton* to refuel. After a few minutes under tow the airship's engine failed and it was becoming difficult to control. The decision was taken to carry out an emergency deflation and part of the envelope slumped onto the deck of the ship along with its car. The other half of the envelope landed in the sea and had to be cut adrift. Further exercises were held with the Grand Fleet on 16 September 1917 and 4 November 1917, but Admiral Beatty was now coming to the conclusion that they may not be suitable for operating in conjunction with his ships. Matters were not helped when another Coastal airship was lost on 22 December 1917 while on its way to take part in exercises with the fleet. The airship C.20 was east off the Berwickshire coast when ordered to return to base. One of the engines ran out of petrol and the crew attempted to land near St Abbs Head. Unfortunately, before it could be secured, the craft was blown back out to sea where its second engine failed. After drifting for a while the crew landed on the water. The destroyer HMS *Oriana* arrived on the scene, rescued the crew and attempted to tow the airship back to the shore. This failed and the envelope was deflated. It refused to sink, so it had to be dispatched by being first rammed by the ship to no avail. The HMS *Oriana* then had to turn its guns on it.

An aerial view of East Fortune Airship Station. A large rigid airship, the R.24 is moored in front of the airship sheds. This airship was built by Beardmore at Inchinnan, after which it was flown to East Fortune, where it carried out its acceptance trials. When these were completed, it was delivered to Howden Airship Station, near Hull, on 22 May 1918. A number of naval aircraft are parked near the tail of the R.24. (© The Trustees of the National Museums of Scotland)

In April 1917 a third airship shed was completed at East Fortune. It dwarfed the other two already there being 700ft long by 180ft wide with a clear height of 100ft. A wide screen was fitted at one end of the shed. It was built to house rigid airships the first of which was delivered here from Inchinnan. The HMA No.24 arrived in December 1917. Prior to this, the first successful British airship, No.9, based at Howden was forced to land at East Fortune on 7 August when it got lost in fog and was running short of fuel. A few days later it took off and flew over the Grand Fleet. HMA No.24 stayed several months at East Fortune to carry out acceptance tests. Whilst at East Fortune the airship suffered from frequent engine failures. On one occasion this rigid airship with a length of 535ft was caught in strong winds near the Bass Rock, and for several hours could not make any headway because of the failure of her port amidships engines. This large airship departed in May 1918 for its new home at Howden, near Hull. The next example to arrive was the HMA R.29 on 29 June 1918. It was the Royal Navy's first successful operational rigid airship and spent most of its life at East Fortune. The highlight of its career came on 29 September 1918 when it became the only example to have taken part in the destruction of a German submarine. Its crew members spotted an oil slick in the water, a tell-tale sign of the presence of a submarine. Bombs were dropped and the destroyer HMS *Ouse* then depth charged the area. A trail of bubbles and oil signified the end of a submarine. It was later confirmed that the German craft UB115 had been sunk off Sunderland.

East Fortune also saw the arrival of new types of non-rigid airships in 1917. Until then it had been the sole preserve of the Coastal Type airship but its replacement, the North Sea class, which could carry a crew of ten, began arriving in the summer. Slightly over 250ft in length, it

Two North Sea class airships, N.S.7 and N.S.8, hover above their base at East Fortune. Both airships were delivered to this station in the summer of 1918. Unlike some of the other classes of non-rigid airships, these had enclosed control cars which could carry a crew of ten men, of which five would be on duty at any one time. In the main car was a large control room. At the back was the living and sleeping compartment. There was a separate small car for the engine. The two cars were linked by a walkway, and some of the crew members can be seen standing on it in this picture. (© The Trustees of the National Museums of Scotland)

North Sea class airship, N.S.3, tethered to the ground at East Fortune. Its control car was modified here by Lt-Cdr Abel and Lt-Cdr Wheelwright (notice the difference compared with N.S.7 above). This craft was later wrecked off Dunbar, East Lothian, in a gale during 1918. (Fleet Air Arm Museum – Bruce/Leslie Collection)

was around 50ft longer than its predecessor. It also had floats and could alight on the sea. One of the early duties for North Sea airship NS.3 was to carry out a co-operation exercise with Edinburgh's anti-aircraft batteries accompanied by a Coastal airship. The newer airships also suffered a number of forced landings and worse while operating from East Lothian.

North Sea airship NS.1, while on patrol off the Farne Islands on 11 December 1917, was unable to make any progress when one of its engines failed, except when it flew at a height exceeding 2,500ft. NS.1 managed to make landfall at Fenwick in Northumberland where her crew landed in a field. The airship was successfully secured with the help of farm workers and soldiers. Later in the day the wind blew up and snapped the mooring rope resulting in the airship's car being damaged. The following day another airship, NS.5 was blown out to sea when her engines stopped functioning. When they restarted, the airship managed to reach the mainland and put down at Ayton, Berwickshire. In the process her envelope was torn on the branches of trees. During 2 June 1918, NS.3 made a night flight over the Grand Fleet at Rosyth Naval Base to give the anti-aircraft batteries practise. When it landed back at East Fortune it was found to have a hole in her envelope, possibly caused by one of the Navy's guns!

Later the same month the same airship took part in towing trials with HMS *Vectis*. On 21 June she was dispatched to Aberdeen to escort a convoy. Off the coast of Angus a patch of oil was spotted on the surface of the sea. It was thought perhaps that a submarine may have been lurking under the waves and the airship dropped two bombs. Later it was discovered the source of the oil was a sunken ship. In the early hours of the morning of 22 June, NS.3 was off May Island in the Firth of Forth not far from East Fortune. A south-west gale had blown up and the North Sea airship found itself unable to reach the safety of the coast. On its sixth attempt to make landfall, a section of the envelope tore and it began losing height, striking the sea a few miles north-east of the Barnes Ness lighthouse. The car containing engines with the two engineers was torn off. The stricken craft then rose a few hundred feet back into the air having lost much weight before hitting the sea for a second time. The car was immediately submerged and the crew were underwater with the envelope spread over them. Five of the crew managed to escape, including Capt. Wheelright and Capt. P. Maitland. They were eventually picked up by the destroyer after clinging to the partly deflated envelope for five hours. The other crew members drowned in the accident. Of the six North Sea airships delivered to East Fortune during 1917 and 1918, one crashed shortly after delivery, one was lost at sea, two were 'mechanically disadvantaged', one remained barely operational, but the final example managed to see it through until the run down of the station in 1920.

During 1918, two further types of non-rigid airships were delivered to East Fortune. The first example of a Coastal Star airship arrived in February 1918. They were developed in response to the problems encountered operating the North Sea class airships. The Coastal Star was related to the Coastal airship, the first type operated at East Fortune. They were smaller in size than the North Sea class with a length of 207ft. A retrograde feature of the design was that they went back to using open cockpits. The second new type to arrive was the Submarine Scout Zero (Sea Scout), which also saw service at Luce Bay. They were much smaller than the other classes of airships being only 145ft in length and were crewed by three men. The idea behind this design was that they were intended to be more agile than their counterparts, enabling them to manoeuvre over narrow shipping lanes in their quest for enemy submarines. The Sea Scout airships frequently operated from the recently established East Fortune substation located at Chathill in Northumberland. This was to counter enemy submarines which were particularly active off the north-east coast of England with its busy shipping lanes. Often the Sea Scouts were unable to carry out their patrols as their envelopes were prone to deflate when the wind rose to any strength. To add to their problems they were propelled by a small engine which was prone to break down.

During the summer of 1918 at least two or three East Fortune airships were on operational duties each day. For example, on 4 July, one Coastal Star airship was airborne for twelve hours over the southern patrol area and a North Sea airship covered the northern sector.

East Fortune Airship Station, *c*.1918, viewed from the north-west. In the foreground is the Silicol plant house and associated facilities for producing hydrogen gas, including two large gas holders. Behind it is the large rigid airship shed flanked on either side by Coastal sheds for non rigid airships. All have been painted in camouflaged colour schemes. Their entrances are all shielded by enormous windbreaks.

After the end of the war, much of the site was demolished, reverting back to farmland. Some buildings were retained for East Fortune Hospital, which was established next to the B1377 road. (Fleet Air Arm Museum)

Non-rigid airship Submarine Scout Zero, S.S.Z.59. from East Fortune, landing on the aircraft carrier HMS *Furious* in 1918. At the end of that year, this airship was based at Chathill Sub-Station in Northumberland. (Fleet Air Arm Museum – Bruce/Leslie Collection)

Submarine Scout Twin class airship S.S.T.2 departing on a flight from East Fortune. Its crew can be seen standing in its control car as it becomes airborne. This type of airship had a top speed of 57mph/91kph. (© The Trustees of the National Museums of Scotland)

On the same day the rigid airship, R.29, arrived back after being airborne for no less than thirty-two hours on patrol and convoy escort duties. The previous day a Coastal Star airship was four miles north-west of the Bell Rock when it's commander observed: '… suspicious submerged object approaching last ship of convoy, about four cables on ships beam. Dropped bomb with delay action. Large whale brought to surface badly wounded. Another bomb dropped to shatter carcass. Signal sent to warn ships of obstruction.' Later in the month North Sea Airship NS.7 was ordered to photograph the aircraft carrier HMS *Furious* involved in torpedo trials off Inchkeith Island.

Patrols were flown from East Fortune up until the end of the war. The following report by Pt. Capt. Chambers in NS.8 gives a good insight into a typical mission:

> 1 August: 15.00hrs, left ground, 15.30hrs, Off May Island. 15.45hrs; dropped three bombs on patch of oil, circled in vicinity til 19.05hrs, a/c to intercept H.Z. Convoy. 19.45hrs; sighted convoy forty ships, five destroyers and trawlers, 20.10hrs, zig-zagging ahead of convoy. 21.55hrs; submarine reported five miles north of Dunbar, increased to full speed and proceed to spot. 22.40hrs five miles North of Dunbar, searched area. 23.33hrs, Strong Telfunken heard probably within a radius of fifty miles. 00.20hrs, 2 August, rejoined convoy twenty miles east of May Island, 02.05hrs, Telfunken last heard very weak. Escorted convoy until 03.15hrs, when it was lost in fog. Visibility about ½mile at 200ft. Endeavoured to find convoy until 05.00hrs. 06.15 landed.

After dropping three bombs on the patch of oil, May Island sent out an armed yacht and motor launches to drop depth charges on the site.

When the war ended, the defeated German Navy was ordered to sail its ships to the Firth of Forth where they would be met by the Grand Fleet. It was one of the largest gatherings of warships in modern times and this dramatic event was filmed and photographed by aircraft and airships from East Fortune. At the end of 1918, six airships were still operational: the rigid airship, the R.29, two North Sea class airships, two Coastal Star airships and one Sea Scout Zero. The future of the station still looked promising in 1919 with the arrival of the HMR R.34 airship.

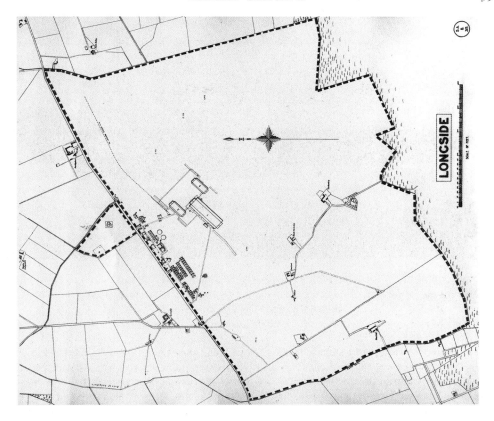

Longside (Lenabo) Airship Station, 1918, was located 7 miles south-west of Peterhead, which then had a population of nearly 17,000. The northern edge of the station is defined by a secondary road that runs from this town westwards to the main Aberdeen–Fraserburgh road. It occupied nearly 1,000 acres of land making it the second largest air station in Scotland, next to East Fortune. Of this total only forty-three acres were occupied by the airship sheds, gas plant and so on. Most of the rest would have remained as open pasture looking much the same as before the military arrived. The airship station was dominated by the large rigid airship shed and two smaller sheds either side of it. They faced into the direction of the south-west wind. To produce the gas to inflate the airships envelope, there was a silicol plant, water gas generating house, cooling towers and gasholder. There was also a blacksmith's shop, engine-testing house and an electric-light and power station. A garage housed the large vehicle fleet attached to the station which included three cars, four motorcycles, an ambulance and sixteen tenders. The buildings to house the 860-odd personnel based here in the latter part of 1918 were located on the north side of the site close to the road that formed the northern perimeter of the station. There were separate quarters to cater for the WRAF, who had their own mess. The station also had a meat store for the officers and separate one for the other ranks! Other facilities for the personnel include a sick bay, first-aid hut and disinfector hut. There was even a boot repair shop. The airship station closed in 1920 and most of the buildings were demolished over the next few years. By the early twenty-first century he site has radically changed, with the once-open meadows being replaced by a large plantation of conifer woodland. In among the trees, some scant traces can be found of the former airship station, including the concrete bases of the sheds, along with the concrete blocks for tying down the airships. The original camp roads also remain and serve as routes for walkers who wish to explore the forest. (The National Archives)

The HMR R.34 went on to make the first return crossing of the Atlantic by air. By the arrived back, East Fortune was in the process of being run down. On 4 February 1920, it closed as an airship station for good with the R.34 and NS.7 being the last craft to depart. The airship sheds were then used for the storage and breaking down of 160 million rounds of ammunition. Once this task was completed no further use for the giant buildings could be found and they were dismantled. The site they occupied has been retuned to agriculture. Some of the other smaller buildings were sold to the South Eastern Counties of Scotland Joint Sanatorium Board, who used them to establish a tuberculosis hospital. A number of the buildings used for this purpose still survive in 2007.

It was planned to establish a second base for rigid airships in Scotland, some six miles west of Peterhead and close to the village of Longside. Construction commenced in 1915 on 950 acres of peat bog. The main contractor was Tawse of Aberdeen, who employed thousands of labourers on the project assisted by bucket cranes and steam engines. The airship station was opened in March 1916, although the first personnel had arrived the previous winter. It was officially known as Longside but is sometimes referred to as Lenabo, the name of the marshy area on which it was built. It is possible that this low lying area was selected as a site suitable for airship operations because hilly ground lay immediately to the west and south sheltering it from the prevailing winds. Initially, the nearest railway station was two miles away at Longside village but this situation was remedied when a light railway line was built from Longside to the airship station in 1916. In November the coastal sheds to house the airships were completed at a cost of £60,000 followed by a shed for rigid airships. The latter measured 711ft in length and was 150ft wide with a clearance height of 105ft. It was not ready until March 1917. Although it was intended to have three or four large rigid airships in operation with the Royal Navy by the summer, various problems delayed deliveries. The large shed never housed these craft on a permanent basis. Wind breaks were built to shelter the entrances to the sheds in the form of a fence constructed from concrete slabs 30ft high, 3ft wide and 1ft thick. Both silicol and water gas plants were installed to produce the means to inflate the airship envelopes. In conjunction with this, deep wells were dug to provide the large quantities of water for this process.

The first airship to arrive is thought to have been a Coastal class, C.5, delivered by rail in March 1916. It did not become airborne until 16 June by which time the airship C.7 had arrived. The locals often referred to the airships as 'Lenabo Soos' (sows). The Longside machines participated in exercises with the Grand Fleet over the next two years. On 16 September 1917, three Coastal airships were joined by a further three airships from East Fortune including two North Sea airships and a Coastal class machine for manoeuvres with Royal Navy ships. The main function of the Longside airships was to patrol the sea off Peterhead, an area in which allied convoys converged from the Atlantic and from Scandinavia, on their way to or from the ports of the east coast of Britain. German submarines which were damaged in operations in the Atlantic would also pass this way in an attempt to reach the safety of their home ports in Germany. Longside's four Coastal airships flew 1,250 hours during 1917. Much of this was done during the summer months when they were airborne round the clock, making use of the very short periods of darkness experienced in these northern latitudes. During July, 382 hours were flown, of which 149 hours were done at night. Thirty patrols were over six hours in length and three exceeded twelve hours. Airships had to go out to sea whenever they were instructed to do so by the Grand Fleet.

While most other airship stations had had their Coastal airships replaced by more modern types, Longside still had five on site in April 1918, namely C.5a, C.7, C.10a, C.14 and C.18. By this time East Fortune only had C.25 remaining. Encounters with the enemy were relatively rare but they did occur from time to time. J. Middleton who flew as an engineer from Longside in the summer of 1916 recounted that, while on one patrol his airship was flying in thick cloud, he climbed up on to the top of the airship. Here there was bright sunshine, but there was also danger. In the distance was a German aeroplane. J. Middleton alerted the pilot to the presence of the enemy and the airship slipped back into the safety of the dense clouds.

B.E.2c No.8720, normally based at East Fortune, is seen here at Longside in August 1916. A smaller number of fixed wing aircraft were deployed to this airship station to provide fighter cover for it. (Fleet Air Arm Museum – Bruce/Leslie Collection)

In what appears to be a placid day at Longside, Coastal class airship C7 floats over Longside in 1917. This airship was built at Kingsnorth and delivered to Longside by rail in May 1916 where it remained until it was withdrawn from use in October 1918. (Fleet Air Arm Museum – Bruce/Leslie Collection)

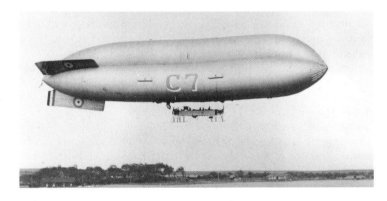

The crew of Coastal class airship C.18 prepare to take-off from Longside. Note that the crew in the control car are exposed to the elements from all directions. This airship was first delivered to Longside in November 1916. Bombs are attached to the car directly under the feet of the man clambering aboard the airship. (Fleet Air Arm Museum – Bruce/Leslie Collection)

Despite the large camouflaged wind break visible behind this Coastal Star class airship, the landing party consisting of several hundred men are having difficulty in bringing it under control during a September gale at Longside in 1918. (Fleet Air Arm Museum – Bruce/Leslie Collection)

Gales and strong winds were the natural adversaries to the airship. When such conditions prevailed it was sometimes necessary to rapidly deflate the airship to stop it from careering out of control across the airship station.

In this picture, a Coastal class airship, is being deflated during gale-force winds at Longside in 1918. Note the man standing in the gap between the two halves of the deflated envelope. (Fleet Air Arm Museum – Bruce/Leslie Collection)

Coastal Star class airship, C★7, flying over Longside. This example arrived here from East Fortune on 31 September 1918. This type of airship was the first to incorporate parachutes for its crew. They were carried externally on lines that could be attached swiftly to the harnesses worn by its crew of five. (Fleet Air Arm Museum – Bruce/ Leslie Collection)

A more alarming experience occurred two years later when North Sea airship, NS.9, was flying over the sea when it found itself being shot at by a German submarine. The airship crew had not seen it as the sea was covered by mist. In this instance they managed to escape after sustaining some minor damage. On 31 July 1918, C.25 from Longside disappeared while on patrol, some sixty miles east of Aberdeen. A damaged enemy submarine had been reported off the East Lothian coast and several airships had taken off to look for it including C.25. Eventually the search for the enemy craft was called off but this airship was never seen again. Only a propeller, which was believed to have come from the airship, was found floating in the sea a few days later. It was generally believed that the C.25 came across an enemy submarine that possibly could not submerge and it shot the airship down with its deck gun. Before the submarine returned to its home port it was probably itself sunk, so the exact nature of the fate to befall C.25 airship and its crew would never be known.

The star on the airship between the C and the number five indicates it is the improved version of the Coastal class airship. Ten of this type of machine were built, which had an excellent safety record, with all of them surviving the War. The example in the picture was based at Longside in 1918. (Fleet Air Arm Museum – Bruce/Leslie Collection)

Delivered in April, 1918 for military service this Submarine Scout Zero class airship, S.S.Z.57 is being handled by its ground crew at Longside. This class of airship was relatively small, being only 145ft in length (44m) compared with some of the other types which were based here. (Fleet Air Arm Museum – Bruce/Leslie Collection)

Submarine Scout Zero class airship, S.S.Z.58, being walked into position by its numerous ground crew who control it by ropes. Four separate parties of men are visible, including one holding onto the nose of the airship and another at its tail. Conditions on this spring day in 1918 look ideal for flying. The Submarine Scout Zero class airship could remain airborne for twenty-four hours when flying at half speed. (Fleet Air Arm Museum – Bruce/Leslie Collection)

This excellent view of Longside shows Submarine Scout Zero class airship S.S.Z.65 handled by its landing party, which includes a dog. An airship shed is clearly visible in the background with its huge doors in the open position. A large windbreak has been constructed to the right of the hangar to make it easier to manoeuvre the craft in and out of it. (Fleet Air Arm Museum – Bruce/Leslie Collection)

Such events were very rare and the main enemy of the airship crews on long missions would have been boredom. The spring saw a spell of good weather over northern Scotland, enabling many patrols to be flown on convoy protection duties. In April 1918, the Coastal class airships made fifty-six patrols, the average length of them being eight hours. On six occasions they were dispatched to investigate reports of enemy submarines off the north-east coast. Although the Coastal class airships had been replaced at other stations, one example continued to operate at Longside until the end of the war. Their place had been taken by the North Sea, Coastal Star and Sea Scout types. In 1918, a sub-station was also created at Auldbar (spelt Aldbar on modern maps), south of Brechin. There were no airship sheds here. Instead of sheds, four large cuttings known as 'nests' were made in the woods where airships could shelter, the trees acting as natural windbreaks. The personnel were housed in huts or tents. The small Sea Scout Zero class airships were often detached here from Longside. One of them, SSZ No.57 had to be ripped after breaking away from its moorings at Auldbar on 2 November 1918. The airship only came to rest after drifting for eight miles. Autumn gales also battered Longside and North Sea airships NS No.9 and NS No.10 had to have their envelopes ripped on 21 September, as it was found impossible to manoeuvre them into the sheds after they had landed.

North Sea class airship N.S.9 at Longside. This machine arrived here in July 1918 after completing its acceptance trials. A short time later it came under fire from a German submarine which surfaced off Aberdeen. The airship escaped with only minor damage. (Fleet Air Arm Museum – Bruce/Leslie Collection)

Auldbar Airship Station near Brechin, Angus, c.1918. This was a sub-station of Longside Airship Station. There were no permanent buildings here with the airships being moored in clearings in the coniferous woodland. The encampment in the forest has a fairy-tale like appearance with some of the tents even possessing small windows. Also, the stones on either side of the path have been whitewashed. The only indication in the early twenty-first century that the area was once home to airships are the remains of some of the mooring pits. (Fleet Air Arm Museum)

Frequent patrols over North Sea convoys were being flown, one even as far as the Orkney Islands, until the end of the war. Afterwards, the run down of this large military complex proceeded fairly rapidly with the last personnel leaving in 1920. The next year the RAF stopped operating airships altogether. No alternative use could be found for the huge airships sheds which were demolished along with most of the other structures in the post-war years.

Longside is sometimes credited as having been the most northerly airship station in Britain. However, in July 1916, Caldale Airship Station was commissioned on the Orkney mainland, giving it this honour. Its main purpose was to provide anti-submarine patrols and convoy protection in the waters around the islands. Cdr Roland Hunt was given the task of finding a suitable area of ground in the Orkney Islands on which to establish a coastal airship station. A couple of locations were recommended to him by Col. Harris who was in command of the Orkney defences. In his report, dated 19 April 1916, Cdr Hunt wrote:

> I visited both these sites and came to the conclusion that the one at A (Caldale) was by far the most suitable. It is situated in a hollow about 2½ miles to the west of Kirkwall and is well protected from south to north through west winds. With the exception of low barbed wire fences the country round here is quite clear for a considerable distance and there is suitable dry level ground for the foundations of a coastal shed.
>
> A road runs to within a quarter of a mile of the site selected for the shed. The chief difficulty is the question of water supply which during the summer months is practically non-existent, the only supply being from a burn which runs through the site and is used by a whisky distillery near the shore. With regard to the general policy of establishing an airship base at Scapa Flow, I was able to see the C-in-C himself and explain to him the limits of a coastal ship. I also told him that it probably be the end of August before the shed could be erected. He expressed the opinion that unless a (air) ship could be provided before September it would be of no practical value this year on account of the strong wind to be expected after September. He appeared anxious to commence experiments in spotting from aircraft as soon as possible, and asked if an SS (Submarine Scout) shed could not be erected on the same site in a shorter time saying that he could always have a destroyer ready in case of engine failure. He proposed to use this (air) ship for sub-calibre firing in the Flow and for full calibre firing in the Pentland Firth while he fully realised that a (air) ship of the SS type would have no military value. With reference to the position of future rigid airship sheds, the C-in-C appeared to consider that they should not be placed very far north as it was improbable that a fleet action would be fought in northern latitude. He also thought they would in the first place work with the cruisers and should therefore precede them to sea. The Firth of Forth be considered, was sufficiently far North under present circumstances but if a site became necessary further north, Cromarty Firth was most suitable owing to the absence of wind near Invergordon. The question of kite balloons was broached and the C-in-C was most anxious to experiment with the one in the Campania. The advisability of putting kite balloons in all the ships of the tenth cruiser squadron with the purpose of extending their limit of search was mentioned. To summarise the results of my interview with the C-in-C, I gathered the impression that he was very strongly in favour of having airships, kite balloons and more seaplane carriers attached to his command as he was of the opinion that they might be of greatest utility for spotting and other purposes.

Two airship sheds were eventually built at Caldale, one a Coastal Type with dimensions of 220ft by 70ft and the other a Submarine Scout which was 150ft by 45ft. The former shed was nearing completion in September 1917. According to Cdr Hunt, 'The actual Coastal shed is now complete but the doors are yet to be hoisted and fitted in position. The recent gales and general bad weather have held up the work considerably.' By the end of that year, work had commenced on constructing a wind break next to it. Its completion was delayed as the metal sheeting had not been delivered by the contractors. Due to its remote location, Caldale Airship Station suffered

The airship sheds of Caldale Airship Station. Two giant windbreaks are visible to the left of the buildings. The picture was probably taken a short time after the end of the First World War, by which time the station had fallen into disuse. (T. Kent, The Orkney Library and Archive)

Caldale Airship Sheds photographed *c.*1920, after the station had been abandoned. They were used to house Coastal Patrol and SS class airships. Note the massive doors at the end of each building. On the left side of the picture are two huge windbreaks to provide protection as the airships were manoeuvred in and out of their accommodation. (© The Trustees of the National Museums of Scotland)

delays in other fields as well Cdr Hunt continued: 'The very greatest difficulty is experienced in obtaining stores which is more especially felt as no other airship station is in close enough contact to fall back on in case of emergency'. The first two airships to arrive at this northerly outpost were Submarine Scouts, SS No.41 and SS No.43. They commenced flying from Caldale in the summer of 1916. By the following year, a more advanced version of this class of airship were delivered in the form of Submarine Scout Pushers, SSP No.2 and SSP No.4. The Orkney Islands were hardly the most suitable environment for airship operation, often being battered by gale force winds that blew straight in off the Atlantic Ocean. Cdr Hunt noted:

> Except for the first week of the month (September 1917), the weather has been the worst experienced while ships have been flying this year. For the last ten days continual depressions have been passing over the island. High winds have resulted and on the 22 September the anemobiograph registered sixty-eight knots. October has been the worst month for flying experienced this year. There have been no settled periods at all and the airship had had to go out at any odd fine moments that came. Pilots complained of the cold if they had to remain on patrol for more than four hours or so.

On 26 November airship SSP No.2 took off on patrol in reasonably calm conditions. Later that morning the wind speed had increased to around forty knots and the airship had difficulty in making headway back to Caldale. At 11.20 a.m. it reported that its engine had stopped and that it was going to make an emergency landing. The airship came down in the sea, north east of the island of Westray. Despite a Royal Navy ship being close by they were unable to save the crew of three as the envelope burst on impact and the craft sank rapidly. HMS *Leopard* searched the area until the light faded but could find no trace of the crew or any wreckage. It was believed that the crew were trapped in their car in the crash. They were the pilot, Ft Lt S.B. Devereaux, PMI A.E. Scott and LMW T.J. Wilson. The wind abetted a short time after the crash and the airship would have also certainly made it back to Caldale had its engine not failed. Disaster struck for the second time in under a month when the SSP No.4 took off for a night flight on 21 December. At 7.20 p.m. the airship was making no headway in heavy snow as it attempted to return to Caldale. The crew sent a message requesting the assistance of a destroyer. Over the next few hours further communications were received from the distressed airship with final contact being lost shortly after 22.00 p.m. The next day the wreckage was washed ashore on the island of Westray but there was no sign of the crew. The station had lost two of its three non-rigid airships and the remaining Sea Scout, SS No.41, could not be flown due to the lack of gas to inflate it!

On 22 January 1918, the Admiralty gave the order to close down the airship station. Caldale, was given a new role as a kite balloon station. In the later part of the nineteenth century tethered spherical balloons had been used to haul artillery observers aloft. Immediately before the First World War, Britain had put most of its effort into developing aircraft to fulfil its reconnaissance requirements. It was found, however, that observation balloons were particularly suited to trench warfare in the open landscape of Northern France. They could monitor a particular area over a long period unlike an aircraft and the observer would gain a detailed knowledge of the area they watched over. At the beginning of the war, Britain sent some vintage spherical balloons to France to assist the artillery units in bombarding enemy positions. This type of balloon could not be used in winds over 20mph and was an unsteady observation platform even in slower wind speeds. Some European armies had solved this problem by using balloons fitted with fins, not unlike a small airship in shape. They thus pointed into the direction of the prevailing wind and were known as kite balloons.

In December 1914, their value came to the notice of the Admiralty. The following year two balloons and an old pattern winch from the French government had left for service in the Dardanelles. Kite balloons had hitherto only been deployed on land but the Royal Navy converted a ship so that they could be operated with the Fleet. In good conditions they would

The officers and men of the recently established kite balloon station at North Queensferry are lined up for inspection by the Commander-in-Chief. The date is 4 May 1917. The huge tent like structures in the background are used to house the kite balloons. (Dunfermline Carnegie Library, Local History Collection)

Officers of North Queensferry Kite Balloon Station pose for their photograph in front of a group of wooden huts used for accommodation of the personnel. The men in civilian clothes have probably been responsible for overseeing the construction of the base. (Dunfermline Carnegie Library, Local History Collection)

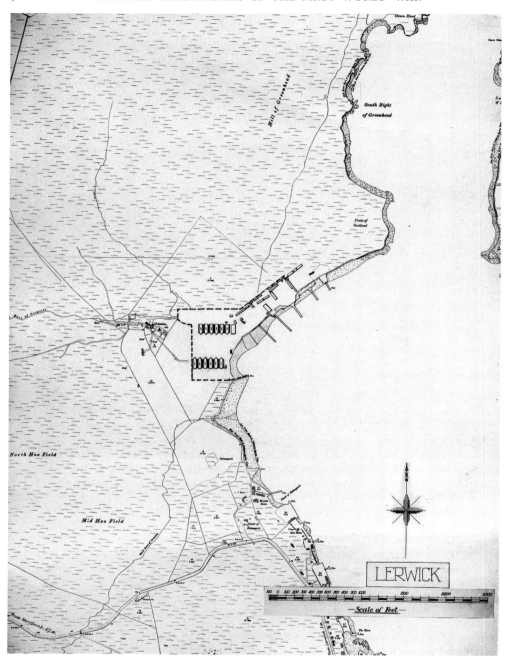

Lerwick Kite Balloon Station, 1918, was two miles north of the town of Lerwick, in the Shetland Islands. It occupied an area of about fifteen acres on the shore of Bressay Sound, which separates the Shetland mainland and Bressay Island. The main feature of the station was the twelve balloon sheds, each 100ft by 36ft in size to house the kite balloons. A hydrogen plant supplied the gas to inflate them. Five piers allowed the kite balloons to be taken down to the seashore for embarkation on board Royal Navy warships. The motor transport shed housed a single motor car and motorcycle, along with three lorries. In October 1918, most of the buildings were complete except for some of the huts for the personnel which would not be finished until the end of the year. (The National Archives)

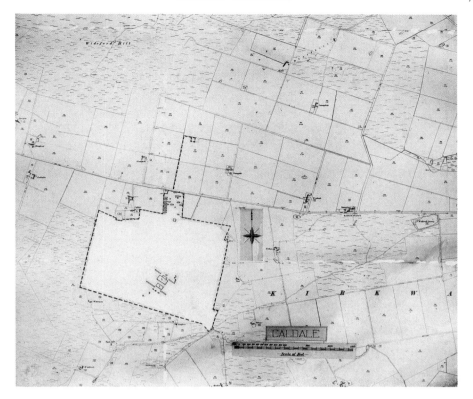

Caldale Airship Station, 1918, was situated on the Orkney mainland, two miles west of Kirkwall. The low lying area of ground was sheltered by Keelylang Hill to the west and Wideford Hill to the north, both rising to slightly over 700ft. The airship station extended across some 146 acres, of what was poorly drained ground. There were two airship sheds here one 200ft by 70ft and the other 150ft by 45ft. In the closing stages of the war they had been vacated by the non-rigid airships, and were used for housing kite balloons. The sheds were protected by no less than six large windbreaks. It appears that unlike other airship stations in Scotland, it did not have the facilities to manufacture gas to inflate the balloons on site. Accommodation for the personnel based here included seven huts for the lower ranks and separate quarters for the officers. Similar to other stations, it had its own transport fleet which included a single motor car, two light lorries and four heavy lorries. It suffered the same fate as the other airship stations in the interwar years with its airship sheds being demolished. (The National Archives)

be winched up to a height of 2,000–3,000ft to observe and direct fire on enemy gun batteries not visible from sea level. Admiral Beatty thought that if the Grand Fleet adopted kite balloons they would offset some of the advantage the German Navy had gathering intelligence with their Zeppelins. On 23 September 1915 Admiral Beatty had a balloon section sent to Rosyth for sea-going experiments under the personal supervision of Rear Admiral Hood. The seaplane carrier HMS *Engadine* was used in these trials and demonstrated that a kite balloon could be successfully towed behind it at speeds of up to twenty-two knots at heights of around 3,000ft. The Royal Navy when proceeded to adapt a number of merchant ships to operate a fleet of kite balloons. When not at sea, a number of shore bases were established to house and maintain them. The former airship station at Caldale was taken over by the Kite Balloon Service in early 1918.

Its function was as a balloon base for convoy duties carried out in co-operation with the navy. There were twelve working balloons. The station was under the control of the Admiral Commanding, Orkneys and Shetlands for Operations. Some 268 personnel were stationed here including forty-nine officers. Scapa Flow Naval Base had a second kite balloon station next to Houton Bay Seaplane Station. The ten balloons here came under the control of the Vice-Admiral, Commanding 2nd Battle Squadron for Operations. Unlike at Caldale, where the balloons were housed in the large airship sheds at Houton Bay they were forced to use ten canvas balloon sheds, each 100ft by 36ft. Crews could make use of the hulk *Latona* to practise launches. The kite balloons themselves were around 80ft long and had a capacity of 28,000cu.ft. The weather conditions, however, were far from ideal for operating the kite balloons, despite the fact that they were tethered either to the ground or a ship. The strong winds often prevented the kite balloons from leaving the ground. On one occasion the rope snapped and the kite balloon, along with its observer, was blown out to sea never to be seen again. Another natural hazard manifested itself in the form of thunderstorms because the electrical charge was prone to discharge itself through the hydrogen filled balloons. A number were ignited by lightning in Scapa Flow but fortunately their crews escaped unscathed.

Further north another kite balloon station was established at Lerwick in the Shetland Islands in early 1918. Personnel were billeted in commandeered huts which formerly housed women connected with the fish processing industry. Balloons were housed in twelve sheds, each 100ft by 36ft. 'Transferring them from shore to ship was a complicated procedure as we had to take them inflated and flying at about 100ft from a winch on a lorry to Lerwick Harbour. The ships we used by RNVR personnel were small and classed as "submarine destroyers" but were outdone for speed by the German submarines' one serviceman crew noted. While some ships carried their own equipment to inflate kite balloons, it was general practise to inflate them at the shore station and then transfer them to vessels anchored nearby.

At the other end of Scotland, a kite balloon base was opened in the summer of 1917 at North Queensferry. It had eight kite balloons for operations carried out in conjunction with the Grand Fleet. While most of the personnel were housed in wooden huts on the site the, officers lived in Ferry Gate House. The kite balloon stations in Scotland were all abandoned shortly after the end of the conflict. Few navies retained their kite balloons for any length of time after this date. Their role was replaced by the aircraft carrier and the long range flying boat. The Forth Rail Bridge and the naval installations were protected by barrage balloons during the Second World War. Although smaller than the kite balloons they were of a very similar appearance.

CHAPTER FOUR

NAVAL AERODROMES

When the First World War was declared the RNAS possessed thirty-nine landplanes and fifty-two seaplanes, in addition to seven airships. Many of their landplanes were stationed at the Royal Naval Flying School at Eastchurch in the south of England. In Scotland there were two seaplane bases, Dundee and Fort George, neither of which had facilities for operating landplanes. The following year a temporary landing ground was established at Barry for landplanes attached to Dundee Seaplane Station, as there was no suitable ground in the immediate vicinity. In the summer of 1915, Dundee had five landplanes on strength. The machines, however, flew from Montrose Broomfield Aerodrome which had been vacated by the RFC when No.2 Squadron moved to France. It was only a matter of time before they wished to repossess this site to expand their flying training programme.

RNAS officers began to scout out new sites where they could feasibly establish a new aerodrome to base their aircraft. In a report to the Admiral Commanding The Coast of Scotland, E. Nanson the Station Commander of Dundee Naval Air Station wrote, 'a very excellent position for an aeroplane base was found near Dunbar'. However, East Fortune was eventually chosen as the most suitable place to create a new aerodrome along with an airship station:

> The grass is short all over and the field is extremely level on the southern side, the surface might be improved by rolling after wet weather but there is no immediate necessity for this. The position of high trees on the western side is disadvantageous, but the field is sufficiently large to allow for landings being made with ordinary aeroplanes with the wind in any direction and in any case a portion of these trees could be easily removed. It is therefore submitted that the proposed shed for aeroplanes should be erected on this field instead of on the site previously inspected near Dunbar.
>
> The shed should be of the ordinary standard type with annex attached and should be capable of accommodating six aeroplanes, it is not considered that the erection of the workshops, petrol store, temporary quarters, and so on would be necessary as those latterly provided for the airship base could be used for both purposes, in the meantime use could be made of some farm buildings in the vicinity.

Finally E. Nanson added in his memo of 26 August 1915:

> In view of the importance of having aeroplanes there as soon as possible for the purpose of attacking enemy's aircraft which may approach the Forth, it is suggested that shed should be erected as soon as is convenient and a temporary base established with the aeroplanes and personnel from Montrose, the aerodrome at Montrose being the property of the Military and its position being of little strategic value.

By mid-September, two Sopwith Two Scouts and a Henri Farman had arrived at East Fortune from Montrose. The first proper RNAS aerodrome for landplanes in Scotland was now in operation. The machines initially were housed in a Piggott tent which was soon blown down in a gale! By the end of 1915, there were a grand total of seven aircraft on strength, including a number of recently delivered Avro 504Cs. In the winter of 1916, three Hervieu tents were put up but stood for less than a week before being blown down by strong winds. For a time the high winds forced a move to the outbuildings adjoining a large house which served as the officers' quarters. More appropriate accommodation for East Fortune's machines arrived in the form of a canvas Bessonneau hangar. A report on the air station in January 1916 stated that:

> A permanent shed is very urgently needed, the large tent that the commanding officer hired and was capable of accommodating four machines has had to be taken down, it proved to be unsafe for housing machines during high winds, this only gives the station accommodation for two machines.

Mention is made of the Sopwith Land Tractor aircraft both of which were in a dismantled state. They were said to be of little use for patrols having little ability to climb rapidly. 'As East Fortune has at present five Avro Tractors, all new machines, it is suggested that the Sopwiths may be returned to store or deleted in order to make room for more useful machines'. Over the summer, construction commenced on permanent aircraft sheds. The aerodrome was officially commissioned on 23 August, 1916. Prior to then it remained a sub-station of Dundee Seaplane Station. New aircraft arrived first in the form of B.E.2s built by Beardmore followed by Bristol Scout Ds and American Curtiss JN4s in the autumn. Many of them were delivered by rail, the aerodrome having its own siding linked to the nearby mainline to Edinburgh.

Throughout 1916, East Fortune remained the sole RNAS aerodrome of any consequence in Scotland. It both trained pilots at its Naval Flying School as well as maintaining air patrols over the strategically important approaches of the Firth of Forth. For example, the station records reveal the following flights took place on 21 August:

> Flt Cdr Beauman flew B.E.2 No.8717 for fifteen minutes on an observation flight with Acting AM1 North as a passenger.
> Flt Lt Routledge flew B.E.2 No.8724 for sixteen minutes on a test flight.
> Flt Sub-Lt Horiman flew B.E.2 No.8718 on a thirty-nine minute flight with L.M.Carr on spotting practise.
> Flt Sub-Lt Horiman then flew B.E.2 No.8720 on a thirty minute flight with C.P.O. Jones as passenger, on gun firing practice.
> Flt Sub-Lt Traynor flew Avro 504C for thirty and sixty-three minute altitude test flights.
> Traynor then flew B.E.2 No.8720, with Sub. Lt Willson, RNVR on an observation flight lasting thirty-four minutes.
> Flt Sub-Lt Gray flew B.E.2 No.8720 on two bomb mirror practise flights, one of twenty-six minutes duration and another of forty-eight minutes.
> Flt Sub-Lt Gray then flew B.E.2 No.8718 on a fifty-three minute patrol flight to St Abbs Head with Flt Sub-Lt Carlin as a passenger.
> Flt Sub-Lt Kirkpatrick flew B.E.2 No.8720 for fifty-four minutes on a practise flight.

The B.E.2s suffered a number of accidents while flying from East Fortune. On 5 August 1916 B.E.2 No.8719 suffered engine failure and had to land near Drem, not far from East Fortune. It had to be transported back to East Fortune. Less lucky was B.E.2 No.8718 which made a forced landing at St Abbs Head later in the same month. Flt Sub-Lt Horniman and AM1 Gridley were on a cross-country flight to Newcastle. While attempting to take off after the forced landing they completely wrecked their aircraft. Another B.E.2 No.8724 was involved in a fatal accident the following year at Edinburgh. The accident which occurred

This Bristol Scout D, No.8991, was delivered to the Naval Fighter School at East Fortune in October 1916. It suffered a burst tyre on landing on 23 May 1917 causing it to overturn. Its pilot FSL A.B. Hill was hurt. The aircraft suffered a second landing accident a couple of months later. (Fleet Air Arm Museum – Bruce/Leslie Collection)

on 10 November 1917 claimed the lives of both its crew members, TFSL R.D. Clive and Plt Off. Reardon.

For the remainder of 1916, the regime of patrols and training flights continued. The latter included dropping dummy bombs and darts on a dummy Zeppelin. A Coastal Type airship assisted in target practise by towing a drogue which the pilots attempted to hit. Most of the practise flights were of a very short duration often only lasting between just ten to thirty minutes. One exception took place on 21 November when Flt Sub-Lt Minifie flew No.8820 on an altitude test flight. He was airborne for eighty-five minutes and managed to climb to a height of 12,000ft.

At the end of the year there were seventeen duty pilots at East Fortune. On 24 December, five machines were recorded as being available for 'defensive purposes'. These aeroplanes consisted of two B.E.2s and three Bristol Scouts. Three Avro 504s and four Curtiss JN4s carried out patrol duties assisted by two Coastal Type airships. Further machines at the station listed as being unavailable for service included two Bristol Scouts, 2 B.E.2s, an Avro 504 and a Curtiss JN4. The beginning of 1917 saw a new type arrive in the form of the Sopwith Pup. Over the next two years the Royal Navy converted more and more of their warships so they could carry and launch land-based aircraft such as this. East Fortune took on a new role as the depot for these machines when they were not deployed at sea. They would be serviced here and a training school was set up for pilots stationed with the Battle Cruiser squadron at Rosyth.

The report for flying on 22 February 1917 at East Fortune, which perhaps was a more active day than most, catalogues the following flights:

Flt Sub. Lt Brewerton flew aeroplanes Sopwith Scout N5400 and Curtiss J.N.4 No.8822 on practise flights lasting thirty-eight minutes and twenty-five minutes respectively.

Brewerton then took up B.E.2c No 8720 on a twenty-three minute bomb mirror practise flight. His day was rounded off with a fifteen minute flight in B.E.2c No.8407 using balloons for air to air gunnery practise.

This Beardmore WB III is undergoing ground tests at East Fortune Aerodrome. Its engine is running, but the aircraft is tethered on a wooden platform with a rope tied to its undercarriage. The Beardmore III was a derivative of the Sopwith Pup designed for operating on aircraft carriers and had folding wings. (© The Trustees of the National Museums of Scotland)

Flt Sub. Lt McLean took B.E.2 No.8724 for a fifty-two minute practise flight. McLean then had some gunnery practise in B.E.2c No.8407, also firing at some balloons. Finally McLean carried out a bomb mirror practise flight lasting twenty-eight minutes in B.E.2 No.8717.

Flt Sub. Lt Enstone flew Bristol Scout N5401, he twice took up B.E.2c No.8720 and then finally a new Sopwith Pup, No.9917. The practise flights were twenty, thirty, fifteen and eighteen minutes in duration.

Flt Sub. Lt Enstone also finished off his day with some gunnery practise in B.E.2c No.8407, again using balloons for target practise.

Flt Sub. Lt Hosking twice flew Sopwith Pup No.9918, and once flew B.E.2c No.8717. The flights lasted thirty, twenty and ten minutes in duration. Then he took up B.E.2c No.8407 for seven minutes and B.E.2c No.8720 for fifteen minutes for firing-in-the-air exercises.

Flt Sub. Lt Ingram made five practise flights. The first was in Sopwith Pup No.9917 lasting only four minutes, then B.E.2c No.8724 for twenty-five minutes, after which he flew another B.E.2, No.8720 for twenty-five minutes. This pilot then flew Sopwith Pup No.9918 on two practise flights, the first only ten minutes and the other of fifteen minutes in duration.

Flt Sub. Lt Ingram finished off by flying B.E.2c No.8717 on a bomb mirror practise flight of twenty minutes duration.

Flt Sub. Lt Mather flew Bristol Scout D N5400 for twenty-five minutes and B.E.2c for fifteen minutes. He then flew B.E.2c on a fourteen minute flight firing at balloons.

Flt Sub. Lt Mathesen (of HMS C Manxman which was equipped with land-based aircraft) flew Sopwith Pup No.9913 three times on practise flights. This aircraft was fitted with rocket armament.

Flt Sub. Lt Smart flew another rocket armed Sopwith Pup on three practise flights, timed as twelve, twenty-three and eight minutes in duration.

What is rather surprising is the fact that in the course of a single day how many different aircraft the pilots often flew. Also, it is interesting how many of the flights only lasted a few

This Avro 504K, H3002, two-seat training aircraft has broken its back in a landing accident at East Fortune. Large numbers of this type of machine were in service as trainers with the RAF when the war came to an end. The Avro 504K also served with Home Defence squadrons including 77 Squadron based in Scotland. (© The Trustees of the National Museums of Scotland)

minutes. Only one operational flight was made on the 22 February and that was by the Coastal Type airship, C.24 which in contrast was airborne for nearly 4½ hours.

Several aircraft were lost over the next few months in accidents. A Bristol Scout burst a tyre on landing on 23 May, damaging its wing and propeller. The pilot, Flt Sub-Lt A. Hill escaped uninjured. On 14 December 1917, B.E.2c of the Naval Fighter School crashed on take-off, badly damaging the machine. Unlike at some RFC training aerodromes, fatal accidents at East Fortune appear to have been remarkably rare.

At the beginning of 1918, there were over forty aircraft in active use here. They included B.E.2s, Bristol Scouts, Avro 504Cs and Sopwith Pups. New models arrived in the course of 1918, including Sopwith Camels and Avro 504Ks. 'F' squadron supplied aircraft for the carrier for HMS *Furious*, which now spent much time in the Firth of Forth. East Fortune witnessed a number of further major upheavals in the course of the year. On 1 April, the RFC and the RNAS were merged to form the Royal Air Force (RAF). Although East Fortune remained dedicated to supporting Royal Navy operations many of the flying units were renamed. In June, the Fleet and Torpedo Pilot Finishing School was formed but it was disbanded on 7 July and reformed as the Fleet Aerial Gunnery School and 1 Torpedo Training Squadron. Another major development was the arrival of large number of Sopwith Cuckoo torpedo bombers. During the early years of the war, the Royal Navy had longed for an aircraft that could deliver a torpedo to attack the enemy fleet at anchorage. After numerous and costly setbacks with aircraft that were not up to the task, the Sopwith Cuckoo was selected as the design most suited for this role. An order for 100 production aircraft was placed with Fairfield Shipbuilding & Engineering Company Ltd, of Glasgow, in August 1917. Admiral Sir David Beatty was anxious to exploit the capabilities of the aircraft and drew up an audacious plan to attack the ships of the German Navy in their harbours. The Operations Committee were less keen on his plan, deeming it impractical, which delayed the order for the machines. Also, Fairfield Shipbuilding's lack of experience in building aircraft resulted in their first machine not being delivered until September 1918. As an interim measure, a small order was placed with Blackburn who were competent aircraft manufacturers. The first Sopwith Cuckoo was delivered on 3 July to

This red painted Sopwith F.1 Camel, F1404 pictured outside the aircraft sheds at East Fortune is thought to be the personal aircraft of Capt. S. Kinkead, D.S.O., D.S.C. & Bar, D.F.C. and Bar. He is credited with over thirty victories while flying with the RNAS. (Courtesy of the Imperial War Museum, HU67917)

Spray rises from a choppy sea as the aptly named Sopwith T.1 Cuckoo, N6954, drops its torpedo in 1918. The outline of Tantallon Castle, near North Berwick, is visible in the background. (© The Trustees of the National Museums of Scotland)

An aerial view of the East Fortune Aerodrome, c.1918. The Edinburgh–London railway line is visible on the right side of the picture. There is a station along with sidings at the edge of the aerodrome. A further siding runs into the aerodrome itself between the aircraft sheds and the accommodation huts. (Fleet Air Arm Museum)

the Torpedo Aeroplane School at East Fortune for torpedo tests in the Firth of Forth. The prototype machine had in fact paid a visit here on 23 September 1917 in conditions of the utmost secrecy. More aircraft arrived over the next few weeks and the operational training of pilots commenced.

A temporary aerodrome was established on Belhaven Sands, immediately to the west of Dunbar. Sopwith Cuckoos landed on the broad beach, its surface considered dense enough for the operation of heavily laden machines. Work had commenced on this temporary landing ground in April 1918. Small huts were erected to provide space for workshops. Servicing of the aircraft was done in a canvas Bessonneau hangar. There was, however, no accommodation for the personnel who travelled the short distance from East Fortune every day. Royal Navy torpedo boat destroyers acted as targets for the pilots of the Sopwith Cuckoos. Numerous small boats of the Marine Section of the RAF were also on hand to recover the torpedoes and rescue any unfortunate pilot who misjudged his launch and crashed into sea. The optimum height for release was no higher than 20ft and no less than 10ft, otherwise the splash may have hit the aircraft.

Until March 1919, there were at least sixteen incidents in which the pilot had to be rescued from the water, although none of them were seriously hurt. Less fortunate was the pilot of a Bristol F2b, B8937 of 1 Torpedo Squadron which spun on take-off on 13 July, killing its pilot, Lt E.F. Kerruish. Although only a handful of these planes ever flew from East Fortune, a second machine, B8942, was lost on 31 October. It stalled in a climbing turn and side slipped to the ground, its smoke bombs exploding on impact. Lt J. Bissell and Lt E.W. Bragg both perished in the crash. On 14 August, 201 Training Squadron was formed at East Fortune, solely equipped with Sopwith Cuckoos. This was followed the next month by 185 Squadron, whose role was to operate these aircraft from the carrier HMS *Argus*. Admiral Beatty's ambition to attack the German High Seas Fleet was brought to a premature end by the signing of the

The crew of Bristol F.2b, E2619, pose beside their aircraft for a photograph at Leuchars in 1918. The aircraft probably is part of the Fleet School of Aerial Fighting and Gunnery's complement, which operated from this aerodrome around this time. (Fleet Air Arm Museum – Bruce/Leslie Collection)

Leuchars Aerodrome shortly after it was completed. It was one of several locations selected for Training Depot Stations, which entailed the building of a brand new aerodrome. From the air it is apparent how well-planned it is compared with some of the earlier aerodromes that evolved in a haphazard fashion. The aircraft sheds and the technical buildings have been built within a short distance of each other. In the end it did not house a Training Depot Squadron but the Grand Fleet School of Aerial Fighting and Gunnery, which moved here from East Fortune at the end of 1918. The aerodrome remained open throughout the interwar years and remained almost unchanged up until the Second World War. (Fleet Air Arm Museum – Bruce/ Leslie Collection)

A Sopwith 1½ Strutter, B2578, was one of several examples delivered to Turnhouse for use by the RAF in support of the Royal Navy in 1918. This type was initially produced as a fighter/reconnaissance aircraft, and was the first British machine already fitted with a synchronised front gun before it entered service. By 1918, most examples had been relegated to the training role but the Royal Navy still had a number of them in operational service on board the carrier HMS *Furious* and other warships. (Fleet Air Arm Museum – Bruce/Leslie Collection)

Armistice. By this time around ninety machines had been delivered, of which twenty-two were based at East Fortune. In the meantime, the Fleet Aerial Gunnery School was disbanded and reformed at the newly completed Leuchars Aerodrome in Fife as the Grand Fleet School of Aerial Fighting and Gunnery on 10 November 1918. The removal of this training unit at East Fortune was undertaken so it could expand its role as a base for torpedo bombers. The East Fortune Christmas card for that year did not exactly convey a message of peace and reconciliation to their fellow men. It featured a picture of a plane dropping a torpedo at the German battle fleet in the Firth of Forth. The wording read 'Would that we two had met. Our weapon. Our objective – But the Huns surrendered'. This expressed a feeling of frustration that the pilots never got the opportunity to drop their torpedoes in anger. Worse was to come, as 185 Squadron, with its Sopwith Cuckoos, only survived until April 1919 when it was disbanded and its aircraft departed for the South Coast of England. This brought East Fortune's role as a naval aerodrome to an end, although the airships continue to operate from here for another year. It is interesting to note that the Japanese went on to purchase a number of Sopwith Cuckoos. They used carrier-based torpedo aircraft to attack Pearl Harbour and in numerous other important battles in the Pacific during the Second World War!

With the expansion of shipborne aviation in the latter stages of the First World War, the RNAS found that East Fortune alone could not cope with the increased demands placed upon it. A fleet practise and aeroplane depot was established at Turnhouse, near Edinburgh in 1918. Its function was as a supply depot for aircraft, a pool of pilots and ratings for the Grand Fleet. This was conveniently situated only five miles to the south east of Rosyth Naval Base. New aircraft were delivered here for assembly and testing. Large numbers of Sopwith Camels arrived in the spring, most having been built by Beardmore, at Dalmuir. The other two main aircraft here were Sopwith Pups and Ships 1½ Strutters. According to one contemporary serviceman, the latter was the main type based here. Turnhouse by this time had a large complement of personnel, numbering around 1,500 officers and men.

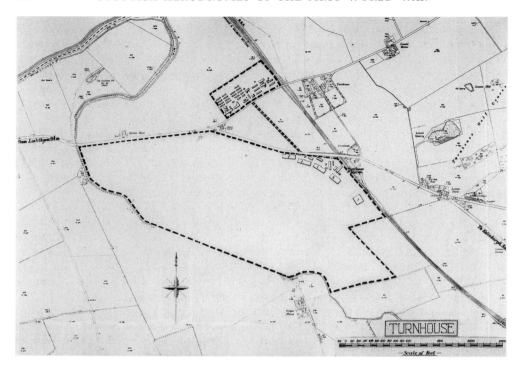

Turnhouse Aerodrome, 1918, near Edinburgh. The aircraft sheds are located in the north-east corner of the aerodrome, close to the railway line, which runs north to Forth Rail Bridge and Fife. The landing area was described as undulating and 'suffering from soft spots' in wet weather, making the surface treacherous. There were five aircraft sheds, several being devoted to repairs. To facilitate the maintenance of the machines, there was a smith's workshop and dope shop. The accommodation consisted of a complex of huts a short distance to the north of the aerodrome. Among them was one occupied by the YMCA. As the century progressed, the aerodrome expanded to become Edinburgh Airport. The area occupied by the First World War base is now devoted to air freight and general aviation. (The National Archives)

Women Members of the armed services on parade at Turnhouse Aerodrome, circa 1918. An early aircraft shed with side-opening doors is visible on the left side of the picture. (Via Eric Simpson)

Opposite: Turnhouse Aerodrome viewed from the south, 20 May 1918. Several types of aircraft sheds are visible. There are three 1915 pattern sheds with the side-opening doors and to their right is a 1916 aircraft shed. Scattered around the aerodrome are about twenty aircraft. Although all the buildings have long since gone, the site they now occupy forms part of Edinburgh Airport. The camp for the personnel is just visible in the top left corner. Some appear to be sleeping in tents which have been put up beside the aircraft sheds. (Fleet Air Arm Museum)

In the summer of 1918, Maj. Geoffrey Moore DSC assumed command of the station. He had previous experience of shipborne aviation as he had served on board the aircraft carrier HMS *Furious*. This ship had been in the vanguard of the attack on the large Zeppelin base at Tondern; the first successful operation of this type in history. The pilots prepared for this mission at Turnhouse Aerodrome where they practised dive bombing with their Sopwith Camels. A target marked out in the shape of an airship shed received the attention of dummy bombs while live ones were dropped on targets in the Firth of Forth.

In addition to the Sopwith Camels operating on HMS *Furious*, there were numerous Royal Navy warships with platforms on their gun turrets from which to launch aircraft. Two aircraft were carried on some of the larger vessels. When not at sea, they underwent servicing and repair at Turnhouse. After returning ashore the aircraft often required extensive work after being exposed to the elements on top of the deck of the warship.

The average lifespan of the Camels and Pups made of wood and fabric was often only three or four months. Maj. Moore, the Station Commander, had no less than three Sopwith Camels for his personnel use. Each one was painted in a striking colour scheme. The first was painted like a Japanese sun, scarlet and white, and the second with a dark blue body with white spots, around four inches in diameter. The third Camel resembled a wasp, with black and yellow vertical stripes on the fuselage and white wings with sepia veins on the top surfaces of the main planes. The insect's eyes and antennae were painted on the engine cowling!

The first machine, painted like a Japanese sun, also had a special harness for aerobatics along with numerous other customised fittings. One day Maj. Moore lent this aircraft, his favourite mount, to a young pilot for gunnery practise, as those in the Fleet Practise Flight were all unserviceable. While diving down and firing at a target, the pilot apparently did not realise how close he was coming to the ground. At the last minute he attempted to full up but the stress put on the Camel tore off its wings. The wreckage plunged to the ground killing its unfortunate occupant. It landed immediately in front of the Fleet Practise Hangar, hitting another Camel whose pilot was sitting in it at the time. He fortunately survived, suffering only from shock.

Sopwith 2F.1 Camels of the Test Flight ARS Turnhouse. Although the picture was taken in 1919, such scenes would have been familiar here in the closing years of the war with numerous examples of this type of aircraft being serviced and flown from the aerodrome. The Camel, N7149, in the foreground bearing the name Swillington is a presentation aircraft and was built by the Arrol-Johnston factory at Dumfries. (Fleet Air Arm Museum – Bruce/Leslie Collection)

One Sunday afternoon Maj. Moore witnessed a Sopwith 1½ Strutter spin into a corn-field:

> The pilot was experienced and in the observer's seat was a well-known and very clever boffin. Neither Fowler nor I had ever seen such a mess-up before, and we had both seen plenty.

Major Moore stated in his book, *Early Bird*, that 'the station seemed to be rather accident prone'. On 4 September, another Sopwith 1½ Strutter, No.9894, collided with Sopwith Pup B8012 over the Firth of Forth, perhaps an indication of the intense aerial activity now occurring in this area. 2nd-Lt R.Payne and Ft Sgt A.Wright on board the first machine, and 2nd-Lt H. Sutherland in the second, were all killed. Another fatal accident occurred on 24 July 1918 when Sopwith Camel C6735 suffered engine failure and spun in, killing its pilot Lt J.A. Rossington–Barnett. Despite being the station commander, Maj. Moore frequently flew and indulged in stunt flying. Moore had a narrow escape, when attempting to loop the centre span of the Forth Rail Bridge in his Camel painted with the Japanese sun scheme. A hazard which Maj. Moore had not taken into account were vertical lines of wire hanging done from the structure supporting anti-submarine nets. Having just caught sight of them at the last minute he managed to steer his aircraft through a gap. The B.E.2, which was slow flying and stalled very gently, unlike the Sopwith Camel, was used to perform another type of stunt by the Turnhouse pilots. They would fly their machines over the Fife countryside approaching the Binn Hill from the north, which towers over the town of Burntisland on the shores of the Firth of Forth. On approaching the high, near-vertical cliffs on its southern side they would stall their machines and float down the rock face only pulling out of the dive as they hurtled towards its base.

Photography became an important element in the First World War, particularly in the role of aerial reconnaissance. Many aerodromes had there own photographic unit and Turnhouse

This de Havilland D.H.9A, E8515, with wing tip floats and hydrovanes served at Turnhouse from 24 October 1918 to December 1918. (Fleet Air Arm Museum – Bruce/Leslie Collection)

was no exception. Here the photographers' duties included recording the new ships of the Grand Fleet as they sailed into the Firth of Forth. Maj. Moore often flew the photographers himself. Torpedo trials and other experiments including aircraft being launched from ships were also recorded. A. MacLean, who was employed in this capacity at Turnhouse, recalled that most photographs were unfortunately thrown out after a period of five or six months. This was apparently standard practise not only at Turnhouse, but at most other aerodromes. Perhaps the most important assignment was to photograph the German High Seas Fleet as it sailed up the Firth of Forth to surrender on 21 November 1918. On this occasion, Capt. Melvin Rattray piloted Sopwith Ship Strutter B4044 with Lt Wilfred Adams acting as the photographer. They returned with a total of ninety-six pictures.

When not carrying out stunt flying Maj. Moore made social calls with his aeroplanes. He landed a B.E.2c in the grounds of Alloa House when he was invited to participate in a grouse shoot with Lady Mar. On other days, after performing stunt flying with his colleagues, they would climb to 5,000ft, then invert their Sopwith Camels and glide over to Donibristle Aerodrome on the opposite shore of the Firth of Forth upside down. The descend was made in spinning nose dives with the aircraft still in formation, until they touched down at this newly opened station. After a short stopover for some refreshments, they then flew their Camels back to Turnhouse.

Donibristle Aerodrome had been constructed to cater for the expansion of naval flying in the Firth of Forth in the latter stages of the First World War. It was situated on the shore of the Firth of Forth and a short distance to the east of Rosyth Naval Base. Warships anchored a short distance offshore from the base. The aerodrome was built on a former landing ground used by 77 Home Defence Squadron. It was located in the grounds of Donibristle House whose owner, the Earl of Moray, was initially reluctant to have aircraft landing on his estate. However, the commanding officer of the unit was a personal friend of the Earl, and managed to appeal to his patriotic instincts. The ground required for the landing strip was adjacent to the main entrance to the park and carriage drive of Donibristle House. Preparations for the site entailed the removal of three plantations. Large trees adjacent to the main road were spared and the guard hut and other buildings were so placed so that they could not be seen from the carriage drive. This night

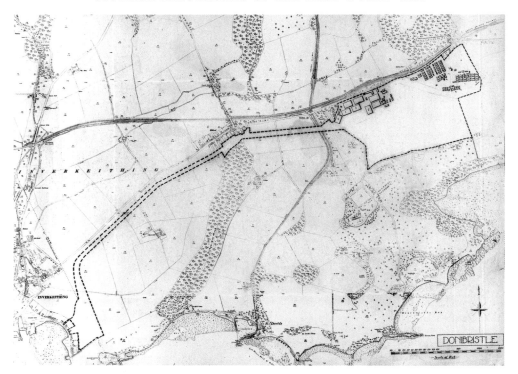

Donibristle Aerodrome, 1918, was located on the edge of the Firth of Forth and close to Rosyth Naval Base. It was built as a shore base for aircraft deployed on aircraft carriers and Royal Navy ships. The maximum dimensions of the station was 1,100 yards by 600 yards. It covered 130 acres of which thirty-five were taken up by the station buildings. There were four aeroplane sheds each 200ft by 100ft, plus an erecting shed with the same dimensions. There was also a large general workshop 240ft by 138ft plus a smiths' and dope shop. Armaments for the aircraft were stored in a bomb store and magazine. Many of these buildings were still under construction when the war ended. The station not only had the task of maintaining and repairing landplanes used by the Royal Navy, but its seaplanes as well. A branch line ran the short distance west to Inverkeithing Bay, where the machines were hauled out the water and loaded on to the back of railway wagons to be transported to the aircraft sheds at Donibristle. The aerodrome also had a siding off the main Edinburgh to Dundee railway line which ran along its northern perimeter. The personnel were housed in huts and brick built buildings in the north-east corner of the base. Unlike most other Scottish First World War Aerodromes, Donibristle did not close after the end of the conflict, but remained in use until the end of the 1950s. In the succeeding years most traces of it have been lost to a major housing development which was built on the site and the area now goes under the name of Dalgety Bay. (The National Archives)

landing ground for 77 Home Defence Squadron's planes based at Turnhouse was never once used in the role it was intended. The RNAS took over the site on 17 September 1917, although the effective change of ownership appears to have taken place some weeks earlier.

A letter dated 20 November 1917 from the Admiralty to the Commander of the Grand Fleet, Admiral Beatty gives an insight into the rapid expansion of Donibristle Naval Air Station. It discloses that due to the decision to equip all light and battle cruisers with aircraft would require the support of extensive shore based facilities. Accommodation for all shipborne aircraft was urgently required, for if the machines were left when the vessels were in port they would experience unnecessary exposure to the elements. It was suggested that mechanics and pilots could obtain practise in their skills at Donibristle while their ship was at anchorage.

No.1 Aircraft Shed (hangar) at Donbristle Aerodrome, December 1918. It uses the same design employed for Admiralty seaplane sheds and was one of very few aerodromes in Scotland to have these distinctive rectangular hangars during the First World War. In the original picture there are a number of aircraft housed inside it, probably Sopwith Camels, including one with a checker board paint scheme. (Via Eric Simpson)

To meet these operational demands the Admiralty gave approval for the erection of one aircraft shed, 200ft by 100ft, plus the accommodation for ten officers 115 men. It was envisaged that this would be insufficient to meet all needs so it was proposed that an additional shed be constructed along with an engine workshop. Accommodation would also be further increased to cater for a complement of fifty officers and 400 men. Two motor lighters were also acquired to transfer aircraft from Donibristle Aerodrome to the ships in the Firth of Forth.

In November 1917 Admiral Beatty requested that yet another aircraft shed, 200ft by 100ft, be erected. The reasoning behind this was that by spring 1918 some fifty aircraft were to be carried on light cruisers and battle cruisers, of which about thirty would not be housed in hangars. If they were not kept ashore they would require frequent overhaul and replacement. By the summer of the same year it was intended that the Grand Fleet would be putting to sea with over 100 aircraft.

On December 1917 the Admiralty wrote to the War Office, who still owned some of the land at Donibristle, requesting for permission to build a railway line and to extend the pier in connection with the launching of seaplanes. It was originally proposed that the railway would be built to Braefoot Point at the eastern end of Dalgety Bay. East Ness Pier, at the mouth of the Inner Bay at Inverkeithing, however, became the terminus of the line which had a length of about two miles. The initial accommodation for personnel at Donibristle consisted of two portable Armstrong canvas huts, one range of corrugated buildings, a meat store, guard hut, dry store and portable latrine. Although most of the aircraft at Donibristle only stayed a brief time before putting to sea again, the station, like almost every other aerodrome in Scotland, had a small number of B.E.2es plus some Sopwith Camels on strength at the beginning of 1918.

By April 1918 the anti-submarine defences in the Firth of Forth were considered to be effective and the Grand Fleet transferred its base to Rosyth. There was now a constant coming

While most new aircraft were ferried by air from the manufacturers aerodromes to their new bases, some were delivered by road and rail. This Sopwith Camel, N6779, seen on the back of a lorry, was delivered to Turnhouse in April 1918, although the picture may depict it on a local journey between aerodromes. The following month the aircraft was deployed on HMS *Calliope*. (Fleet Air Arm Museum – Bruce/Leslie Collection)

Sopwith Camel N6779 on a launch platform on HMS *Calliope* while at Rosyth. Later, platforms were placed on warships' large gun turrets so the aircraft could be pointed into the wind without the need for the ship to change course. This Camel, when not on board ship, spent time at Turnhouse and Donibristle aerodromes. The photograph was probably taken in spring 1918, when this machine is recorded as operating from HMS *Calliope*. (Fleet Air Arm Museum – Bruce/Leslie Collection)

and going of Sopwith Camels, Strutters and Pups between their parent ships and Donibristle. A couple of examples are listed below, with such movements being repeated many times over:

> Sopwith 2F.1 Camel N6604, delivered to Donibristle,week ending (w/e) 3 November 1917: to HMS *Nairana* w/e 8 November 1917: to Rosyth w/e 23 November 1917: to Donibristle w/e 7 December 1917: to Rosyth w/e 13 December 1917: to HMS *Nairana* w/e 14 December 1917: to HMS *Lion* 19 December 1917: to Rosyth w/e 20 December 1917: to Donibristle w/e 28 December 1917: to Rosyth by 11 January 1918: to HMS *Pegasus* w/e 11 January 1918: Donibristle to Rosyth 8 February 1918: to Donibristle w/e 16 March 1918: to Rosyth w/e 21 March 1918: to HMS *Princess Royal* by 25 April 1918: to HMS *Nairana* w/e 9 May 1918: to HMS *Glorious* w/e May 1918: For deletion at Rosyth by 16 May, 1918 – crashed HMS *Nairana*, engine to Donibristle by 23 May 1918.

> Sopwith Pup N6446, Arrived at East Fortune by rail 8 September 1917: to Donibristle 15 September 1917: to Rosyth 16 September 1917: to Donibristle w/e 15 November 1917: Rosyth w/e 13 December 1917: to HMS *Pegasus* w/e 14 December 1917: Rosyth to Donibristle w/e 14 December 1917: to HMAS *Australia* w/e 20 December 1917: to HMS *Pegasus* January 1918: to HMS *Repulse* 3 January 1918: to Donibristle w/e 18 January 1918: to Rosyth w/e 18 January 1918: to HMS *Pegasus* 13 January 1918: to Donibristle by February 1918: to Turnhouse w/e 21 February to 1 March 1918: Rosyth to HMS *Furious* w/e 4 April 1918: to Rosyth w/e 5 May 1918: to HMS *Furious* w/e 11 May 1918: to Rosyth w/e 18 May 1918: deleted 20 June, 1918. (Taken from *Royal Navy Aircraft Serials & Units 1911-1919* by Ray Sturtivant and Gordon Page)

These large earthworks at Donibristle Aerodrome have been raised to form firing butts for testing aircraft armaments. This was taken in December 1918. (Via Eric Simpson)

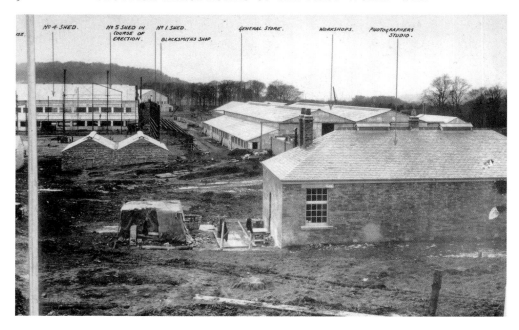

A general view of Donibristle Aerodrome taken in December, 1918. It shows an extensive complex of hangars and workshops including a blacksmiths' and photographers' studio. They appear to be in the final stages of construction. (Via Eric Simpson)

During the last year of the War Donibristle played host to aircraft from numerous other ships including HMS *Indomitable*, HMS *Renown*, HMS *Royalist*, HMS *Lion*, and the world's first true aircraft carrier, HMS *Argus*. There were very few fatal accidents at this aerodrome but one exception took place when a Sopwith Camel from HMS *Galatea* struck a treetop when coming into land. Its pilot Flt Sub-Lt M. Trendall died from his injuries the following day, 19 May 1918.

The diaries of Capt. Melvin H. Rattray give some indication of aerial activity over the Firth of Forth at this time. His first flight from a warship was made on 26 September 1917 when he took off from HMS *Nairana* in a Sopwith Pup and subsequently landed at Donibristle. Two months later he landed here again after taking off from the gun turret of the battle cruiser HMS *Repulse*. In May 1918, Capt. Rattray flew a Sopwith 1½ Strutter from the deck of the aircraft carrier HMS *Furious* which was at anchor in the Firth of Forth. Later in the same month, accompanied with 2nd-Lt Wilkens as the observer, he departed from Donibristle Aerodrome on a reconnaissance flight to Heligoland Bight off the coast of Germany. Not having the range to return home, the plane was ditched in the North Sea which was successfully recovered by the destroyer HMS *Verulam* along with its pilot and observer.

Capt. Rattray's diary also records some of the other numerous activities he participated in while attached to the Grand Fleet in the Firth of Forth. They included searching for lost or crashed aircraft, mock combat with other pilots, formation and cross country flights, testing, ferrying, wireless telegraphy, carrying bombs to and from various naval stations, spotting for the 2nd and 3rd Divisions and anti-aircraft practise with HMS *Furious*. Low-level flying referred to as daisy cutting was also undertaken along with the unofficial activity of attempting to roll the aircraft's undercarriage wheels on the roofs of aircraft sheds.

A considerable amount of construction work was in progress at Donibristle Aerodrome when the war came to an end. In the immediate post-war years, large numbers of aircraft and engines were scrapped here. It also took over the work previously done at Rosyth. Two seaplane sheds had been erected on the quays in the docks, next to the River Forth. By 1918,

This Beardmore WBIII, N6102, a naval version of the Sopwith Pup, was delivered to Rosyth by rail on 12 December 1917. It then moved to Turnhouse, but was engine-less by the end of March 1918. The airframe remained here until early the following year. (Fleet Air Arm Museum – Bruce/Leslie Collection)

they were handling far more landplanes than seaplanes. Like Turnhouse, it too assembled Sopwith Pups and Camels delivered from their manufacturers. They included machines manufactured by Beardmore which arrived by rail. Other aircraft which had undergone maintenance at Turnhouse and East Fortune were sometimes transported here by lorry. Despite the large number of movements between Turnhouse, Rosyth and Donibristle, there was no official landing ground at the naval base. It appears that aircraft improvised by using the playing fields at Rosyth when the need arose. For example, Sopwith 2F.1 Camel N6639, crashed while attempting to take off in the snow from the football ground during January 1918. A contemporary newspaper article published in June 1919 reported that:

> The seaplane shed which was a hive of great activity during the latter stages of the war, has now been vacated by the airmen. The building, a huge structure of timber and corrugated iron standing at the waterside near the historic Rosyth Castle will be used as a victualling store. The airmen with their goods and chattels have removed to the aerodrome at Donibristle.

In the First World War all the major naval aerodromes were located in the vicinity of the Firth of Forth. Further north there was a small landing ground at Delny House, to the north of Invergordon. It was used by aircraft flying off Royal Naval warships anchored in the Cromarty Firth. This location was still in use in June 1920, when D.H.9a undertook wireless and range finding experiments with HMS *Barham* and HMS *Warspite* on moving targets. No trace of this little known aerodrome remains. Rather surprisingly there was again only a minor aerodrome for the Grand Fleet in the Orkney Islands. It was called Smoogroo, and located on the northern shore of Scapa Flow. With the experimentation of flying land-based aircraft from ships being initially conducted in these northern waters, there was a need for a location where the pilots could touch down on solid ground. There were no landing decks for them to return to their vessel. Hence Smoogroo began to be used for this purpose in 1917, although it had no facilities of any sort initially. It was designated as a fleet practice station.

Sopwith Ships Pup, N6453, built by Beardmore & Co. Ltd, seen at Smoogroo Aerodrome in the Orkney Islands. This aerodrome was hastily established for pilots practicing take-offs from the carrier HMS *Furious* while at anchor in Scapa Flow. Initially, they could not land back on the ship, so the aircraft had to put down on dry land. Sqn Cdr Dunning, however, made the first successful landing on HMS *Furious* forward deck while flying Pup N6453. (Fleet Air Arm Museum)

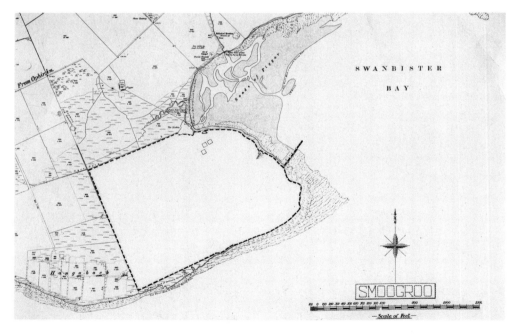

Smoogroo Aerodrome, 1918, was situated on the northern shore of Scapa Flow on the Orkney mainland. This small aerodrome was used as a shore base for aircraft that were deployed on aircraft carriers and other warships. There were precious few facilities here, with shelter for the aircraft being provided by three canvas Bessonneaux hangars located in the north-east corner. Repairs had to be carried out at Scapa Flow Seaplane base some eight miles to the east. There was a jetty next to the aerodrome and aircraft could be transferred there by sea. A contemporary account gives an unenthusiastic description of the site: 'The aerodrome is small and the surface is very rough and uneven in places. Full advantage, however, can be taken of the total surface available for landing as the approaches are good'. All traces of this long disused aerodrome have disappeared. (The National Archives)

Later, three Bessonneaux tents were put up on the edge of the landing ground. There were also a pier from which the aircraft were ferried back out to their ships anchored in Scapa Flow. If repairs were required the machines would be taken to Houton Bay or Scapa Flow seaplane bases. Sopwith Camels, Pups and Strutters were the main types to use Smoogroo Aerodrome. Towards the end of the war construction was started on a new aerodrome at Swanbister immediately to the north of it. Even after the Armistice, work continued but it was never completed. Smoogroo Aerodrome closed for good shortly after the end of the war. For several years after the end of hostilities, civilian aircraft were banned from flying over nearly all of the Orkney Islands at altitudes of less than 6,000ft. With large numbers of ships being sunk by submarines within sight of the British coast in 1918, plans were drawn up to use large numbers of landplanes for maritime patrol work. Up until then this role had mainly been the preserve of seaplanes and non-rigid airships. At the end of January 1918 it was requested that additional aircraft be made available to patrol the waters between Newcastle-upon-Tyne and Sunderland, where losses of ships were particularly high. De Havilland D.H.6 were made available for this task. The Air Ministry then proceeded to offer the Admiralty enough aircraft to form a further thirty-two flights for anti-submarine patrol work. Of these, twenty-seven were established at various coastal aerodromes and the remaining five flights were operated by the US Naval Air Service for patrols off the Irish Coast. The anti-submarine D.H.6 were often flown in adverse weather conditions and many hardships were suffered by the airmen

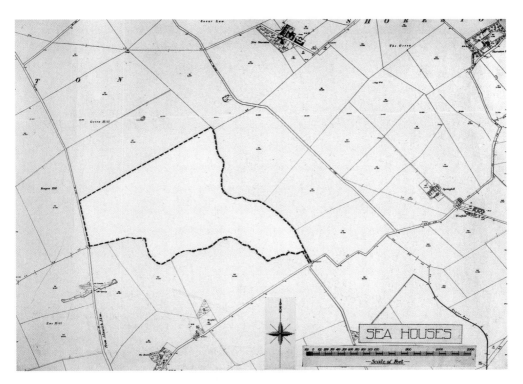

Seahouses Aerodrome, 1918, lay a short distance inland from the village of Seahouses and twelve miles north of Alnwick, Northumberland. This small aerodrome extended across ninety-two acres and had the dimensions of 800 yards by 550 yards. The D.H.6 aircraft based here were housed in canvas Bessonneaux hangars. Around 130 personnel manned the aerodrome in the autumn of 1918, and living in Armstrong houses or billeted in the village of Seahouses. The site is now farmland. (The National Archives)

In April 1918, the RAF inherited from the RNAS their de Havilland D.H.6 used for anti-submarine patrols around the British coast. They were basically trainers that had been converted to light bomb carrying anti-submarine patrol aircraft. The example in this photograph, C7794, was flown by 244 Squadron and based at Luce Bay. (Fleet Air Arm Museum – Bruce/Leslie Collection)

A de Havilland D.H.6, C7863, used for anti-submarine patrols by 244 Squadron during 1918. This example was based at Bangor, Ireland, and was photographed on a visit to Luce Bay. It was powered by a 90hp Curtiss OX-5 engine. (Fleet Air Arm Museum – Bruce/Leslie Collection)

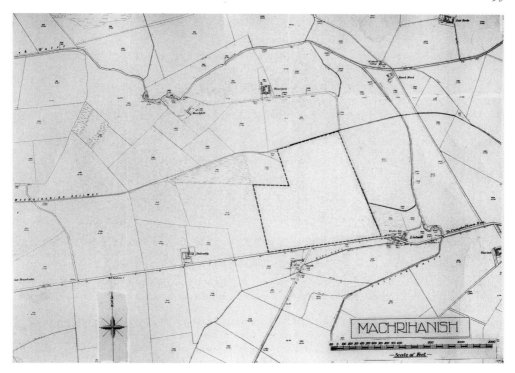

Machrihanish Aerodrome and Airship Sub-Station, 1918, located two miles to the west to Campbeltown on the Kintyre Peninsula. This base provided a bolt hole for Luce Bay airships should adverse weather conditions prevent them returning there. There are no buildings shown on the site, which was 600 yards by 550 yards in size and covered some sixty-five acres. 'Surface moderate, fairly level with slight slope towards the east. General surroundings, open, slightly undulating country with large fields. There is marshy country towards the north'. In the closing stages of the war, D.H.6 aircraft were based at Machrihanish Aerodrome to carry out anti-submarine patrol flights. They were housed in canvas Bessonneaux hangars with Armstrong huts providing the accommodation for the personnel. The Campbeltown to Machrihanish light railway ran along the northern edge of the base. This long closed railway only had two stations, one at either end of the line. As the aerodrome sat equidistant between the two locations, this mode of transport was not much use. It is perhaps one reason why there were no less than twelve motorcycles assigned here with four sidecars. There was also a car and eleven tenders. Although flying ceased here at the end of the war, a large modern airfield now exists a short distance to the north-west. (National Archives).

that flew in them. The aircraft was far from ideal for this role and was known by a number of uncomplimentary nicknames including 'Clutching Hand' or due to its slab-sided appearance the 'Orange Box'. Although it was designed to carry a crew of two, it often only carried the pilot as it could not carry a full load of bombs as well as the observer.

Seahouses Aerodrome in Northumberland acted as the headquarters for 256 Squadron's D.H.6 operations in this area. There were detachments at New Haggerston Aerodrome, a short distance to the south of Berwick-Upon-Tweed and close to the Great North road (A1). On the opposite side of the Border there were a small number of D.H.6 aircraft based at a small aerodrome close to the village of Cairncross in Berwickshire. The aerodrome was 1,000 yards by 750 yards in size and occupied 115 acres.

On the opposite side of the country, 524/529 Flights of 258 Squadron operated alongside the airships of Luce Bay. There were eight examples of the D.H.6 here in August 1918 flying what were sometimes sarcastically referred to as 'scarecrow patrols' due to their questionable effectiveness. On 30 September Sea Scout airships SSZ No.11 and SSZ No.12 carried out an integrated patrol with four aircraft. Further up the coast, the approaches to the Firth of Clyde were protected by the D.H.6s of 272 Squadron. Machrihanish Aerodrome on the tip of the Kintyre Peninsular acted as their base. Conditions here were primitive with both aircraft and personnel housed in tents and other temporary accommodation. At least two of its aircraft had to make forced landings in the sea, including C2111 which was rescued from a watery fate along with its pilot by SS *Agate*.

Most of the units operating the D.H.6 on anti-submarine patrols were rapidly disbanded by the end of 1918. Even while the conflict was raging they had a low priority and were often short of aircraft and personnel.

CHAPTER FIVE

AIR DEFENCE AERODROMES

While several devastating wars had been fought on continental Europe in the eighteenth and nineteenth centuries, Britain had escaped the ravages of conflict thanks to her geography. Due to the invention of flying machines, it was recognised in some quarters of government that the country may not remain invulnerable to an enemy onslaught for much longer. At the beginning of the twentieth century, science fiction writers such as H.G. Wells in his book *War in the Air* predicted the Zeppelins' potential as a war machine. There were ominous predictions that the government may have to be evacuated from London if war broke out.

Hence it came as rather a surprise when shortly after the outbreak of the First World War the Germans launched a seaborne attack on the towns of North-East England. Over 100 people were killed when three enemy warships bombarded Hartlepool on 16 December 1914. While there had been some doubt about who had domination of the air, it was assumed that the Royal Navy had control of the seas. The following January it was the turn of the Zeppelin to strike fear into the heart of British civilians. Despite flying at speeds of around 50mph and measuring several hundred feet long, they roamed the skies at will in the early stages of the war. While the Royal Navy could challenge attacks on the British coast with its warships, there was little the RFC could do initially to confront the airship. The early aircraft only carried rifles or other personal weapons of the pilot. Gen. Henderson, who commanded the RFC in the field, was asked by his airmen if it were their duty to ram the Zeppelin and destroy it. When he replied that it should only be attacked with the weapons at their disposal, some of the pilots were disappointed, even though it would almost certainly mean death for them. No matter how eager the pilots were to destroy such enemy craft, their attempts would have been handicapped by the performance of their aircraft. The Zeppelins could cruise at altitudes of around 10,000ft, which was out of reach of most aircraft in the RFC. Even if they were caught flying at much lower heights by allied aircraft, they could escape by dropping their ballast and out climbing their attacker. Over the next two years all of this would change as the performance of aircraft was improved immensely. They were also armed with munitions designed to inflict maximum damage on a hull filled with hydrogen gas.

At the outbreak of the First World War there were no squadrons or aerodromes dedicated to the air defence of the country. Over the next couple of years, the RNAS established a chain of aerodromes along the coast of Britain and carried out patrols over the sea to protect both the sea lanes and the airspace. There were constant arguments between the War Office, the Army and Royal Navy as to who should be responsible for providing aircraft to protect Britain's airspace from enemy air raids. In Scotland, this task fell squarely on the shoulders of the RNAS as there were no operational RFC squadrons north of the border in the early stages of the war. In a discussion held in the autumn of 1913, there was particular concern that the Crombie magazine on the River Forth and the oil storage tanks at Invergordon may be high on the list of potential enemy targets. It was concluded that:

The Navy might do the scouting work and the army the protecting of vulnerable spots for which large numbers of machines would be required to render attacks improbable. For example, it is anticipated that some 20 machines on the Forth to protect the Crombie magazine and the oil tanks.

The War Office also drew up another plan to form six squadrons with 162 aircraft to protect the skies over Britain. It was intended to base two squadrons in Scotland. Nothing came of these two ambitious plans and, up until 1916, only a handful of RNAS aircraft were available to protect the Firth of Forth.

The nearest RNAS base of any consequence was, in fact, Dundee Seaplane Station. To enhance their ability to patrol the mouth of the Firth of Forth and Tay, they received five land-based aircraft in May 1915. Seaplanes took a long time to respond to any alarm as they had to be launched into the water, and were only able to take off if the water was not too rough. As there was no suitable landing ground in the vicinity of Dundee Seaplane Station, the newly delivered machines operated from Montrose Broomfield Aerodrome. They included:

…one dear old Bristol 'Balloon', brand-new, and a beauty, a Henri Farman pusher, an 80hp Gnome, very delicate machine, very nice machine to fly. And three of the well-known Sopwiths, they called them Spinning Jennys because they were a little bit tricky to handle on the ground. But they were very, very efficient 'planes. Exceedingly good.

They were not, however, the first aircraft to use Montrose Aerodrome since the departure of No.2 Squadron at the beginning on the war. In early 1915, there were two aircraft including a Bristol Scout, flown by the RNAS for use with the Army as target spotters on the Barry Range at Buddon Ness.

Capt. Grahame Donald was appointed commander of this small detachment. Despite having only five aircraft, he was the only pilot there and took turns in flying each one of them! There was a great shortage of pilots in the summer 1915. Capt. Grahame Donald was on permanent call to respond to any submarine or Zeppelin sighting.

The trouble about the Zeppelin alarm, it usually came during the night because Zeppelins only came over in the hours of darkness. It was rather absurd but to please everybody you had to put a show of going out to chase Zeppelins. I mean you'd about as much chance in those days when there was no radar, no anything, no night landing facilities – you'd as much chance of spotting a Zeppelin in the dark as going round catching a black cat in the Albert Hall in the dark. But the fact remains that you could take off hoping the sun would rise before you ran out of petrol because it was just too bad if you'd to make a landing. We didn't have any night landing facilities. But I was very lucky, the few times I had to go out at night the dawn had broken so you were able to see what you were landing on – otherwise it would've been a bit awkward.

Capt. Donald also flew routine patrols 'mostly covering the area off the Firth of Tay and the Firth of Forth because the battle cruisers were using the Firth of Forth and there was an awful lot of merchant shipping going into the Firth of Tay'.
Some days the flights extended as far north as Stonehaven, and on others as far south as St Abbs. The aircrafts' sole armament was a rifle with explosive ammunition!

In the summer of 1915, the RFC had plans to use Montrose Broomfield Aerodrome for flying training and the RNAS detachment was required to move out. The Royal Navy were not altogether unhappy with having to relocate as an extract from A.C. Rosyth shows:

Naval Air Station-Montrose. This station which is equipped with five aeroplanes, may be well suited for training or other military purposes, but is in my opinion, too far distant to co-operate successfully with the defences of the Forth for attacking enemy aircraft which if operating off the Scottish Coast would probably make Rosyth and Edinburgh the object of their attack. The most suitable position for our aeroplanes to operate from, both from a geographical and tactical point of view is in the neighbourhood of North Berwick.

On 12 September, Spinning Jennys No.1059, No.1067 and No.1068 departed from Montrose for the new aerodrome at East Fortune, close to the Firth of Forth. None completed their journey that day. One suffered engine failure and damaged its undercarriage on landing. Another descended and landed at Dundee because of bad weather and the third aircraft returned to Montrose for the same reason. The weather finally improved two days later. While attempting to take off from Dundee, Spinning Jenny No.1067 collided with a tree and was completely wrecked. Of the original three aircraft, only No.1068 completed its journey. Henry Farman Pusher No.1454, also arrived at East Fortune on the 14 September, 1915 having departed earlier the same day from Montrose. It had to land briefly en route at Kirkcaldy owing to fog.

Further aircraft were delivered to East Fortune to enhance its ability to protect the Scottish east coast. Seaplanes were still called on to assist in the role of air defence despite their sluggish performance. In early 1916 Zeppelin raids were no longer confined to southern England. On the evening of 2 April, a message was received at Dundee Seaplane Station that four Zeppelins were crossing the North Sea. At 7.15 p.m. they were reported to be eighty-seven miles east of Alnmouth in Northumberland. Three seaplanes were armed with Ranken darts, and rifles which fired both explosive and ordinary .303 ammunition. It was pointed out to the Extended Defence Officer that these machines were not considered suitable for attacking Zeppelins at night, due to their poor climbing powers. Despite this, a message came through from the Extended Defence Officer at 9.15 p.m. saying 'send one machine up'. It was impossible to launch it for another hour due to the fact that is was low tide and there was no water at the end of the slipway. A short time later a second seaplane followed. A third aircraft was in the process of being launched when the order came from the Extended Defence Officer to cancel the order. It is thought that neither of the first two aircraft actually took off from the water. Later, the Commanding Officer wrote to the Admiralty in Whitehall, London:

With reference to the use of this type of machine for a Zeppelin attack at night, it is pointed out that they are most unsuitable on account of the extremely bad rate of climbing when loaded for a flight as on this occasion and also the absolute invisibility of any object directly ahead.

The night was clear overhead but with a medium ground mist and it was not possible on the water to distinguish any object more than a quarter of a mile ahead. Both machines, once they got away from the slipway were quite invisible and there was no means of telling whether they had got off the water or not. Wireless operators were not carried as it was considered that in the event of the machines finding a Zeppelin, good marksmen would have been more use.

The sighting of a Zeppelin at a height of 5,000ft on a pitch dark night, from the ground when the observer has nothing else to think about, is not an easy thing to do, and to try and achieve the same object from a machine, the view ahead of which is extremely bad, is almost impossibility.

It is submitted that if this station is regarded as an anti-Zeppelin station, it is considered essential that a different type of machine be allocated, more especially as these attacks will probably always take place during the night, observing that:

1.   The area of patrol is sixty to seventy miles away from the Base.
2.   Visibility directly ahead and on either side and vertically downwards and upwards, is essential.

German Naval Zeppelin L.14 coming into land. Its crew of eighteen men were carried in the two cars which are visible underneath its hull. The airship was over 530ft long and could fly at 60mph. Its range was 2,672 miles on the night of 2 April 1916 this Zeppelin in the company of L.22 bombed Edinburgh. It returned a month later to attack Rosyth naval base but got lost and dropped its bombs harmlessly near Arbroath. (Archiv Der Luftschiffbau Zeppelin Gmbh, Friedrichshaven)

Many of the problems mentioned also applied to land planes although their performance was superior to those of seaplanes. The same night an Avro 504C Scout, No.8589, took off from East Fortune in an attempt to intercept the same enemy Zeppelins whose intended target was Rosyth Naval Base and the Forth Railway Bridge. The RNAS aircraft attempted to catch one of the hostile craft that was heading in the direction of East Lothian but was unsuccessful. On landing back at East Fortune, the RNAS Avro 504C crashed on landing, badly injuring its pilot Flt Sub-Lt G.A. Cox. This frequently happened when aircraft attempted to intercept Zeppelins in the hours of darkness.

The four Zeppelins reported off the north east coast of England to Dundee Seaplane Station were L.13, L.14, L.16 and L.22 operated by the German Navy. One of them, L.13, developed engine trouble a short time later and turned back for home. L.16 crossed over the coast near Northumberland, failing to take into account the strength of the northerly wind and dropped its bombs on what it believed to be Tyneside factories. None of them did any damage, although eleven fell on Cramlington Aerodrome. Two of the aircraft stationed there chased after the raider, but failed to catch it. Further to the north, Zeppelin L.22 dropped its bombs in fields close to Berwick-Upon-Tweed under the belief they too were attacking Tyneside industrial targets. It then flew back out to sea before reappearing over Edinburgh where it dropped some more bombs which shattered a few windows. Around the same time the fourth Zeppelin in the fleet, L.14 commanded by Kpt. A. Bocker, also arrived over the city. Bocker's L.14 had shaken off gunfire from destroyers as he moved inland via St Abbs Head fixing his position by the lights of Leith and Edinburgh. He failed to locate the intended target of the naval base at Rosyth and flew over the Firth of Forth to launch an attack on Leith instead. Bombs fell on the docks but the greatest loss occurred when the Innes and Grieve whisky bond went up in flames.

This memorial plaque is located in West Princes Street Gardens close to Johnston Terrace. The bomb dropped here by the Zeppelin narrowly missed Edinburgh Castle, landing on the rocks immediately under its walls. The plaque is very hard to find as it is situated some distance above the public footpaths on a steep slope. (Malcolm Fife)

L.14 then flew south and proceeded to attack Scotland's capital city. A bomb narrowly missed Edinburgh Castle and others landed on the Grassmarket. David Robertson, a discharged soldier was struck in the stomach by a piece of shrapnel and later died in hospital. The Royal Infirmary had many of its windows blown out. Further bombs fell on tenements on the south side of Edinburgh causing further damage to property.

The greatest loss of life that night occurred when a bomb was fell on Marshall Street, close to Edinburgh University. Six people died instantly and a further seven injured. The Zeppelin, L.14, then flew eastwards across Arthur's Seat where it was fired on by machine-guns. A Mrs Lawson, who resided at Prestonfield Lodge, reported that on this bright moonlit night she had seen two airships at 12.15 a.m., one a little higher than the other. The witness also stated that a 'strong blinding light' had been displayed by one of them. The Naval C-in-C also received a report 'that when the Zeppelins visited the Firth of Forth they effectually blocked the Service Wireless'. Zeppelin L.14 broke off its attack at 00.55 a.m. on 3 April 1916. It had dropped a total of twenty-four bombs on Edinburgh killing eleven persons and injuring a further twenty-four. Numerous properties had been damaged including three hotels. A further nine high explosive and eleven incendiary bombs had fallen on Leith claiming two more lives. It was, however, the only air raid on the city in First World War.

A month earlier, Zeppelins L.11, L.13 and L.14 had been instructed to: 'Attack England North, chief target Firth of Forth'. All three airships were forced to abandon the plan when they encountered unexpected snow showers and north-westerly winds of up to fifty mph and instead changed course for Yorkshire.

A further attempt to inflict damage on Rosyth Naval Base and the near by Forth Rail Bridge was planned for the night of 2/3 May 1916. The Royal Naval Admirals were unenthusiastic about their new base. One of the main reasons was their concern that if the Forth Rail Bridge was damaged in an attack, parts of it may fall into the waters below, with this planned attack blocking their warships' path to the sea. Up to a point their fears appear to have been justified. Weather again played havoc on the German's ambitious plans to attack the bridge and the naval Base with no less than eight Zeppelins. Strong winds were encountered well off the

Scottish coast which caused all but two Zeppelins, L.14 and L.20, to abort their mission. Heavy cloud also created navigational problems for the entire force. By the time the Zeppelins had reached Scotland they had become completely lost. L.14 passed over the coast near St Abbs Head at 8.25 p.m. and missed the Firth of Forth. The same airship that had created terror in Edinburgh only a month before, discharged its load of bombs harmlessly on fishing boats near Arbroath. Bocker, its commander, mis-identified the Firth of Tay for the Firth of Forth. L.14 was last seen heading out to sea off Fifeness around 1.00 a.m. The other Zeppelin L.20 crossed the Scottish coast five miles south of Montrose at 9.55 p.m. heading inland. It was unable to obtain radio bearings from its base and finally managed to establish its position at midnight when it was over Loch Ness. Its commander, Franz Stabbert, then steered towards the North Sea arriving over Peterhead at 2.40 a.m. On route Zeppelin L.20 dropped some its bombs over the Scottish countryside, one landing close to Craig Castle near Rhynie.

A further eight fell in the fields around Insch and Old Rayne. Local rumour has it that Craig Castle, which had its own generating plant was lit up brightly for a party being held there at the time of the attack. It is possible that the Zeppelin did regard it as an opportunist target, but more probably was just jettisoning its bombs to lose weight. Stabbert realised that he could not reach his home base so he headed for the coast of Norway. His Zeppelin, L.20, crash-landed near Stavanger and the crew were placed in captivity. Both Stabbert and his crew eventually escaped and returned to flying.

Perhaps his exploits inspired the British film *Zeppelin*, made in 1971. Its plot entailed a raid on a castle in the Scottish Highlands where the national treasures were being stored for safekeeping! After the incursions of L.14 and L.20, Zeppelins were rarely seen over Scotland. The former craft did put in appearance over Berwick-Upon-Tweed at 12.25 a.m. on 9 August 1916 and departed over Alnwick at 2.00 a.m. There was, however, at least one false alarm in the subsequent months. During October 1916 a Zeppelin was reported to have reportedly crossed over Newcastle and was heading towards Edinburgh. At that time Turnhouse was a training aerodrome but all the instructors were told to report for duty by the Scottish Command. The only aircraft that were available were Farman Shorthorns, whose ceiling was around 5,000ft and they could take up to an hour to reach this height. The Zeppelin would probably be flying at twice this height. The Squadron Commander was not very happy with his pilots flying at night and with no armament other than rifles. He contacted the Wing Commander at Newcastle, and by the time the pilots had arrived at Turnhouse the order for them to take off had been cancelled. The Zeppelin never materialised.

At the beginning of the First World War some consideration was given to using 'killer airships', which would fight air battles in the sky with the Zeppelins. Known as the Macmechan Zeppelin Destroyer or the Marshall–Fox Airship, it was developed in conditions of great secrecy. It was intended to be 236ft in length and have a range of 300 miles. The airship would have a crew of four. Plans were made for an initial fleet of five killer airships, and a shed was constructed in Barking, London to house them. The Admiralty took over the building in June 1916, and nothing more was heard of the scheme. By this time, the performance of aircraft was rapidly improving enabling them to be capable of challenging the Zeppelin in the air and, as a result, there was no longer a need for a killer airship.

After the first eighteen months of war, with the threat of air attacks now very real, plans were made to radically reorganise Britain's air defences. The War Office now took over responsibility for this role. They had allowed six months for planning and preparation, after provisionally agreeing to take over the Home Defence. It was accepted that flying aircraft on dark nights against Zeppelins, unassisted by searchlights, was not practical. When there were lights or when there was bright moonlit it may be possible to undertake interception missions.

On 1 February 1916, the first Home Defence Squadron was formed at Cramlington near Newcastle-upon-Tyne. By 5 June this unit was equipped with B.E.2c and Bristol Scouts. Going under the designation of 36 (H.D.) Squadron flights were detached to Ashington and

A B.E.2 of 36 Home Defence Squadron at Turnhouse. On the Western Front this type of aircraft was used operationally in reconnaissance and, sometimes, a bombing role. As the war progressed increasing numbers of the B.E.2s fell victim to enemy fighters as it flew slowly and was not very agile. In the role as a fighter on the Home Front, its only opposition until the arrival of the Gotha bomber was the even less manoeuvrable Zeppelin, of which five examples fell victim to its guns. The B.E.2, despite its shortcoming as a fighter, remained in service in the Home Defence role to the end of the War. (Fleet Air Arm Museum – Bruce/Leslie Collection)

Seaton Carew. Turnhouse Aerodrome was intended to be a flight station at one stage but was in the end not used. In October 1916, however, it became the Headquarters for 77 Home Defence Squadron responsible for protecting the Firth of Forth area and the coast as far south as Berwick-Upon-Tweed. Detachments of aircraft were based at Whiteburn (B Flight) and New Haggerston (C Flight) aerodromes. By the beginning of 1917 there were eleven full-time Home Defence Squadrons extending from Edinburgh to Sussex. They, however, had a low priority and in February serious consideration was given to disbanding two of them including 77 Squadron. It escaped this fate but at this time only had a meagre number of planes. The squadron should have had eighteen machines on strength on 7 March 1917, but in reality only had five. Over the course of the next year the situation appears to have improved. While some Home Defence Squadrons in southern England received modern equipment in the form of Sopwith Camels and Pups, 77 Squadron had to make do with the B.E.2c, B.E.2d, B.E.2e and the B.E.12. Although these aircraft were slow-flying they were very stable, which gave them an advantage as a weapons platforms from which to shoot at Zeppelins. Their low stalling speed was an asset when having to fly at night. The B.E.12 was in fact a development of the B.E.2 but had twice the rate of climb. Small numbers of D.H.6s, R.E.7s and R.E.8s were also flown by this unit. Squadrons at aerodromes from Lincoln to the Firth of Forth were in communication with area warning controllers and their commanders receiving information from them before being ordered to take off. If a Zeppelin was reported, two aircraft from each flight took off to patrol a designated area with orders to fly as high as possible.

In the latter stages of the war, Zeppelins had become notable by their absence over Scotland. 77 Squadron's aircraft had other duties allocated to them, in addition to protecting the air space over south-east Scotland. In the event of a German invasion they were to provide support for

A B.E.12 fighter, R.F.C. seen ready to take off from Penston Aerodrome East Lothian, c.1917. The B.E.12 was a developed of the widely used B.E.2 but was a failure as a fighter on the Western Front but around a hundred were delivered to Home Defence Squadrons. In the latter role they had some success, shooting down Zeppelin L48 over Southern England. (Fleet Air Arm Museum – Bruce/Leslie Collection)

the army, carrying out aerial reconnaissance, the bombing of hostile transports, photography and artillery co-operation. The bombardment of Hartlepool and Scarborough by German warships at the beginning of the war had caused much public indignation. Coastal artillery batteries were upgraded and their guns could fire shells some thirteen miles out to sea. It was decided at a conference, in November 1916, that the Home Defence Squadrons would provide one aeroplane and one wireless receiving station at each 9.2in battery on the east coast. By the end of the war, 77 Squadron had wireless stations at Inchkeith and Kinghorn Batteries.

On 10 August 1917, 77 Squadron moved most of the aircraft it had based at Turnhouse to Penston Aerodrome, around twelve miles to the east of Edinburgh. It was also joined by C Flight from New Haggerston, near Berwick-Upon-Tweed. Early the following year, the squadron headquarters also moved from Turnhouse to Penston. This rural aerodrome was now the centre for air defence of the Firth of Forth. It was staffed by around twenty officers and 200 other ranks in the autumn of 1918. They had a sizeable transport fleet at their disposal including one car, eleven light tenders, six heavy tenders, eight motorcycles and three ambulances.

At this point in time, there was also a detachment of 77 Squadron aircraft at Whiteburn Aerodrome in Berwickshire. There were only fifty-one personnel here, including seven officers. The official number of aircraft allocated to A Flight was eight Avro 504K night fighters. This type began to be delivered to 77 Squadron in the autumn of 1918 and over the next few months replaced their B.E.2c and B.E.12. The squadron also had some searchlights at this site to aid their interception of enemy airships. Other examples were situated at Cockburnspath, Innerwick and at New Haggerston Aerodrome in Northumberland. Whiteburn Aerodrome was situated on the edge of the Lammermuir Hills, very exposed to the elements of nature. Lt Sydney Lawrence was delivering an Avro 504 aircraft from Catterick to Ayr when the following happened:

Near St Abb's Head, the wind was very strong and I was only going very slowly near the ground. As darkness was approaching I landed at a landing ground near Dunbar, right on the coast. When I found they had no sheds or stores I decided to go on another ten miles to the next place. I found that beyond there was a mist and it was getting very dark so I came back to Skateraw. I got a guard and had the machine made secure. After sending off wires and arranging for petrol and so on, in the morning, the people from a small drome at Whiteburn, nine miles inland and 800ft up in the hills sent a side car for me. I had a fine moonlight ride. I stayed at the mess. That night was bitter and I slept very little. Next morning there was a foot of snow on the ground and more coming down. Flying was out of the question so I had to amuse myself as best I could.

Next morning it was a little better and by lunch time I decided to go. I got a tender and men with petrol, etc. This got stuck three times in the snow drifts. We helped it out twice but the third time we gave up and decided to go back and go round another way. This delayed my start, however, I flew over Edinburgh just as dusk was falling and landed safely at Turnhouse at 5.30 p.m.

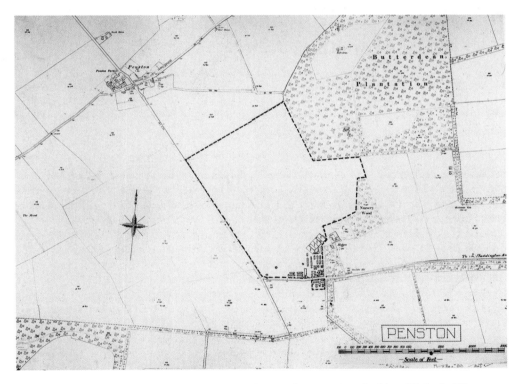

Penston Aerodrome, 1918, was situated to the south-east of Tranent, East Lothian. All the buildings are clustered together in the south-east corner. Among them are two aeroplane sheds, each 130ft by 60ft, along with a workshop, 90ft by 28ft. There was also an ammunition and bomb store. Communications were operated from a wireless telegraphy hut. The dimensions of the aerodrome were 900 yards by 700 yards covering just 106 acres. The station buildings occupied ten of them. From meteorological observations made at the station between March 1917 and November 1918, it was calculated that it was possible to fly on 708 out of 1,622 daylight hours (43.6 per cent). During daytime there were 153 hours of mist and thirty-six hours of fog. All traces of the aerodrome on this site have disappeared and the land has long since been returned to agriculture. The rural road that formed the western boundary of the aerodrome is still there in the form of the B6363. Little else in the immediate area has changed in the last century. (The National Archives)

Crews of 77 Home Defence Squadron seated for their Christmas Lunch. (Imperial War Museum, Q113024)

Some fifty miles south-east of Ayr, Lt Lawrence's aircraft suffered engine failure and he had to make a forced landing in a field. The Avro completed the final section of its journey to Ayr Aerodrome on the back of a large lorry. In fact, only about a third of the batch of aircraft that were being delivered here had turned up intact!

As flying at night was a hazardous undertaking, 77 Home Defence Squadron had numerous sites where their aircraft could put down if their engines failed or if the weather prevented them from returning to their base. The landing grounds were established on requisitioned farmland that was required to be cleared of animals or other hazards when flying was notified. In areas where the ground was undulating the highest area of level ground was selected for use. They were divided into three categories:

> *1st Class* could have flares set out for landing in any direction, had a good surface and no flight path obstructions.
>
> *2nd Class* had irregularities in surface or obstructions which restricted approaches from some directions.
>
> *3rd Class* usually allowed approaches along a single axis and were only taken up when no better local alternative was available.

Early in the war, petrol cans containing cotton waste provided the lighting for aerodromes at night. They were succeeded from 1916 onwards by the Money Flare which burned less fuel. Towards the end of the war, aerial lighthouses began to appear at the major aerodromes which flashed recognition letters.

A number of 77 Home Defence Squadron's landing grounds were eventually expanded into proper aerodromes. They included Cairncross in Berwickshire, Donibristle, Fife and West Fenton,(Gullane) in East Lothian. The other sites included Colinton, Gilmerton and Granton

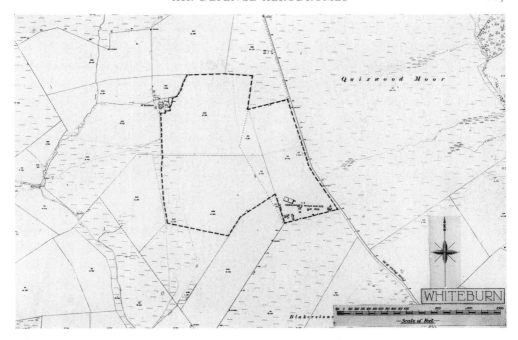

Whiteburn Aerodrome, 1918, was located some four miles west of Grantshouse village in Berwickshire. It is sometimes known by the name of this settlement. The aerodrome was 750ft above sea level and situated on an area of open moorland on the edge of the Lammermuir Hills. It was 120 acres in size of which only three had station buildings on them. They included a single aeroplane shed, 125ft by 60ft, along with a workshop. In addition there was a technical store as well as offices. The aerodrome had its own boiler and powerhouse. Other facilities included a compass platform and a machine-gun range. To arm the aircraft operating from here, there was an ammunition store and a bombstore. There was an officers' mess and quarters and three huts for the other personnel. Meteorological observations made over the winter of 1917/18 came to the conclusion that flying could only be carried out during 25 per cent of daylight hours. All traces of the aerodrome have long since disappeared with the land being used as pasture for livestock. The minor road which formed the eastern boundary is still there, as is Whiteburn Farm. (The National Archives)

Floodlights illuminate Four B.E.12 and B.E.12b which stand ready to be scrambled at Penston Aerodrome, near Tranent, East Lothian, c.1918. These ungainly fighter aircraft belong to 77 Home Defence Squadron which was responsible for the air defence of Edinburgh and south-east Scotland. The B.E.12 was based on the B.E.2 design. (Fleet Air Arm Museum – Bruce/Leslie Collection)

B.E.12bs and Avro 504s of 77 Home Defence Squadrons undergoing maintenance in an aircraft shed at Turnhouse Aerodrome, early 1918. (Permission of Farnborough Air Sciences Trust)

Photographs taken of aircraft at night are a rarity in the early years of the twentieth century. Here a Parnell-bult Avro 504K, E 3273, prepared to take-off from Penston Aerodrome in early 1919. It has been converted to the Home Defence role by doing away with the front cockpit and a Lewis machine-gun has been fitted over the top wing. (Fleet Air Arm Museum – Bruce/Leslie Collection)

near Edinburgh. To the north, there were landing grounds at Kilconquar in Fife, and South Kilduff in Kinross. Both were in the 3rd class category. Close to the southern entrance to the Firth of Forth lay South Belton some two miles from Dunbar. It covered forty-four acres and measured 480 yards by 450 yards. Its category was 2nd class by day and 3rd class by night. Further south and next to the coast was the 3rd class site of Skateraw 'on cliffs of sea coast' extending across fifty-three acres with the following dimensions 650 yards by 400 yards. Inland lay landing sites at Townhead, 1½ miles to the east of the village of Gifford in East Lothian. This landing ground was thirty-five acres in size and 700 yards by 400 yards. It again was in the 3rd class category. At Tynehead in Midlothian there was a much larger site of 114 acres, 850 yards by 650 yards. It was in the category of 1st class landing ground. On the opposite side of the Lammermuirs there were several more 77 Squadron sites including Eccles Tofts some three miles from Greenlaw. It also came into the category of 1st class landing ground. Most of these locations were probably little-used and hardly ever saw an aircraft. While many of the sites mentioned above were never used by aircraft once they were finished, Eccles Torts became the site of Charterhall airfield in the Second World War. Nearby Horndean landing ground became the site for Winfield airfield.

77 Home Defence Squadron was eventually disbanded on 13 June 1919 and its main aerodrome at Penston was abandoned. Although it was the only squadron of its type in Scotland, Montrose Aerodrome formed a War Flight for anti-Zeppelin and anti-submarine patrols. It was probably formed in late 1917 and continued until November 1918. Flying instructors based at the aerodrome flew the aircraft which were drawn from the advanced training machines based here.

CHAPTER SIX

TRAINING AERODROMES

In the early days of military flying in Britain all the recruits who wished to become pilots were trained at the Central Flying School at Upavon in Wiltshire. At the beginning of First World War the applicants generally had an interest in aviation and in fact, most had already taught themselves to fly. Up until 1916 no one would be accepted for pilot training unless he already had a pilot's licence. With the rapid expansion of the RFC this requirement was dropped and appeals for volunteers were made in the infantry and other army units. In some cases, when a unit had someone they disliked he would be encouraged to transfer to this newly formed organisation. Although all applicants had to undergo a medical, few in fact failed. The same applied when the recruits underwent pilot training. Due to the insatiable demand for aircrew few would not pass their course. As late as 1917, Sefton Brancker, who was an experienced pilot and Director of Air Organisation, gives an insight into the thinking behind the requirements of a new recruit held by some senior officers:

> There are very few Englishmen who won't make good pilots so long as they have sufficient experience. Flying is perhaps easier than riding a horse because you sit in a comfortable armchair in a quiet machine instead of a slippery saddle on a lively horse.

With such attitudes held by those in authority it is not surprising that the training of potential pilots left a lot to be desired. Many of the early instructors themselves were not up to the job. Some had returned from France after being injured or with battle fatigue and been delegated to this task. Others were poor pilots who were unsuitable for front line duties. The aircraft employed in the training role were not much better either. The Maurice Farman Shorthorns and Longhorns were particularly favoured for this role. The former aircraft was underpowered and had a very high drag factor, having a large number of rigging wires. It would be prone to stall at a speed of 5mph less than its top speed. Until 1917 it was thought it was impossible to recover from a stall which often had fatal consequences. Trainee pilots were given a few flights with an instructor and then allowed to go solo and teach themselves. Communication between the trainee and his instructor was almost impossible in most training aircraft. In the Shorthorn the instructor would often kick the back of the pupil's seat if his actions did not meet with his approval.

Some instructors 'were known to stand up and hit the cadet on the head with a monkey wrench or anything available' if the pupil froze at the controls. Although many of the shortcomings in training were rectified in the latter stages of the war, pupils still were posted to operational squadrons with the minimum of flying experience. Official figures show that more than 14,000 British pilots died during the conflict of whom 8,000 were killed during training. Being an instructor was an unpopular duty and often they referred to their pupils as the 'Huns', derived from being placed in more danger from the rookies than the Germans.

It is therefore not surprising that every training unit had its own funeral fund. One cadet based at Cranwell in England wrote:

> We had a good day on 1 March, eleven crashes, one poor devil went west during his 13th loop, we bedded him out today. It rather put people off doing stunts the next day but they were all hard at it on Saturday.

Often training aerodromes had the wreckage of numerous aircraft scattered around them. The only positive aspect of witnessing so many accidents was that it would have prepared the pupils for the carnage at the Front. The RFC appear to have been particularly accident prone as the attrition rate for pilots trained in Canada was a small fraction of that in Britain. They used more appropriate machines for flight training and ambulances were always on stand by to attend to any casualties. The Germans' accident rate was about a quarter of that experienced by British flying schools.

For the first year of the First World War, the RFC had no presence in Scotland. Since No.2 Squadron left Montrose for France in 1914, the aerodrome had remained vacant except for a temporary deployment of a small number of RNAS aircraft. The aerodromes in southern England were becoming increasingly crowded and it was decided to disperse flying training throughout Great Britain.

In early 1915, a number of Reserve Aeroplane Squadrons were created. They had the dual role of training pilots for existing service squadrons as well as forming the core of a new active service squadron. In July 1915, a letter from the Deputy Director of Military Aeronautics to the Officer Commanding the Administrative Wing at Farnborough instructed that:

> In consequence of the arrival of a number of experienced pilots from overseas, it is considered possible to start another elementary training centre and with this object I am to request you to form No.6 Reserve Aeroplane Squadron which will be stationed at Montrose.
>
> In view of the fact that the RFC barracks at Montrose are at present occupied by other units for whom it may prove difficult to obtain other accommodation the barracks will be handed over to you gradually and not more than one flight should be despatched in the first instance to this station.
>
> Major A.C. Maclean, at present commanding No.3 Reserve Aeroplane Squadron, will be appointed to command No.6 Reserve Aeroplane Squadron and the senior flight commander at Shoreham will command there as a temporary measure. A further communication as to the status of the Officer Commanding No.6 Reserve Aeroplane Squadron will be addressed to you. It is for consideration whether the new squadron will form part of your Wing or whether, in view of the distance from your headquarters to Montrose and consequent administrative difficulties, it will not be preferable to make Montrose an independent command.
>
> For the present No.6 Reserve Aeroplane Squadron will be equipped with Maurice Farmans and Cauldrons. It is not considered desirable that pilots should be graduated on these machines alone without experience of others and pupils trained in this squadron will, therefore, be posted to service squadrons for further instruction before graduation.

On 31 August, 1915, plans were drawn up to send 'four Curtiss machines' to No.6 Reserve Aeroplane Squadron. For this purpose 2nd-Lt V.W. Eyre, with his trained men, would proceed to Montrose for the purpose of erecting the machines which would come up by goods train. The whole operation should not take more than a week at most. At the same time it was suggested that two or more Armstrong–Whiteworth aircraft should be allotted for advanced instruction.

> The weather there will shortly become too boisterous for preliminary instruction of beginners and the only flying possible will be that done by very advanced pupils. Such being the case it seems desirable that they should be provided as soon as possible with fast tractors of the above type.

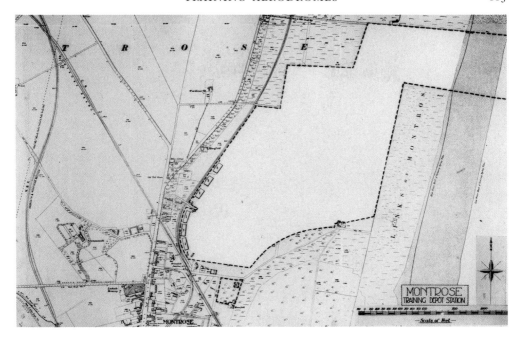

Montrose (Broomfield) Aerodrome, 1918, was situated on the northern edge of the town of Montrose in Angus. Its aeroplane sheds were situated on its western perimeter close to a now disused railway line. They numbered six in all, three with dimensions of 170ft by 80ft and the remaining three were 210ft by 65ft. Rather surprisingly, the aeroplane workshops were situated at Panmure Barracks, two miles from the aerodrome. Most of the personnel were also housed there. A large number of vehicles were assigned to Montrose Aerodrome. Its fleet included a car, ten light tenders, ten heavy tenders and eight motorcycles with sidecars. The landing ground was described as: 'surface fair, but gives a lot of trouble, owing to the sandy soil, by wearing and blowing into holes by wind action. Improvements are being made by adding clay, etc. and seeding'. The seashore lay on the eastern boundary of the aerodrome. The maximum dimensions of the base was 1,000 yards by 900 yards extending across nearly 190 acres. Meteorological measurements made from October 1917 to March 1918 concluded that flying could be carried out on slightly more than half of all daylight hours. No fog was recorded at this site but there were 123 hours of mist. Like many First World War aerodromes it closed not long after the end of the war. However, it re-opened in 1936 to train pilots. Fortunately, it did not suffer the comprehensive redevelopment that occurred at many other locations and several First and Second World War hangars have survived into the following century. In April 1983, a group of local enthusiasts banded together and went on to found the Montrose Air Station Heritage Centre, housed in the former air station headquarters. (The National Archives)

The weather was in fact the main reason given for forming 25 Squadron from No.6 Reserve Squadron and that the latter would be then re-formed at another aerodrome. Often training planes would be grounded if the winds were more than 5–6mph as the pupils could not cope with anything more. Training aerodromes usually commenced their flying programme very early in the mornings when the air was often very calm. There was a memo written in defence of Montrose highlighting the fact that the average number of flying days here is probably not below that of most other aerodromes. It was stated that the greatest disadvantage was the shortage of daylight hours this far north.

The formation of 25 Squadron went ahead and elementary flying training ceased at Montrose for the immediate future. The unit operated Shorthorns, Caudron G.III, Curtiss JN 4, Martinsyde S.1, Avro 504 and B.E.2c for the remainder of 1915.

Flying instructors at Montrose Broomfield. The pilot standing on the far right is wearing a tartan bonnet and kilt. (Fleet Air Arm Museum – Bruce/Leslie Collection)

On 31 December the squadron moved south to Thetford where it re-equipped with Vickers F.B.5. No sooner had it departed that 18 Reserve Aeroplane Squadron was formed at Montrose and remained here until the summer of 1918. As in common with many other training units it operated a motley collection of aircraft which included, F.E.2b, B.E.2b, B.E.12, Martinsyde S.1, JN3, Martinsyde Elephants, F.K.3, Scout D, Pups, Camels and Avro 504A, 504J and 504Ks. Later in the summer of 1916, 39 Training Squadron was formed here. Shorthorns, JN.4, Caudron G.III, Longhorns, B.E.2c, Avro 504, R.E.8 and Martinsyde Elephants were all on its inventory. Finding spares for such a variety of aircraft must have been a nightmare. Montrose Aerodrome, however, had its own workshops that could carry out major repairs and probably could improvise if the correct part was not available. 39 Training Squadron moved to South Carlton in England in autumn 1917. Several new aircraft sheds were built in 1916 to cope with the ever increasing numbers of aircraft being used for training.

1917 saw the formation or arrival of several more training units. They included 82 and 85 Canadian Reserve Squadrons who were created here and then migrated to their home country. Towards the end of the year, two further reserve squadrons arrived from other aerodromes. The first was 52 Squadron which arrived from Raploch Aerodrome, Stirling, at the beginning of September 1917. They were followed by 36 Reserve Training Squadron which arrived three months later and their machines included F.K.3, B.E.2c, Sopwith Pups and Camels.

In the course of the same year two front line squadrons also came into being at Montrose. At the beginning of 1917, 18 Reserve Squadron provided the nucleus for 83 Squadron. After a brief stay it moved to Spittlegate Aerodrome on 15 January. August saw the arrival of the newly formed 80 Squadron. It flew aircraft issued to the training units until it left for Beverley in Yorkshire in November where it was equipped with Sopwith Camels.

The last year of the war saw the arrival of numerous Americans at Montrose. The 41st, 138th and 176th Aero Squadrons (Pursuit) US Army Air Service all passed through here in the early months of 1918. They, however, possessed no aircraft at this stage and their personnel came here for ground instruction. Among them was Sgt Wilfred Mack of the 41st Aero Wing who was a flight rigger and underwent instruction on British aircraft including the Sopwith Camel

This B.E.2c, A8948, was used as a training aircraft at Montrose Broomfield Aerodrome in 1918. It has been totally rebuilt by the workshops here which had the ability to carry out extensive repairs and modifications to their aircraft. (Fleet Air Arm Museum – Bruce/Leslie Collection)

Montrose Aerodrome seen from the air, c.1918. The original aircraft sheds are visible on the top right of the picture. In the foreground are a complex of huts which were used to house some of the servicemen. Over twenty aircraft are scattered across the aerodrome. (Montrose Air Station Trust/ SCRAN)

which was flown by some US squadrons. His job was to carry out repairs on the aircrafts' wires which were used in different parts of the machine both bracing and operating the flying controls. Daily checks were carried out on them and if they looked slightly perished they would be replaced. The planes the Americans worked on had been involved in accidents. Most of the instructors were men who had been wounded in the early days of the war and were of no further use as combat soldiers and others who were rejected for such service, due to some physical handicap or other. 18 Repair Station was based at Montrose, its function was to return the large number of crashed and damaged aircraft back to service. Such were their skills that they built twelve 'new' B.E.2c and a Bristol Scout from the remains of written-off machines.

Bristol Scout D, No.5598, of 18 Training School based at Montrose Broomfield in 1918. The aircraft is painted in fish scale markings. It may also have 'eyes' painted on to its nose. This Bristol Scout was also flown by 2 T.D.S. at Gullane, East Lothian. (Fleet Air Arm Museum – Bruce/Leslie Collection)

Two airmen pose for their photograph sitting on top of the cockpit of unarmed Sopwith Camel C6753, which was flown by 32 Training Squadron at Montrose Broomfield in the summer of 1918. Although the Sopwith Camel was a single-seat fighter, a number of two-seat examples were constructed for training purposes. (Fleet Air Arm Museum – Bruce/Leslie Collection)

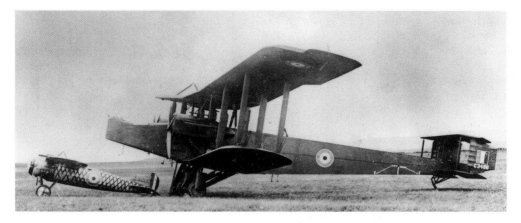

Bristol M.1C, C5014 and Handley Page 0/400 C3498 at Montrose, Broomfield in 1918. The large bomber may well have been participating in exercises with the training units based here. (Imperial War Museum, HU76142)

Sgt Wilfred Mack and his colleagues were housed in a disused flax mill which was not very comfortable. There was no heating and many of its windows were missing. He was more impressed with Montrose Aerodrome stating:

> This was an immense field where a large number of British pilots received their flying instructions including aerial gunnery, photography, etc. Should they qualify on all instructions they were given their wings and assigned to various combat squadrons at the Front where needed. Many looked very young, some looked too young to shave.

In April 1918, Nos 6, 18 and 36 Training Squadrons were based at the aerodrome along with the 30th Wing Headquarters. The latter squadron moved to the newly completed aerodrome at Edzell in the summer. The remaining two squadrons were merged to form 32 Training Depot Station. Accompanying this re-organisation of training units throughout Britain, efforts were made to standardise the aircraft used for instruction. Gone were the vast variety of types which were often handed down from front line squadrons. The official number of aircraft allocated to Montrose Aerodrome in the latter part of 1918 was thirty-six Avro 504 and thirty-six Sopwith Camels. In reality the situation on the ground was probably somewhat different with some of the older types still soldiering on.

Even with the introduction of new training techniques and aircraft there were numerous crashes at Montrose in the closing stages of the war. On 16 October 1917, D.H.4 of 52 Training Squadron suffered an engine failure. Its pilot, Lt W.C. Thomson attempted to turn back to the aerodrome but his aircraft stalled and dived into the ground, killing him. Many lives were lost when the aircraft's engine failed shortly after take-off and the pilot attempted to turn round and try to land back at his aerodrome. Pupils were told never to do this, but continue to fly straight ahead even if this meant coming down on the roof of a house. However, they frequently ignored this advice with fatal consequences. 2nd-Lt P.S. Gaster died when his Sopwith Camel C.6 stalled while performing a turn and spun in from 500ft on 21 April 1918. The following month, Sopwith Camel C111 suffered a choked engine. The pilot 2nd-Lt R.P. Walker performed a turn causing his machine to stall and spin into the ground. He died later from the injuries he sustained in the crash. 2nd-Lt G. Marriott's Sopwith Camel, E1448 hit telegraph wires during formation flying. He died from the injuries he received in the subsequent crash. On 8 July, Sopwith Pup B7485 was involved in a mid-air collision with C.381. Both pilots, 2nd-Lt L.M. Frederick and 2nd-Lt G.H Grimshaw, were killed. Another Sopwith Pup, D4025, crashed while low flying seriously injuring its pilot, 2nd-Lt O.S. Parker.

The pilot, 2nd Lt J. Walker escaped from this crash without injury. His Sopwith Camel, E1449, of 32 T.D.S., Montrose made a heavy landing: its impact resulted in one of the wheels falling off and the machine tipping over onto its nose. (Fleet Air Arm Museum – Bruce/Leslie Collection)

Crashes frequently occurred to Montrose Broomfield-based aircraft. Fortunately, as was the case in this instant, there was often little damage to the aircraft or its occupants. Here a B.E.2c has come down on top of a cottage on the boundary of the airfield whilst on a training flight during 1918. Four men are on the roof of the building examining the machine, including one who is standing rather precariously on its nose! (Fleet Air Arm Museum – Bruce/Leslie Collection)

A more unusual accident occurred to Flt Cdt W.D. Henderson while performing stunts in Sopwith Camel F4207. His seat belt broke, and he fell out his machine to his death. Another Sopwith Camel, C80, broke up while pulling out of a steep dive on 20 June 1918. The same happened to Sopwith Camel D6676 two months later, killing its pilot, 2nd-Lt Cangiamila. Yet another aircraft, D9556, suffered structural failure on 9 September 1918, when its wing broke up killing NCO Cdt C. Reid. A Sopwith Camel was lost when its pilot, 2nd-Lt F.A. Lewis, fainted while flying. He spun in and was killed. Sopwith Pup D4030 flew into a mountain in heavy mist while on a cross-country flight, killing its pilot 2nd-Lt J.H. Hall. The wreckage was found the following day; 26 August 1918. In contrast, Sopwith Pup D8131 was destroyed when it spun off a roll and crashed into the sea.

Many of the deceased pilots were buried in Sleepyhillock cemetery. Amongst them are two Australians, an American, a South African and three Canadians, along with the first RFC pilot to die at Montrose, Desmond Arthur, who gave rise to the ghost stories.

When the First World War ended, 32 Training Depot Squadron was the only flying unit left at the aerodrome. It was disbanded in May 1919. A year later Montrose Aerodrome was officially closed. Its equipment and stores were transferred to the recently opened Leuchars aerodrome. The domestic site which lay to the south of the aerodrome was sold and the aerodrome returned to the army. Maj. Burke's three original sheds and the three more recent aircraft sheds were used to store tanks and artillery pieces. In 1936, the site was reopened as an aerodrome and resumed its role of training pilots for the RAF.

At the beginning of 1916, Montrose was the only RFC aerodrome in Scotland. During the course of that year, two further stations were opened, namely Raploch at Stirling and Turnhouse near Edinburgh. Both were used for training purposes but neither attained

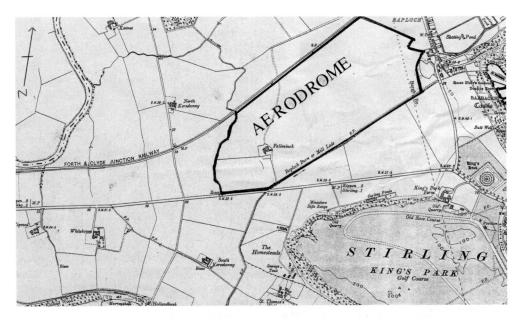

Stirling (Raploch) Aerodrome, 1916, occupied on area of low-lying ground immediately to the west of Stirling Castle. It was centred on Fallininch Farm which was used as the officers' quarters. A number of wooden hangars were erected to house the aircraft but most of the other facilities and accommodation was under canvas. The aerodrome had a brief existence, closing in 1918. Although no trace of it remains in the early years of the twenty-first century, the land on which it stood has altered little in the intervening years, despite its close proximity to the town of Stirling. (© The Trustees of the National Library of Scotland)

anything like the importance of Montrose in this role. Few aerodromes, however, could have a more dramatic setting than that of Raploch. A few hundred yards to its east was Stirling Castle, perched on its rocky outcrop. Appropriately, it was here that Scotland's first recorded attempt at manned flight took place. John Damian, was a French, or possibly Italian, alchemist and court favourite of King James IV. Among the skills he claimed was the ability to turn lead into gold. Damian also claimed he had discovered the secret of flight. In 1507, a practical demonstration of his mastery of the air was arranged. In front of a large crowd, John Damian leapt from the castle's battlements with wings of feathers strapped to his arms. Instead of heading in the direction of France, his intended destination, the birdman fell straight down to the ground landing in a pigs midden. John Damian was lucky to survive this experience with nothing more than a broken leg. He attributed his failure to the use of chickens' feathers in his wings and the fact that this creature could not fly!

A somewhat more successful venture was the establishment of the aerodrome in spring 1916. It was centred on Falleninch Farmhouse, which was requisitioned by the military. The landing ground was immediately to the east. To facilitate flying operations, the Forth and Clyde Junction Railway had to shorten all the telegraph poles on the railway line that ran along its northern edge by 2ft.

No.18 Reserve Squadron at Montrose provided a nucleus of mechanics and motor transport for the formation of 43 Squadron at Stirling. The first motor transport vehicle, a Leyland repair lorry, arrived on 22 April. It was another month, however, before the first aircraft arrived in the form of a B.E.2c borrowed from 18 Reserve Squadron. Four days later, an Armstrong Whitworth F.K.3 was delivered, the first machine allocated to the squadron.

By June 1916 there were eight aircraft on strength. During their short stay at Raploch Aerodrome, 43 Squadron operated a total of eight Avro 504s, eight Armstrong Whitworth F.K.3s, three B.E.2cs, two B.E.2ds and two B.E.2es. Of these, five Armstrong Whitworth F.K.3s, two Avro 504s and a B.E.2es were written off between May and August. The Commanding Officer's orders were: 'get the squadron trained to a standard fit to take to France before the

Armstrong Whitworth F.K.3 No.5512 sits outside the wooden hangars at Raploch Aerodrome. These were the only permanent structures at this short-lived landing ground. (Fleet Air Arm Museum – Bruce/Leslie Collection)

Bearing a distinctive white cross on its rear fuselage, this de Havilland D.H.4, A7779, served at both Montrose and Stirling Raploch aerodromes. The D.H.4 was designed as a day bomber but went on to serve with the Home Defence Squadrons. It was also used in a variety of training roles, including bomb dropping and photography. (Fleet Air Arm Museum – Bruce/Leslie Collection)

year is out'. The unit, however, left in August for Netheravon on Salisbury Plain where they were to receive Sopwith 1½ Strutters. They left their Armstrong Whitworth F.K.3s, B.E.2 and Avro 504 at Stirling to be used to train pilots of the newly formed 63 Squadron. Two new types also arrived here in the form of D.H.4 and B.E.12. When this squadron was only three months old it departed for Cramlington in North-East England.

The following year, 52 Training Squadron arrived from England with B.E.2 and D.H.4. on 18 March 1917. After a stay of less than six months their aircraft left for Montrose Aerodrome on 1 September. This was the last time aircraft were permanently based at Raploch Aerodrome. It boasted few permanent structures other than some wooden hangars and many of the personnel were housed under canvas. Large new training aerodromes were shortly to be built at several other locations in Scotland and there was probably no need to retain this landing ground. In 1933, private aircraft were allowed to land on the former site of the aerodrome if they paid the farmer at Fallininch Farm one shilling.

43 Squadron eventually went on to become one of the RAF's premier fighter squadrons. It was based at Drem Airfield in East Lothian in the early years of the Second World War. Flying Hawker Hurricanes, the squadron shot down numerous enemy bombers that attempted to penetrate Scottish airspace. From 1950 onwards, 43 Squadron has spent most of its existence at RAF Leuchars in Fife flying jet fighters. Its birthplace was not forgotten; in 1991 a formation of Tornado aircraft flew over the site of Raploch Aerodrome, Stirling, on the 75th anniversary of 43 Squadron's creation here.

The other training aerodrome established at Turnhouse, however, had a very different fate. From the time it opened in 1916, it remained in continuous use throughout the twentieth century, eventually graduating to become Edinburgh Airport. Flying here commenced in spring 1916 with one flight of Maurice Farman Shorthorns and one flight of Longhorns, which were initially housed in canvas hangars. Instructors lived in bell tents and messed in a marquee. Pupils only flew when there was little wind.

A general view of Turnhouse Aerodrome, c.1917. Four Sopwith Camels of 73 Training Squadron are parked in front of the aircraft shed in the centre of the picture. (Fleet Air Arm Museum – Bruce/Leslie Collection)

W.D. Patrick wrote in a pre-war 603 Squadron newsletter:

At Turnhouse in my time there were more pupils than the instructors could keep employed and I managed to get a good deal of shooting and amusement. We were extraordinarily ignorant, judged by modern standards, of all but the elements of the art of flying and did the strangest things with our antiquated machines because we knew no better. There was continually some strange incident happening, one pupil who was trying his first solo landing, flew right in a hangar door, crashed three machines and escaped without a scratch, another thought he would like to show his nice new toy to some pals at the depot of his old regiment. He tried to land on the barrack-square at Redford, crashed his machine to ribbons, telephoned for a breakdown gang and walked into the Mess".

As the year progressed construction began on permanent accommodation for the aircraft. In time, two 1915 pattern sheds with dimensions, 200ft by 70ft, plus a further one 150ft by 70ft were erected. They were followed by one 1916 pattern shed, 170ft by 80ft and one HD pattern shed, 130ft by 120ft. The first unit to be based at Turnhouse was 26 Reserve Squadron. It left for Harlaxton in autumn 1917. Shortly before it left 73 Training Squadron arrived with Avro 504J, a Sopwith Camel and Sopwith 1½ Strutters. This unit taught recently graduated pilots how to fly in formation, spins, stalls, vertical banks, Immelmann turns and so on. Its commanding officer was Maj. P.C. Maltby who undertook the instruction of numerous pupils himself and assessing the suitability of some to become 'scout pilots'. When not undertaking training flights he often tested recently repaired aircrafts for the Aeroplane Repair Section. Maj. Maltby also performed stunts over the fleet in the Firth of Forth and the Mound in Edinburgh. On 30 January 1918, he performed a pamphlet-dropping flight over the city. On some winter days Turnhouse Aerodrome was covered in water, but this did not deter Maj. Maltby from flying. During its time here a number of its machines were involved in serious accidents. 2nd-Lt P.A. Anderson was killed when the propeller of his Sopwith Pup, B2247, parted company with the rest of the aircraft. It should be noted that during the First World War pilots did not carry parachutes. On 14 November 1917, Sopwith Camel B6262 was practicing landings when it was involved in a mid-air collision with B.E.2e B4011. Its pilot 2nd-Lt H.M. Armstrong was killed. The previous month, Sopwith Camel, D9525, nosedived and spun in killing its pilot 2nd-Lt H. Monk. More fortunate was 2nd-Lt H.G. MacKintosh who survived with serious injuries when his Sopwith Camel, went into a spinning nosedive from 500ft. 73 Training Squadron eventually departed for Thetford on 20 February 1918. For the remainder of the war, Turnhouse Aerodrome provided a shore base for aircraft operated on Royal Navy Ships.

THE TRAINING DEPOT STATIONS

The latter stages of the war saw dramatic changes in the way aircrew were trained. In the summer of 1917 a School of Special Flying was created at Gosport in southern England. Its Commanding Officer, Maj. R. Smith-Barry developed a training course based on the experiences of numerous other pilots. Prior to then, trainee pilots were taught little about the theory and mechanics of flights. The skill of how to recover an aircraft from a stall now became an essential part of the new syllabus. New pilots were also taught how to land and take off in a wind, as well as how to extradite themselves from numerous other difficult situations they may encounter. This in turn created far more competent flyers, who now could devote far more of their effort in combating the enemy instead of worrying how to control their machines. The Gosport Training System was eventually adopted by air forces all over the world and many of its techniques are still in use today. Another of Gosport's contribution to flight training was that aircraft now began to be fitted with a tube between the two cockpits enabling the instructor to speak to his pupil while in flight.

At the same time as new methods of instruction were being introduced there was a rapid expansion in the flying training programme. Early in 1917, it was planned to have a total of ninety-seven reserve squadrons serving in this role. Later in the year these units were simply referred to as training squadrons. Another major development that took place around the same time was the establishment of training depot stations. Flying instruction would be concentrated at these aerodromes to economise in personnel and transport. There also had been concern about the amount of agricultural land being consumed by new aerodromes and it was hoped that this new policy would go some way to solve the problem. By the end of the First World War, around sixty training depot stations had been created the length and breadth of Britain. Many of them were built to a standard specification and all those in Scotland built in 1918, had six aeroplane sheds, wood and metal workshops along with several instruction huts for general lectures, gunnery, bombing and wireless lessons.

The first new training depot station to open in Scotland was at Gullane, East Lothian. The aerodrome was also sometimes known as West Fenton, taking this name from the hamlet that stood next to it. There had been a small landing ground here which was probably established in late 1915 for use by RNAS aircraft based at East Fortune aerodrome which lay a short distance to the south east. Later the same site was allocated for use by 77 Home Defence Squadron, operating from Turnhouse. Nos 9, 19 and 35 Training Squadrons were initially merged to form No.2 Training Depot Station at Lake Down Aerodrome, England, in August 1917 which then transferred to Gullane on 15 April 1918. A large building programme was initiated constructing a facility that dwarfed the previous landing ground on this site.

The designated function of No.2 Training Depot Stations was to train pilots to fly single-seat fighter aircraft. Its strength on paper was thirty-six Royal Aircraft Factory S.E.5s and thirty-six Avro 504A/J/Ks. Other types were also used here including Bristol F.2bs, Bristol Scouts, Sopwith Camels and Pups. New recruits usually first flew the Avro 504, before graduating to Sopwith Pups and S.E.5s.

On completion of their training, some of the pilots were posted to No.27 Training Depot Station at RAF Crail on the opposite side of the Firth of Forth. Here they received instruction on fighter reconnaissance aircraft.

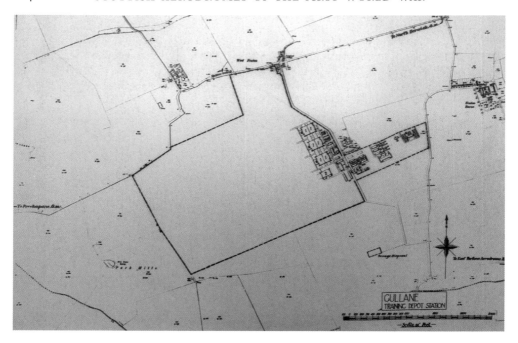

Gullane (West Fenton) Aerodrome, 1918, was located four miles south-west of North Berwick in East Lothian. Although there was a landing ground here by 1916, the site underwent a major expansion in the final year of the war. By this time the maximum dimensions of the site occupied by the aerodrome was 1,100 yards by 900 yards, covering 186 acres. The technical buildings took up some thirty-three acres. They included six aeroplane sheds, each 170ft by 100ft, plus the aeroplane repair shed in a similar building. Gullane Aerodrome had comprehensive facilities from the maintenance and repair of its aircraft. They included a engine workshop, a smiths' workshop, sailmakers' workshop for repairing the aircraft's fabric and a dope shop for treating the material. The unit commander had his own office and there was a separate one for the training depot. Trainee pilots, while not flying, were given instruction in the general lecture hut. There was also a gunnery instruction hut, a gunnery workshop, a wireless and bombing hut and a buzzing and picture target hut. The latter formed the function of an early flight simulator. For gunnery practice there was a machine-gun range. The personnel were housed in a complex of huts immediately to the east of the technical site. Gullane had a large fleet of motor vehicles to meet its transport needs. They included a car, ten light tenders, ten heavy tenders and eight motorcycles with sidecars. By August 1918 all construction work on the aerodrome buildings was nearing completion. The aerodrome suffered the usual fate when the war ended, functioning for a few more months before being closed. Many of the structures including the aeroplane sheds survived up until the end of the 1930s being used as giant barns for livestock and harvested crops. A new aerodrome was established on the site in the year before war broke out again. The First World War buildings were demolished, including the aeroplane sheds which were replaced by more modern examples. Unusually, the site was no longer known as its old name of Gullane but was now referred to as Drem Aerodrome. It went on to become one of Scotland's most famous Second World War stations, its Spitfires and Hurricanes being engaged in numerous air battles in the opening stages of the war. In 1946, the aerodrome closed again, never to re-open. The land was returned to farming but many of the Second World War buildings still stand. A handful of First World War accommodation blocks that escaped demolition also remain and have been turned into a farm shop and a variety of other retail outlets at Fenton Barnes. (The National Archives)

An aerial view of 2 Training Depot Station, Gullane, RAF, taken on its southern edge on 16 November 1918. A line-up of aircraft is visible in the centre of the picture and includes Avro 504s and Sopwith Camels. (Courtesy of Imperial War Museum, No.HU91007)

The large scale size of the aerodrome at Gullane, or West Fenton as it was sometimes known, is apparent from this aerial view taken from the south-east corner. Most of the buildings were demolished at the beginning of the Second World War when the airfield was rebuilt and renamed Drem. This view was also taken on 16 November 1918. (Courtesy of Imperial War Museum, No.HU91006.)

A Maurice Farman A.11 Shorthorn, A2206, is prepared for take-off by a group of boy trainees in January 1918 at Gullane Aerodrome. (Courtesy of the Imperial War Museum, No.HU91008)

Boy trainees manoeuvre Maurice Farman Se11 Shorthorn, A2206, into position for take-off at Gullane Aerodrome, January 1918. This type was originally designed primarily for observation duties but was also used as a bomber. Towards the end of the war it was becoming obsolete and relegated to the training role like the example in the photograph. (Courtesy of the Imperial War Museum, No.HU91009)

Lectures played an important role in the training of potential aircrew. Hanging on the wall in the back of this classroom at Gullane Aerodrome is a large poster on the Lewis machine-gun. This along with the Vickers machine-gun was the primary armament on British aircraft during the First World War. Hence much time was spent on the ground teaching about the intricacies of these weapons. (Courtesy of the Imperial War Museum, No.Q108880)

By 1 August 1918, Gullane Aerodrome had a large implement of personnel numbering 839 in total. This included 120 officers, plus a further sixty NCOs who were under instruction. Among them was Air Mechanic William Smith who joined the RFC at the age of sixteen. After completing his training he was posted to Gullane in early 1918. He recalled that the landing ground was 'V-shaped with a dip in the middle'. The mechanics slept in a large barracks and worked mainly in canvas Bessonneaux hangars. In winter, when the canvas doors froze, the Bessonneaux hangars were cursed by all, but they played a vital role in protecting the flimsy aircraft. The permanent brick-built sheds would not be ready until the summer.

The cadets at RAF Gullane were mostly new pilots undergoing initial training so there were numerous accidents, but due to the low-flying speeds of the biplanes the pilots often escaped with nothing more than a few cuts and bruises. Several machines crashed into the waters of the near by Firth of Forth. The open cockpit enabled the airmen to usually escape from their sinking aircraft without too much difficulty. There were exceptions: 2nd-Lt William Hunter was drowned on 3 July 1918 when his Sopwith Camel D6680 landed in the sea after aerial gun firing practise. The flyers' luck sometimes gave out and there were several fatalities in the 18 months of No.2 Training Depot's existence. One day Air Mechanic William Smith was sitting in the mess eating his meal. Suddenly there was a large noise and everybody rushed out the building to see what had happened. A student pilot, flying low over the airfield had misjudged his height and flown straight into the side of a disused concrete building. He was killed instantly. Apparently the pilot had been due to go on leave and had been showing off to his friends on the ground.

During the First World War it was the general practice for the deceased to be shipped home for burial ony if they were natives of mainland Britain. This is why there are numerous Canadian airmen interred in graveyards near training bases but with few British examples. Capt. Glanville was the only No.2 Training Depot Station fatality to be buried near the airfield at Dirleton because he was resident overseas when he enlisted. The pilots whose bodies were not returned to their families were buried at Comely Bank Cemetery in Edinburgh, where their last resting place is today marked by a simple white headstone. They are accompanied by several other RFC aircrew killed at Turnhouse Aerodrome and elsewhere.

Not only were airmen from the Commonwealth countries trained at No.2 Training Depot Station, but when the USA entered the war in 1917 it sent both soldiers and sailors to assist the Allies fighting on the Western Front. This included 41 US Aero Squadron which had been formed at Kelly Field, Texas, in July 1917, and was posted to Britain in the spring of the following year. The squadron spent some time at RAF Montrose before arriving at Gullane aerodrome.

Sgt Wilfred Mack, a flight rigger, was among them and fortunately recorded his experiences for posterity. His diaries give an interesting insight into life here in a way that is not conveyed in official records:

> Our airdrome at Gullane, Scotland, was situated far out in the hills with no town within miles. The only railroad track was about two miles or more away. From our barracks we could see the Edinburgh Express train at is passed by on its way to Edinburgh which was about twice daily. From the distance it appeared to be a miniature train with the light or dark smoke puffing from its chimney.
>
> From this airdrome we could plainly see the British Royal Naval air station which houses quite a few dirigibles or blimps (airships at East Fortune Station) and other naval craft, used in patrolling the surrounding area as well as the North Sea area, weather permitting. Our food at Gullane was much better than at Montrose. When they served oatmeal for breakfast, they served jam with it and not milk. Then as the troops were eating, the Officer of the Day, (British Orderly Officer) on his rounds would enter the mess hall and the mess sergeant would yell out: 'Orderly Officer, will one man stand up at the end of each table'. This was to hear the complaints, if any. I wouldn't want to be in the shoes of the Tommy who would stand up. He could be in the kitchen for a month perhaps, just for complaining. Therefore no one would stand up.
>
> War or no war, these same British Tommies always knocked off for their tea and cakes twice daily, morning and afternoon. This was their custom.

When the 41st Aero Squadron arrived at Gullane from Montrose the unit was divided into two flights. The squadron was given complete charge of the flights and the maintenance facilities but the British had overall control of the training programme. After the first week the total number of flying hours and the number of aircraft repaired by the 41st exceeded that of the British Flight which was serviced entirely by British mechanics. Following an inspection by Col. Mitchell, Inspector General for the American Expeditionary Forces in Britain, the 41st Squadron received a mark of 85 per cent, the highest grade received by any squadron in Britain:

> The mechanics for the 41st Aero Squadron were housed in Bessonneaux hangars made from heavy canvas, which in turn was supported by heavy wood uprights and had a cathedral type roof support. The hangars were very large but could be dismantled and moved whenever necessary.

Sgt Wilfred Mack also recollected that:

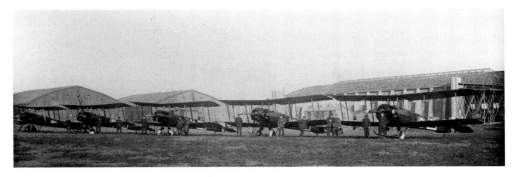

A line up of RFC Avro 504K two-seat training aircraft and their crews at No.2 Training Depot at Gullane Aerodrome in 1918. Bessonneaux hangars are visible in the background on the left hand side. On the right is a general aeroplane shed which appears to be in the final stages of construction. (© The Trustees of the National Museums of Scotland)

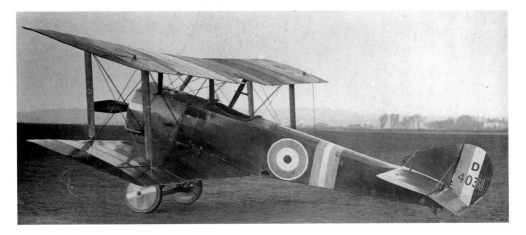

Amongst the aircraft used for advanced pilot training at 2 Training Depot, Gullane, was this Sopwith Pup D4031. Initially this machine was delivered to 30 Wing A.R.S. Montrose before being transferred to Gullane in the summer of 1918. (© The Trustees of the National Museums of Scotland)

> We usually stored six or seven planes in each hangar which gave us ample room to do our work without congestion. Our repairs were limited to small crashes of all types. In very severe crashes the planes were sent to the main reclamation depot for overhaul.

Wilfred Mack witnessed at least one fatal accident during his stay at Gullane Aerodrome. The undercarriage of a Sopwith Camel which was coming into land struck a string of high tension cables. This caused the pilot to loose control and hit a stream engine that was still hot from its day's labours. The Sopwith Camel burst into flames on contact and...:

> ...in a few seconds nothing remained except a charred form of a man and a few pieces of wood and wires. We couldn't get near enough to do anything as it happened so fast. There was no such fire-fighting equipment in those days as we see being used in similar crashes today. As we tried to recover the remains, they simply disintegrated but we recovered whatever was possible.

Sometime later a friend of the deceased pilot crashed into the hills near the aerodrome. The mechanics who salvaged the wreckage of aircraft involved in accidents would sometimes 'liberate' the more valuable parts, particularly the propellers which were French polished for potential buyers! Other crashes involving 2 Training Depot Station aircraft included Sopwith Camel D6670 which crashed out of control from 2,000ft on 18 June 1918 killing 2nd-Lt Wilkinson. Another Sopwith Camel, C6750, which suffered engine failure as it came out of a spin on 3 September 1918. Its pilot 2nd-Lt H. Roper was slightly injured. Less lucky was 2nd-Lt G.W. MacAllister who was killed when his Camel went into a spin on 12 August 1918. A further machine was lost when D9535 suffered engine failure on take-off. It spun in killing its pilot, 2nd-Lt G.L. Coffey. This happened three months after the end of the War on 24 February 1919.

With the end of hostilities there was a rapid contraction of the newly created RAF. 151 and 152 squadrons arrived at Gullane as cadres from Liettes on 21 February 1919. The squadrons were disbanded there on 10 September and 30 June respectively. No.2 Training Depot Station was the last service unit at Gullane and it soldiered on until 21 November 1919 when it,

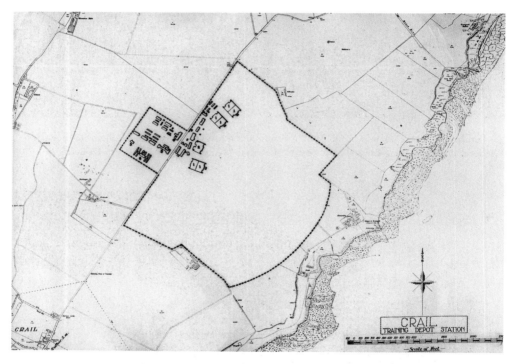

Crail Aerodrome, 1918, in Fife. It was located overlooking the shore of the Firth of Forth next to Crail village. The personnel were billeted in huts on the north side of a minor road that ran past the station. The technical buildings and landing ground were located on the opposite side. There were six aeroplane sheds, each 170ft by 100ft with an additional shed functioning as the Aircraft Repair Shed. Workshops existed for wood and metal work, housing carpenters, sailmakers, coppersmiths and smiths. Instruction was carried out in a lecture hut. Other lessons took place in the gunnery instruction hut, wireless and bombing hut and buzzing and picture target hut. The technical buildings extended across thirty-five acres. On 1 August 1918 much of the aerodrome was still under construction. In the interwar years most traces of the station were swept away. A new aerodrome was built on top of the earlier example at the outbreak of the Second World War. Much of it survives at the beginning of the twenty-first century, albeit in a derelict state. (The National Archives)

too, was dissolved. The aerodrome closed a short time later. The station, however, re-opened shortly before the Second World War, under the name of Drem. Initially it resumed its role in the training of new pilots but was soon taken over by Fighter Command in whose domain it remained until the closing stages of the conflict.

On the opposite side of the Firth of Forth, a large new aerodrome was constructed next to Crail village in Fife during the early part of 1918. It was built by Laing, who employed a large workforce on the project including around 300 tradesmen. No less than 100 horse-drawn vehicles were used to haul the materials. By the summer the project was nearing completion. The first flying units to arrive were 50 Training Squadron from Spittlegate and 64 Training Squadron from Harlaxton. Three days after their arrival from England, the two units were disbanded to form 27 Training Depot Squadron (TDS) on 18 July 1918. Its function was to train Fighter Reconnaissance pilots on the two seat Bristol Fighter F.2. A total of thirty-six of

The aircraft sheds at Crail Aerodrome, 1918. The aerodrome had seven 1917 pattern sheds in three pairs. The remaining single one served as the Aeroplane Repair Section. (Via the late Bruce Robertson)

Airmen stand in front of a Bristol F2B fighter at 27 Training Depot Station at Crail, Fife. The man standing on the second to the left is brandishing a Very pistol! (Fleet Air Arm Museum – Bruce/Leslie Collection)

these aircraft were to be allocated to this unit plus a further thirty-six Avro 504s. Other types based here in small numbers included R.E.8s and Sopwith Camels.

As was common with all training units, there were numerous accidents. Miss Janet Wilson, a member of the Women's Auxiliary Air Force (WAAF), saw one pilot smash his aircraft into the Sergeants' Mess and another narrowly miss the women's living quarters. During its existence, 27 Training Depot suffered at least six fatalities while based at Crail Aerodrome. The first involved a R.E.8, B6638, a type usually used for aerial reconnaissance. It crashed near its base on 9th September 1918 killing Flt Cdt A. Winstanley. The next fatality was Flt Cdt A. Kettlewood who was killed when his Bristol Fighter lost speed and stalled on 20 November 1918. Another Bristol Fighter crashed on 23 December, when it spun in from a low height. Its occupants; instructor Lt C.R. Mundy, along with his passenger, fitter F. Green, both perished and were buried locally. A few days later, an Avro 504K, H218, stalled while turning and spun in, killing Flt Cdt J.A. Scarratt in the process. The new year was only a few days old when yet another Avro 504K, came to grief. This accident took place on 6 January 1919, killing Instructor J.A. Bruce. His pupil, H.M. Brodie was more fortunate, escaping alive but injured.

During August 1918, the Americans had a detachment based at the aerodrome in the form of 120th Aero Squadron. Their personnel were trained to fly in Avro and Sopwith Aircraft. 27 Training Squadron was disbanded on 31 March 1919. During the same month, 104 Squadron moved from Turnhouse to Crail. It is not clear if they were still equipped with aircraft or if it was just a movement of personnel. The unit completely disbanded on 30 June 1919 and the aerodrome closed shortly afterwards. The land was returned to agriculture and the large aircraft sheds were eventually demolished. A large new aerodrome was constructed on its site at the beginning of the Second World War to house Fleet Air Arm Squadrons. Much of it still survives in 2007, including the control tower and a large hangar.

Further up the Fife coast another Training Depot Station was established at Leuchars. The area's association with aviation dated as far back as 1911 when a balloon squadron of the Royal Engineers set up a training camp in Tentsmuir Forest. Work began on establishing an aerodrome at Leuchars in 1916 with the levelling of the ground. It was intended to be used for single-seater fighter training. As it neared completion in November 1918, the Grand Fleet School of Aerial Fighting and Gunnery transferred here from East Fortune Aerodrome. Unlike most other units it continued to function until 1920 and continued in a different guise after that date. Crashes of First World War types continued after the end of the conflict. A Sopwith Camel, attempted a slow roll too near the ground and it killed its pilot Lt D. Cooper in May 1919. Avro 504, H3007, suffered engine failure on landing on 23 August 1921 and collided with a railway signal and crashed at Guardbridge, next to Leuchars Aerodrome.

A further new aerodrome was built to the north of Edzell next to the hamlet of Greendykes, Aberdeenshire to house a training depot for training pilots of single-seat fighters. Unlike most other aerodromes, which were situated close to the coast, this was situated in the heart of the Scottish countryside with the Grampian Highlands looming in the distance. It was intended to base thirty-six Avro 504s and thirty-six S.E.5 fighters here but it is unlikely that anything like these numbers were achieved. On 15 July 1918, 26 Training Depot Station was formed from 36 and 74 Training Squadrons. The types operated at Edzell included R.E.8s, F.E.2b, Avro 504, S.E.5a and Sopwith Camels and Pups. Many of the aircraft came from Montrose Aerodrome situated only a few miles away. The location of the grass runways varied depending on the crop rotation of what was still an agricultural field system.

One of the Sopwith Camels, C6752, was destroyed on 14 October, 1918 when it stalled while making a turn and spun in. Its pilot, Lt E.C. Derwin was killed. Similar to most of the other Training Depot Stations in Scotland, it closed during 1919. The site where the the First World War Aerodrome stood was not used again but a new airfield was built a short distance to the south of it at the beginning of the Second World War.

Above left: Leuchars Aerodrome, 1918, was established on the banks of the of the River Eden around five miles north of St Andrews in Fife. Nearly ninety years after it first opened, it still functions as a military aerodrome. The original site was 1,250 yards by 900 yards. It covered 221 acres of which twenty were taken up by the aircraft sheds and other technical buildings grouped together on the northern edge of the station. There were six aircraft sheds, each 170ft by 100ft. Situated immediately behind them was a seventh example, designated the ARS (aircraft repair shed). Like other recently established training stations, it had well-equipped workshops which housed smiths, carpenters, sailmakers, and coppersmiths. Other buildings were used to teach the trainee pilots various skills. They included a gunnery instruction hut, a gunnery workshop hut, a wireless and bombing hut and a buzzing and picture target hut. Leuchars also had a machine-gun range and a bomb dropping tower. The accommodation quarters were on the western perimeter of the site close to the Edinburgh to Dundee railway line. On 1 August 1918 construction of the aircraft sheds and technical buildings had just begun. Work was scheduled to be completed by 1 November illustrating the rapid timescale in which many of the Scottish aerodromes were built. (The National Archives)

Above right: Edzell Aerodrome, 1918, was situated some fifteen miles inland from Montrose Aerodrome. Access was by a second class road from Edzell Village, which was also the nearest railhead. The dimensions of the aerodrome was 1,200 yards by 900 yards extending across some 211 acres. Around forty acres were occupied by the technical buildings which included a carpenters', sailmakers', dope, engine, smiths' and coppersmiths' workshops. The accommodation for the aircraft consisted of six aeroplane sheds, each measuring 170ft by 100ft, plus an aircraft repair shed and a salvage shed. For tuition of the trainee pilots there was a gunnery workshop, lecture hut, photographic hut and a wireless and bombing hut. Administration was carried out in the unit commanders and depot offices. In August 1918 work had just commenced on the aircraft sheds, but the accommodation for the personnel was ready to be occupied. In the Second World War a new airfield was built a short distance to the south of the original one. (The National Archives)

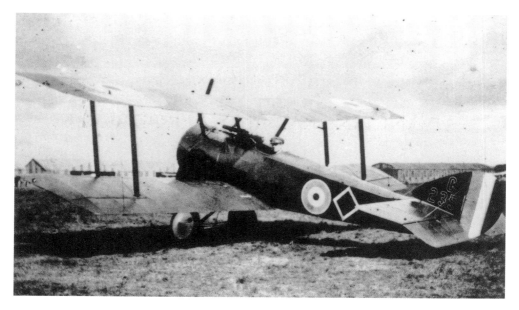

Sopwith Pup C235, with a diamond marking on its rear fuselage, was flown by 32 Training Depot Station at Montrose-Broomfield. It was then transferred to 26 Training Depot Station at Edzell, where it crashed on 12 August 1918 after it went into a spin. Its pilot, 2nd-Lt J.A. Potts, was seriously injured. (Fleet Air Arm Museum – Bruce/Leslie Collection)

A highly unconventional checkerboard paint scheme has been applied to this Sopwith Pup B7575, of 26 Training Depot Station based at Edzell, in Angus. On 1 October 1918 it suffered an engine failure and had to make a forced landing. (Fleet Air Arm Museum – Bruce/Leslie Collection)

CHAPTER SEVEN

ADVANCED TRAINING AERODROMES

At the beginning of the war, military aircraft were only used to carry out reconnaissance work. Pilot training for this task was fairly rudimentary as it was only necessary to master the basic flying skills before being posted to the Front. As the conflict ground on, aircraft began to be used in increasingly specialised roles. To meet these new requirements, flying schools were created to teach aerial navigation, wireless operation, bomb dropping photography and artillery co-operation and so on. Several aerodromes were given over to the essential task of aerial gunnery instruction.

No.2 Auxiliary School of Aerial Gunnery was formed at the newly opened Turnberry Aerodrome in January 1917. While No.1 School based at Hythe in Kent was responsible for training observers in the use of the Lewis machine-gun, No.2 School gave final gunnery instruction to fighter pilots. Until that time, most of the aerodromes were situated on the east coast of Scotland. Turnberry was the first major one on the west coast. Its centrepiece was the hotel constructed in 1906 to cater for golfers wanting to play on the great Ayrshire courses.

The aerodrome was in fact constructed on the golf course that lay next to Turnberry Hotel. It was probably this area of relatively flat ground, with the ready availability of accommodation close by, that attracted the RFC to this location. Both the British and Germans often requisitioned large houses or hotels near their aerodromes in France to billet their personnel. Turnberry Hotel had over 200 rooms and it also had its own railway station. The Ayrshire coast experienced a mild climate and, even in those days, snow was practically unknown. The building stood on a rising ground overlooking the landing ground. According to Robert Todd, an American airman:

> The Hotel was half way up the side of a mountain, looking over the aerodrome and into the bay, a most beautiful spot. All our meals were served in the main dining room and we were introduced to several Scottish dishes immediately, kippered herring with our eggs and treacle for our cereal. The aerodrome was the golf course complete with bunkers, sand traps, and a dandy water hazard that circled the whole field. This was a brook, a typical Scot hazard on a golf course. The prevailing wind came off the sea which was not bad for take-offs but to land, we had to come down the mountain where the hotel was and sideslip in for a very short landing strip to avoid the brook and other hazards.

Robert Todd was less impressed with the aircraft, complaining that they were not maintained to the same standards as the ones he had flown at an English aerodrome. The training here must have had some positive influence on Robert Todd, as he went on to become an ace flying Sopwith Camels. Another American pupil, who arrived in early March 1918, wrote unenthusiastically about the place:

A ramshackle collection of buildings and wooden huts at Turnberry Aerodrome. Not the luxury accommodation of the hotel for the lower ranks! In the background several large aircraft sheds are also visible. This official US photograph is dated February 1919. (Courtesy of Imperial War Museum, MH23385)

Turnberry Hotel, which provided accommodation for the officers that served at Turnberry Aerodrome, would still be recognisable to them nearly a century later, although it has since been greatly extended. This is a picture of the hotel in 1919. (Courtesy of the Imperial War Museum, MH29384.)

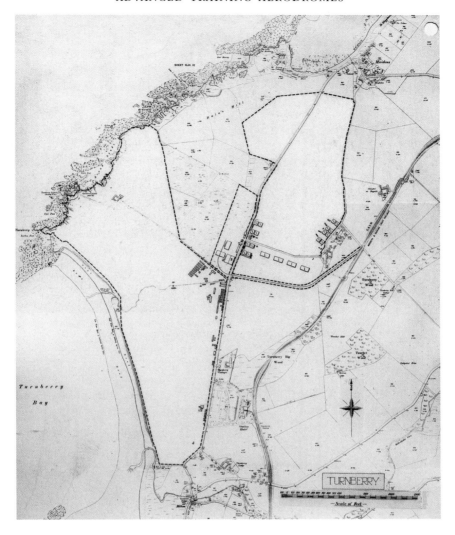

Turnberry Aerodrome, 1918, was located to the north of Girvan in Ayrshire. The aerodrome was established on the golf course of the Turnberry Hotel. The aerodrome is cut in two by the Girvan to Ayr coastal road, a feature which is still present in the twenty-first century. In those days there was also a railway line which followed a similar route and a siding was constructed to serve the aerodrome. The maximum dimensions of the base were 1,800 yards by 1,250 yards, occupying 370 acres. Thirty-five acres were used for aerodrome buildings. There were four aeroplane sheds, each 150ft by 80ft, plus an aeroplane repair shed and a salvage shed. In addition there were no less than sixteen canvas Bessonneaux hangars, each 80ft by 60ft. For repairing the aircraft there was a carpenters' workshop along with a sailmakers' for replacing the damaged canvas covering and a dope shop to treat the material. For training the new aircrew there were four huts for instructional purposes along with gun and sea ranges. The officers' mess and quarters was located in the Turnberry Hotel. The other ranks were allocated twenty-five huts. Transport allocated to the aerodrome included a car, three motorcycles, a 'charabanc', a float lorry and two ambulances. In the Second World War a new airfield was constructed on the same site. After hostilities ended the site was returned with some difficultly to the golfers. In the early twenty-first century the Turnberry Hotel remains a major Ayrshire landmark, and has been greatly extended since the time it played host to RFC pilots. (The National Archives)

Here we are at Turnberry in Scotland. It's on the coast and is cold as hell. We go to machine gun classes for ten hours a day for ten days. They run us to death and we freeze and starve.

The Gunnery School was equipped with Sopwith Camels, Vickers F.B.9, D.H.2s, Armstrong Whitworth F.K.3s, Maurice Farman Shorthorns and Royal Aircraft Factory B.E.2e, B.E.2c and F.E.2b. The pilots fought mock air battles between themselves. Some aircraft were equipped with camera guns so the results could be analysed at the end of the day when flying had ceased. Live firing was practised on silhouettes of aircraft laid out on the near by beach or on drogues towed behind R.E.7 aircraft which were employed as target tugs.

In the autumn of 1917 a second training aerodrome was established at Ayr Racecourse, some 12 miles to the north-east. Unlike Turnberry, this station was close to the town of Ayr and occupied a relatively confined area. The landing ground was restricted to the area encircled by the race track. Although it may seem an odd choice for an aerodrome, several other racecourses in Britain were put to the same use. In Ireland, the Curragh Racecourse was requisitioned for the RFC. Rather appropriately, the word aerodrome is derived from the Greek words meaning 'aerial racecourse'. No.1 School of Aerial Fighting was formed here on 17 September 1917. Its function was to train pilots in the skills of aerial combat being posted to France. The RFC were losing large numbers of pilots to the enemy due to their inexperience in air combat when they arrived at the Front. The instructors at Ayr all had been in combat in France and were expected to pass on their knowledge to their pupils. Each course lasted only a few days and up to a maximum of one week. Despite its brief length was successful in reducing the casualty rate of new pilots posted to operational squadrons on the Front. At Ayr, its pupils were taught to fly and shoot in combat so it became a reflex reaction and therefore reduced their response time when engaged in aerial combat with the German aircraft. When they first arrived here, the instructors checked that the new arrivals flying skills were up to the minimum standards required. The pupils were then flown by their instructor in a two-seat aircraft which would carry out mock attacks on other machines. They were then given the opportunity to put into practise what they had been taught by flying a fighter against the instructors. Pupils also tested their newly acquired skills by engaging in mock aerial combat with each other. This was followed by live firing practise against both targets in the air and on the ground. Stunt flying was also encouraged to give the pupil confidence in the handling of his aircraft. In the first few years of the war, this activity had actively been discouraged at flying training establishments.

Col. Rees is in charge here and he tried to put pep in the boys by giving a stunting exhibition below 500ft. He certainly did fight the tree tops and he wouldn't come out of spin above 50ft. Then he made all the instructors go up in Camels and do the same thing. It was a wonderful exhibition and then he made us a little speech and told us there was nothing to worry about, to go to it. Several of the boys were so encouraged that they took off in Camels and tried to do the same thing. Only one was killed!

The aircraft operated by No.1 School of Aerial Fighting included Sopwith Camels, D.H.2s, SPAD S7s, S.E.5s, Bristol M1cs and Bristol F.2Bs. More usually there were also several captured German aircraft for the pilots fight against. These machines were painted in RFC markings. They were probably the only German aircraft to be seen in Scottish skies in the First World War!

Lt Bogart Rogers was one of over 300 Americans who joined the RFC in 1917. He wrote home in one of his letters that:

The aerodrome is an old race track and not too good. But the machines make up for all other deficiencies, for they are in good condition and almost every type including some captured German machines. The instructors have all had a great deal of experience and most of them are decorated from V.C.s down. One pilot in particular is now the ace of aces and has over fifty Huns to his credit and just about all the decorations in the category.

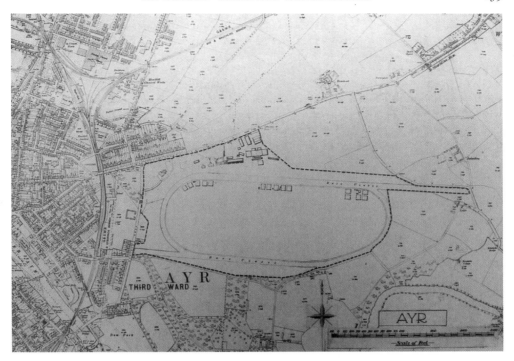

Ayr (Racecourse) Aerodrome, 1918, made use of the flat area of land that had been used for horse-racing. Aircraft landed and took off within the area enclosed by the oval racetrack. The site was 1,250 yards by 670 yards extending across 138 acres, including some fifteen acres on which stood the aerodrome buildings. There was a single large aeroplane shed measuring 170ft by 80ft located on the north side of the station. This was supplemented by a further fifteen canvas Bessonneaux hangars, each 70ft by 60ft. There were several other large structures, including workshops for wood and metal, and an engine shop. All were over 100ft in length. One feature missing from this aerodrome were the rows of huts to house the military personnel. Everybody who worked here was billeted in houses in Ayr. The large aeroplane shed, which was built next to the grandstand, survived until 1991 when it was demolished. In the latter part of its life it had been adapted to be serve as the tearoom for Ayr Racecourse. (The National Archives)

This is a reference to James Byford McCudden who served as an instructor at both Ayr and Turnberry. Unusually, there was no accommodation for personnel at Ayr Aerodrome and they were billeted in houses and hotels in the town. The Women's Auxiliary Army Corps (WAAC) assisted with the catering in some of them. One of the favourite activities of the pilots was for two of them to go for a flight over the countryside looking for large country houses. When they found a suitable example they would land their aircraft in its grounds. The owner would usually arrive on the scene to investigate what had happened and the pilots then pretend that they had to make a forced landing due to engine trouble. Often they would be invited back to the country house for tea which was the idea behind this ruse. When the pilots returned to their machine it was found that the engine trouble had sorted itself out and their aircraft would take off for Ayr Aerodrome.

Lt Bogart Rogers left for France at the end of April 1918. This was not before he witnessed one of the numerous crashes to befall the aircraft operating from Ayr Aerodrome. In mid April a Bristol Fighter took off and then did a steep climbing turn down wind 'which is generally a foolish thing to do'. A moment later, the aircraft lost all its flying speed, side slipped and crashed into the centre of the aerodrome. Everybody came out from the aircraft sheds and

A Sopwith F.1 Camel of No.1 Fighting School at Ayr in 1917. It is painted in a striped colour scheme. Like many air aces of the First World War, flying instructors often had their aircraft painted with distinctive markings. (Fleet Air Arm Museum – Bruce/Leslie Collection)

ran towards the wreckage. Before they could reach it, flames began rising from the crash site. The observer managed to crawl clear of the aircraft's remains with his clothes on fire. To extinguish the fire he rolled on the ground and then pulled his unconscious pilot clear of scene. Both of the crew, thought to be Americans, suffered serious burns. Fire was the main fear of the early aviators. In those days aircraft did not carry parachutes and many would rather jump out of their machines and fall to their deaths than be burnt alive.

Other accidents included an S.E.5, D3436, whose left wing fell off in a manoeuvre killing Cdt T.C. Mathau of the US Air Service on 20 March 1918. Another S.E.5, flown by George Vaughn, suffered engine failure while flying over Ayr. The aircraft made a forced landing in a vacant lot but the machine eventually came to rest on the roof of a building. George Vaughn escaped unhurt, but later injured his arm when someone asked him to pose for a picture in the wrecked aircraft and the fuselage toppled over. Cuth Nathan was not so lucky when the wings of his S.E.5 parted company with the rest of his aircraft at 5,000ft on 20 March 1918. He went into the roof of a three storey house and his body had to be dug of the basement.

Sopwith Camels were notoriously difficult to fly and often came to grief in the hands of inexperienced pilots. It had a sensitive rotary engine and the pupils were often unable to react quickly enough when the fine-adjustment fuel control had to be altered soon after take-off. If the engine's faltering loss of power was not immediately corrected, the aircraft could stall and go into a spin at an altitude at which it was too low to make a recovery. Six American Naval pilots were sent to Ayr Aerodrome for the Aerial Fighting course. They had previously flown Hanriots and thought the Sopwith Camel would not be any more difficult to handle and did not listen to the advice of their instructors. Within the week three of them had come to grief. Ens. F.W. Hough of the US Naval Air Service died when his Sopwith Camel, B5562, stalled and spun in on 3 March 1918 followed by Ens. H.G. Velde on 7 March in B7420. More fortunate was 2nd-Lt H. Chambers, who was only injured when the engine on his Sopwith Camel, B5557, choked on take-off and spun into trees. Five months later, on 5 May 1918, a Sopwith Camel, B9258, flown by Sgt A.J. Messer suffered a similar problem. The aircraft stalled and crashed, seriously injuring its pilot. Lt A. Ortmayer of the US Air Service, however, died from his injuries when the engine of his Sopwith Camel choked at 150ft and his machine spun in off a flat turn. He was an experienced pilot and former instructor with over 300 flying hours. Lt T.S. Dealy died on 7 March 1918 when his Sopwith Camel, B7418, spun in. The following month 2nd-Lt H. Dixon was killed when he lost control of Sopwith Camel B7465 in a dive. On April 1918, Sopwith Camel C8207 collided with B5563 at 3,000ft killing both the pilots, Lt R.E. Brooks and 2nd-Lt F.E. Ball. Another pilot, Capt. V.G.A. Bush was killed when his Sopwith Camel broke up in the air on 8 February 1918. In the early twentieth century the skylines of the towns of Britain were punctuated by tall industrial chimneys. They could be a hazard to the early flyers and at least one Sopwith Camel based at Ayr was destroyed when it collided with one. Ira Jones, who was chosen for 74 Squadron and was sent here along with many of his colleagues before being posted to France, wrote:

No.74 Squadron was to be equipped with S.E.5 single-seater Scouts. While at Ayr I did all my flying in this type of machine. Pupils who were to go to France with Sopwith Camels rotary-engined, single-seater scouts with exceptionally fast manoeuvreability-had to fly that type. The accidents were many. I remember seven funerals in one week as the result of the right hand turn close to the ground. Dozens of pilots were killed by the Camel.

One American pilot named Springs took a quart bottle of eggnog to drink when he went for a flight in a Spad fighter. At the end of his flight he decided to touch down on the disused horse racing track at the aerodrome. When he attempted to negotiate a bend on the course his top wing got caught on some telephone wires. The Spad then went straight up in the air to a height of around 300ft before plunging back to the ground. Realising he was going to crash, Springs threw his bottle of eggnog out the cockpit. The aeroplane was a complete write-off but the pilot walked away unhurt. Capt. Foggin had actually encouraged Springs to fly that day hoping that he would actually crash the Spad so the parts on it could be cannibalised for other aircraft. There was a great shortage of magnetos and the only way they could be obtained was from wrecked machines!

After only being in existence for eight months, No.1 School of Aerial Fighting moved to Turnberry Aerodrome where it merged with the gunnery school there to form the No.1 School of Aerial Fighting and Gunnery on 10 May 1918. By the end of the month it had changed its name yet again to No.1 Fighting School. Ayr Aerodrome continued in use. 105 and 106 Squadrons with their R.E.8s stayed there in May while on their way to Ireland for operational duties. Flying Instructors Schools (FIS) were set up by each of the Area Commands of the new RAF, the North-West Area FIS forming at Ayr on 1 July 1918. Contemporary documents outline the functions of the School as follows:

Subjects taught – The intention of the course at this School is to train pupil instructors in the latest methods of instruction, such as the use of the telephone between pupil and instructor, orders and terms employed, side slipping, vertical turns, forced landings, the proportion of dual and solo to be given to pupils and so on.

Supply of Pupils – Instructors are trained from two sources:
1. Pilots returning from overseas for a tour of duty on the Home Establishment.
2. Pupil instructors i.e. promising pupils at Training Units recommended by the Wing Examining Officer to be retained at their Training Unit as Instructors after having passed through the Course at a Flying Instructors' School.
The establishment of machines at an Instructor's School is nineteen Avros (Avro 504s), the Avro being the standard training machine for all service types, also two machines of each service type of training in the area concerned. The pupil during his fortnight's course is taught up-to-date instruction on the training machines and acquires a satisfactory knowledge of the flying capacity of the service type employed in this Training Unit.

On passing out of this school, an instructor is categorised 1A, 1B or 2 according to his merits. Any pupil failing to reach one of these standards is not employed as an instructor.
Length of Course: two weeks.
Estimated output: fifty-four per month.
Pupil capacity: there are nine instructors and twenty-eight pupils, an average of three per instructor, with an extra to allow for temporary unfitness, etc.

A pilot poses for his photograph in front of a Bristol M.1, C4940, at Turnberry. The sleek shape of the airframe of this machine is apparent in this photograph. The Bristol M.1c had a performance that was comparable to many German fighters. Rather surprisingly, only 125 examples were built which was later regarded as a major mistake. The skies over Ayrshire were one of the few locations in Britain where the Bristol M.1c could be seen flying in 1918. (Fleet Air Arm Museum – Bruce/Leslie Collection)

The most famous pilot to serve at Turnberry and probably in the whole of Scotland was air ace Capt. James McCudden, V.C. After a brief posting here as an instructor in spring 1918, he returned to France to take command of 60 Squadron. Rather ironically, he perished when his aircraft crashed on take-off from Auxi-le-Château. At the time of his death he had shot down nearly fifty enemy aircraft. In this photograph he is standing beside a Bristol M.1c, C4955. (Fleet Air Arm Museum – Bruce/Leslie Collection)

Another picture of Capt. James McCudden, V.C. at Turnberry in 1918. Here he is seen standing beside his Vickers FB16D, A8963, which he used as his personal transport. Although this fighter had a performance equal to any of its contemporaries, it did not progress beyond the prototype stage due to the engine being inaccessible and difficult to replace. This aircraft was painted dark red and was named the 'pot-belly' on account of the shape of its fuselage. Capt. McCudden made an emergency landing at Closeburn, eleven miles north of Dumfries while flying from Liverpool to Ayr, as he was having problems with the engine. (Fleet Air Arm Museum – Bruce/Leslie Collection)

In the autumn of 1918, Ayr Aerodrome had fourteen officers and a further twenty-eight officers under going instruction. There were 145 other ranks, including forty-eight women including eighteen who were employed on household duties.

The North-West Area Flying Instructors School was disbanded on 15 January 1919 with numerous other specialist flying training units going the same way after the war ended.

By the late summer of 1918, Turnberry Aerodrome was among the largest in Scotland. There were 1,215 personnel here consisting of sixty-one officers, with a further 204 officers under instruction. In addition it had seventy-two NCOs and WOs above the rank of Corporal, sixty-eight Corporals, 597 rank-and-file, eight boys, 145 women with a further sixty employed on household duties. In command was Lionel Rees V.C., one of Britain's first fighter pilots.

While flying alone on 1 July 1916, he spotted four enemy aircraft. Rees then engaged them only to be attacked by a further two or three German machines. Despite the overwhelming odds he downed two of them and drove the others off but was injured in the process. For this action he was awarded the Victoria Cross. The leg injury which he received in this action precluded him from further operation flying and on 7 March 1918, Lionel Rees V.C. was appointed Commander of No.1 School of Aerial Fighting at Ayr. When it transferred to Turnberry Aerodrome in May he moved with it and remained in charge until 1919. Renamed No1. Fighting School, it operated most of the major types of fighter aircraft. There were four flights each equipped with Sopwith Camels, S.E.5as, Bristol Fighters and D.H.9s. A new function was the training of two-seater fighter pilots, observers and the crews of bombers. This was one of the reasons why the aerial fighting school transferred from the small aerodrome at Ayr to the more spacious one at Turnberry. Additional types included Sopwith Pups, Dolphin Snipes, D.H.2 and D.H.5s.

Bristol M.1c at Turnberry in 1918. It was used by No.1 Fighting School. The armament on this aircraft consisted of a single Vickers machine-gun mounted just behind the propeller. The examples used in Britain, however, only had camera guns. (Fleet Air Arm Museum – Bruce/Leslie Collection)

A wintery scene at Turnberry, c.1918, with snow lying on the ground. Several different types of aircraft are visible including a Bristol M.1c, C5013 in the foreground and an Avro 504 to its right. (Fleet Air Arm Museum – Bruce/Leslie Collection)

Although no hostile German aircraft are known to have flown over Scotland in the First World War, a number of captured German machines bearing RAF markings were flown by No.1 Fighting School at Turnberry. They gave Allied pilots an opportunity to test their flying skills against enemy machines. The aircraft in the photograph is an Albatross D.V, which was given captured aircraft serial G144. (Photograph courtesy of Imperial War Museum, HU67914)

There was also at least one Handley Page 0/400 Bomber. Such large land-based aircraft were a rarity at Scottish aerodromes. In addition there was captured German Albatros Scout aircraft. The official number of machines to be allocated to this aerodrome in autumn 1918 was:

24 Avro 504s.
8 Bristol Fighters.
16 D.H.4 or D.H.9
20 Sopwith Camels.
12 S.E.5
12 Sopwith Dolphins.
Total – 96 aircraft.

There was probably a considerable difference as to what was to be officially allocated and what in reality was available on the ground. The large fleet of aircraft based at Turnberry were housed in four aircraft sheds and sixteen canvas Bessonneaux hangars, each 80ft by 60ft. The function of No.1 Fighting School was stated as follows:

The School receives as pupils pilots who have graduated 'B' at their Training Station. The instruction given is a finishing course and passes out the pupil as a service pilot entitled to wear Wings and fit to proceed for service work. The course combines Aerial Gunnery and Aerial Fighting instruction. Subjects taught:
1. The advanced use of sights, guns, and gears both on the ground and in the air.
2. Advanced formation flying at service heights, and low formation flying in the case of Scout Pilots.
3. Fighting in the air, at first dual control with an instructor, then one pupil against another and finally, pupil against instructor, and Scouts against two seaters Capacity – 160 pupils.

Length of Course – Three weeks with average weather.

Monthly output – About 200 finished pilots.

A line up of aircraft and personnel at Turnberry Aerodrome in 1918 in far from ideal conditions. It appears to be raining heavily with the men in the foreground sheltering under the wing of the Bristol M.1 which is at the front of the line. Behind it are several Sopwith Camels. (Fleet Air Arm Museum – Bruce/Leslie Collection)

J. Leacroft, who was an instructor at Turnberry, poses in front of a Bristol M.1c in 1918. He later returned to operational service to become a leading British ace, claiming over twenty enemy aircraft. In 1937 J. Leacroft left the RAF, but returned at the outbreak of the Second World War. (Fleet Air Arm Museum – Bruce/Leslie Collection)

Instructors of No.1 Fighting School, RAF Turnberry in 1918. Gen. Caley is sitting in the centre of the front row, looking to the left. On his right is Col Rees, V.C. This flight of stairs leading up to the Turnberry Hotel was a favourite location for group photographs of airmen. (Fleet Air Arm Museum – Bruce/Leslie Collection)

S.E.5a, C5323 flying over Turnberry Aerodrome in 1918. (From an original colour painting by Dugald Cameron)

Instructors at Turnberry pose for their photograph. On the left is R.W. Chappell of 41 Squadron and
H.W.L. Saunders of 84 Squadron. The small man in the centre is J.V. Sorsoleil, a Canadian. (Fleet Air
Arm Museum – Bruce/Leslie Collection)

Royal Aircraft Factory R.E.7, with a target drogue being held out to display the cartoon target design
painted onto the sleeve target fabric. The location is Turnberry in 1917. The R.E.7 had been used as a
bomber in 1916 but many ended their days as target tugs for aerial gunnery practice, one of the first
ever aircraft types to be used in this role. The aircraft in the photograph carries the name 'Accra II'
which indicates it was a presentation aircraft donated by this African city. (Margaret Morrell/SCRAN)

Pilots not only faced danger in the air but on the ground as well. An Avro 504J, D7583, has collided with an S.E.5a, D411, at Turnberry Aerodrome in 1918. The Avro 504 on the left seems to have come out the worst from this confrontation. (Fleet Air Arm Museum – Bruce/Leslie Collection)

Pupils commenced their course with intensive instruction in ground firing including firing at small model aircraft from a mock-up fuselage. They then took to the air where they got the chance to shoot at targets moored in the sea.

Turnberry Aerodrome had a lighthouse on its western edge. There was once a castle here where it is believed the Scottish King Robert Bruce was born in 1274. He went on to secure Scottish Independence by defeating the English at the Battle of Bannockburn. A fleet of motor boats was operated by Turnberry Aerodrome to maintain the offshore target range. Obsolete types such as the R.E.7 towed targets which gave the pupils the chance of air-to-air firing although it was not unknown for the aircraft acting in this role to be hit instead of a drogue behind it.

Proceedings were sometimes livened up when pilots from the North Western Area Flying Instructors School now based at Ayr Aerodrome would perform mock raids on their colleagues down the coast. The officers staying in Turnberry Hotel would also sometimes be treated to the sight of an aircraft flying past the building up side down below the level of the roof. This stunt was discontinued when it cost the life of one of the pilots attempting it.

As at Ayr Aerodrome, there were numerous accidents. They included the S.E.5 D1762, which turned downwind near the ground with insufficient bank and spun in on 5 April 1918. Its pilot, Cdt G.A. Brader, US Army Air Service was killed. There was another fatal accident involving an S.E.5, E3954, which spun in with Sgt Lilley on 28 November 1918. A number of two-seat D.H.9s were also involved in crashes. C1333 took off in a crosswind and turned downwind at which point it stalled and spun in from 30ft. Flt Cdt A. McLean and 2nd-Lt W. Rymal both perished, despite the low altitude involved. A few weeks later on 20 October 1918 D.H.9, C1372, stalled on a climbing turn and plunged into the sea. Lt J.S. Brown and 2nd-Lt C.A. Fletcher both lost their lives. Lt K.F. Piper and Ft Cdt J. Hughes flying D.H.9 C1374 crashed after making a forced landing when its engine began vibrating violently. Both crew were seriously injured and taken to hospital. On arrival, someone struck a match setting fire to Ft Cdt J. Hughes's petrol soaked clothing. He later died from his injuries. Another D.H.9,

Above: Avro 504 J D4421 of No. 1 Fighting School at Turnberry impaled on the roof of a Bessonneau hangar. These aircraft shelters were little more than giant canvas tents. It was probably very fortunate for the pilot, for if he had struck the roof of a more solid structure the damage to the aircraft would have been far worse. (Margaret Morrell/SCRAN)

Left: Lt Roberts poses for his picture beside Bristol M.1C C5019, of No. 1 Fighting School, Turnberry. The fuselage sports a red skull and crossbones. (Courtesy of the Imperial War Museum, HU67906)

C1231, was flying over the sea on 5 June 1918 when it broke up killing both airmen, Lt H.W. Elloitt and Lt R.B. Reed of the US Service Signal Corps. Two months later D.H.9 C1334 was involved in a mid-air collision killing both its occupants 2nd-Lt A. McFarlan and Ft Cdt A.Hepburn. The latter's body was found in Ballochneil Wood, around a mile away from the site of the crash.

As at other training aerodromes, a high portion of the crashes involved Sopwith Camels that went into unrecoverable spins. 2nd-Lt H. Butler died in this manner on 2 June 1918 in B9262 as did 2nd-Lt H.R. Smith, US Army Air Service, in B7467 on 8 October 1918 and 2nd-Lt C.H. Godfrey in F1408 on 11 December 1918. During a mock combat exercise on 6 November 1918, Sopwith Camel B7470 got caught in the slipstream of the opposing aeroplane, causing it to spin into a wood near Turnberry. Its pilot 2nd-Lt E.V. Ruben of the US Army Air Service was seriously injured. Another machine, B9210, went out of control at 200ft while firing at a target on a raft on 11 April 1918. It came down near Turnberry Lighthouse and struck submerged rocks killing its pilot 2nd-Lt C.W. Janes. Sopwith Camel F1410 was looped to near the ground leading to the death of its pilot on 30 September 1918.

No.1 Fighting School did not last long after the end of the First World War, being disbanded on 25 January 1919. By that time, some 5,000 officers, non-commissioned officers and men from Britain, its Commonwealth and America had been trained at Turnberry Aerodrome in its two years of existence. The other four RAF Fighting Schools had also all disappeared by 1920.

The numerous makeshift buildings which had housed the aircraft and the airmen were rapidly removed and the links were reinstated as a golf course. The residents of Turnberry did not, however, forget the airmen who had been posted here. A memorial to them was unveiled on 28 April 1923 in front of a large crowd. *The Carrick Gazette* on 4 May 1923 described it as follows:

> The monument is erected on a rocky mound commanding a magnificent view of the isle-studded Firth of Clyde and is 22ft in height on a square base with a tall pillar, surmounted by a double Celtic Cross, on one of which is sculptured the Air Craft Badge and on the column there is device of the Crusaders Sword. It is absolutely original in conception and was designed by Colonel H.R. Wallace of Busby. It is composed entirely of grey granite and the sculpturing and work of erection was carried out by Mr. Robert Gray.

The inscription on it reads:

> To the memory of the Officers, non-commissioned Officers and Men of the RFC, RAF, and the Australian and United States Air Services who gave their lives for their country while serving in the School of Aerial Gunnery and Fighting at Turnberry, 1917-1918, Their name liveth for evermore.

There then follows the names of ten members of the RFC, twenty-three members of the RAF, two members of the Australian Flying Corps and four members of USA Aviation. The actual death toll is thought to have been actually much higher and some sources put it as over sixty. The memorial still stands on the 12th green of the Ailsa golf course and is one of a very small number of tributes to be found in Scotland to the First World War flyers. More lives would be claimed here as the site was re-opened as a training aerodrome in the Second World War. The golf courses also suffered badly as they were buried under thousands of tons of concrete used to construct the runways. It took and great deal of time and effort to recreate the golf courses once hostilities ended in 1945.

THE LOCH DOON GUNNERY RANGE.

If everything had gone according to plan, Ayrshire would have had a third major training aerodrome in operation in the latter stages of the war. No.2 School of Aerial Gunnery was formed at Turnberry in early 1917 for the final gunnery instruction of fighter pilots. It was intended that the No.1 School of Aerial Gunnery at Hythe, responsible for training observers in the use of Lewis machine-gun, would also transfer to Scotland and be based at Loch Doon, some twenty miles to the east of its sister unit. The move, however, was postponed indefinitely due to problems with the site.

While most aerodromes in early 1917 were built on a very limited budget and consisted of nothing more than a few brick or wooden structures of modest size, there were ambitious plans for the site at Loch Doon and money for this scheme seemed no object. From the outset, the project had a major flaw, its location. One of the legacies of the First World War was that many of the sites picked for aerodromes eventually became major airports or military stations. Ayr and Turnberry Aerodromes were situated next to the coast and experienced mild winters with little snow or fog. In contrast, Loch Doon, the largest inland body of water in south-west Scotland was some 600ft up and exposed to the rain bearing winds. It was also surrounded by hills, some nearly 2,000ft high. The area could easily be mistaken for a landscape in the Scottish Highlands. It was not exactly an environment conducive for flying operations. Brig. Sefton Brancker, Director of Air Organisation, was the main driving force behind the project

Looking south from the head of Loch Doon. Seaplanes operated briefly from the Loch and it was intended to establish an aerodrome on its banks as part of the scheme to establish a school of aerial gunnery. Note the inhospitable terrain for aircraft in the form of a range of hills in the background. (Malcolm Fife)

This B.E.2c, No.4721, has been fitted with centre floats and is seen here in 1917 on the banks of Loch Doon. Although B.E.2cs were used extensively by the RFC in Scotland, all others operated from dry land. Note the makeshift wooden trolley used to haul the aircraft in and out of the water. (Fleet Air Arm Museum – Bruce/Leslie Collection)

Another view of B.E.2c, No.4721, experimental floatplane on to the shore of Loch Doon in November 1917. Short Seaplane 827, A9920, also operated from this body of water, probably for trials in conjunction with the gunnery range that was being constructed at that time. (Fleet Air Arm Museum – Bruce/Leslie Collection)

Despite laying large numbers of pipes in an effort to transform this area of marshy ground on the west bank of Loch Doon into a site on which a large aerodrome could be built, the attempt eventually had to be abandoned. The soil proved to be too damp for adequate drainage, and an alternative site was found a short distance to the north at Dalmellington. (Malcolm Fife)

to establish a new gunnery school. Brancker's biography gives some insight as to why he selected this site:

> I had come back from France obsessed with the importance of giving pilots a proper training in air fighting. Here again we studied French methods and I received full reports about the most efficient aerial fighting school which they had set up at Cazaux on one of the big lakes near Arcachon (near Bordeaux). A suitable place for an aerial gunnery school is very difficult to find. A land-locked lake presenting a wide surface of smooth water in an uninhabited country offers the best possible site. We tried to find something of this sort in the British Isles. I had officers reconnoitring all over Scotland, Ireland and the Norfolk Broads to find a suitable place in which to develop our first school of aerial gunnery. The most promising site we could find anywhere was at Loch Doon, Ayrshire and there we set to work to develop a school of aerial gunnery. It, however, presented great physical difficulties and the engineers whom we consulted were a little too optimistic regarding the possibility of making suitable aerodromes in the vicinity.

> Had those in authority heeded the advice of local farmers and others familiar with the terrain, the enterprise may never have commenced. Even some senior Army officers expressed doubts at an early stage. Col. McAdam of the Directorate of Fortifications wrote that he thought that flying conditions here were questionable and that this fact should be

An Armstrong Whitworth FK3, A1505, poses in a static position at Bogton Aerodrome, Dalmellington. The aircraft's tail has been raised by placing a wooden trestle under it. This type of aircraft was also used by the School of Aerial Gunnery at Turnberry. (Fleet Air Arm Museum – Bruce/Leslie Collection)

fully taken into account. His view was supported by Maj. Gen. Sir George Scott-Moncrieff who wanted the scheme postponed 'until it is definitely ascertained whether no alternative is possible.

Brig. Sefton Brancker dismissed these concerns: 'I am not apprehensive regarding mists, bumps, snow or wind which are equally more prevalent in any uninhabited part of the country'. In August 1916, the sum of £150,000 was approved to finance the construction of the new Aerial Gunnery School. The main civilian contractor was R.McAlpine & Sons. Many of their workers were housed in a town of huts on the banks of Loch Doon. Others were lodged as far away as Ayr and travelled each day to site by train or lorry. The large civilian workforce was assisted by members of the Royal Engineers and RFC. They were later joined by German prisoners of war who were held in a large camp which was also erected on the edge of the Loch.

A long row of concrete blocks were laid in the north-east corner of Loch Doon. It was intended that they would support a track which would transport moving targets. Further south, on the steep faces of Craigencolon and the Black Craig, standard gauge railways in horse shoe and zig-zag forms were erected to carry more targets. This goes some way to explain why an upland area surrounded by hills was selected for the gunnery school. A hydroelectric dam was built at the head of the Loch to provide power for them.

By early the spring of 1917 there were over three thousand of men toiling on the project. All attempts to drain the flat area to the south of Garpel, burn and convert it into a landing ground failed. Thousands of yards of pipes were laid and grass seed sown on the ground but to no avail. Next to the site of the intended aerodrome, a double seaplane shed was built on the banks of Loch Doon. A small number of these machines did carry out trials from here. Other structures built here to house the gunnery school included storehouses, a hospital, quarters to house eighty officers and a cinema with seating for 400 persons.

At the beginning of March, the challenge of trying to convert a peat bog into a large aerodrome proved too much. Another site was selected at Bogton next to the village of

Dalmellington, five miles to the north. As indicated by its name, the location was not much improvement on the original choice being prone to flooding from the adjoining loch. Lt Lewis wrote on 8 April that:

> We are making quite a nice temporary aerodrome outside Dalmellington, it is a bit small and rather marshy but will improve in both respects in time. There are two hangars up already and we have the best part of two flying animals here. One is a two-seater very like a B.E.2c made by Armstrong Whitworth and the other a D.H. Scout. I hope we shall get them into the air in a week or two, it is a bit difficult starting without any spares as they will take some time to get. Newling and I are working on the aerodrome, the D.H. is not very nice for this part of the world unless you have very skilled mechanics in case of a forced landing.

By the summer, Bogton Aerodrome had taken on a permanent appearance with several centrally heated aeroplane sheds, workshops, stores, vehicle sheds and eighteen brick huts, each providing accommodation for thirty men. There was also a railway line that ran onto the site and was used to deliver aeroplanes. Despite the formation of Y Squadron, the aerial gunnery range was still a long way off from being completed. The apparatus to carry the targets was not yet in place and the targets still had to be delivered. With over £350,000 spent on construction work by May 1917 questions began to be asked about the whole idea. Some of the critics pointed out that targets which ran down tracks on steep hillsides at 50 to 60mph bore still resemblance to the movements of enemy aircraft. One of the first actions taken by the Air Ministry, which was formed in December 1917, was to call a halt to the project. Two senior officials visited Loch Doon early the next year and their report lead to all work ceasing on the site.

By that time, some 50,000 tons of materials had been handled by the construction firm, McAlpines. Some 25,000 tons of stones had also been used to construct roads. The buildings at Loch Doon lay abandoned for a long time but all were eventually demolished under an agreement with the proprietors that required their land had to be restored to its original state once the war had finished. The foundations of some buildings are still visible in the early twenty-first century along with some of the concrete blocks for the intended target range.

Bogton Aerodrome remained in commission until the end of the war. It was little used and its sheds were used to store aircraft. It is thought as much as £3 million may have been spent on the Aerial Gunnery School. Sefton Brancker, who by 1921 had become a major-general, took much of the blame for the scheme. In his biography he stated in his defence:

> We had endless trouble over the enterprise and as each new difficulty cropped up the expense involved grew to alarming proportions and the hoped for date for opening the school for active training receded. Eventually it was abandoned in 1918 on the score of expense and bad climate. It had, however, exceptional geographical advantages for a school of aerial gunnery and I still believe that if we could have pushed it through it would have been a most valuable asset to our training. While this unfortunate station was being developed we already started temporary gunnery schools at Hythe and Turnberry and from these schools machine gun practise from the air was carried out over the sea, neither however offered the advantages possessed by the French school at Cazaux.

Sefton Brancker, by a strange twist of fate, perished when the airship R101 crashed. This was another expensive, ill-conceived British project.

CHAPTER EIGHT

The Manufacturers' Aerodromes

A government report written in 1909 stated that 'great progress has been made towards the successful employment of aeroplanes within the last year, they can scarcely yet be considered to have emerged from the experimental stage. Aeroplanes may already be purchase for £1,000 and could probably be constructed in large numbers for much less.' These were prophetic words. The First World War would soon create an insatiable demand for aircraft. To feed the demands of the War Machine, the techniques of mass production would be applied to the fledgling aviation industry.

In the years before the war, the manufacture of aircraft was little more than a cottage industry with a handful of enthusiasts building many of the flying machines. Among them were Frank and Harold Barnwell who designed and constructed their own monoplane at their Causewayhead engineering works, Stirling in 1908. It, however, failed to leave the ground. Their next aircraft had a 48ft wingspan and was powered by a Humber car engine driving two propellers with a 10ft diameter. It was only able to make a few short hops but this did not dampen the Barnwells' pioneering spirit. In 1911, their persistence was rewarded when they won the Scottish Aeronautical Society Law Prize of £50 for the first Scottish half-mile flight with their third machine. The same aircraft went on to fly a distance of over five miles at Blair Drummond, located to the north-west of Stirling. The brothers left Scotland soon after to take up posts with the aircraft manufactures in England. Harold went to Vickers and Frank took up a post with Sir George White's & Colonial Aeroplane Company which later was named the Bristol Aeroplane Company. The latter company built some of the most successful First World War warplanes including the Bristol Scout and the F.2. These machines, along with many less known types, were designed by Frank Barnwell.

In 1913 a report on the construction of aircraft in this country stated that:

Some considerable progress has during 1912 been made with aeroplanes and hydroaeroplane construction in this country. There are some sixteen firms and the Royal Aircraft Factory capable of turning out good and reliable machines. No progress had been made with the manufacture of airships.

The Royal Aircraft Factory located at Farnborough would have a major influence on the production of aircraft during the First World War. They designed new aircraft and flew prototypes but did not manufacture machines themselves. This work was farmed out to commercial companies who built their designs under licence. Critics of this system accused it of stifling innovation of new types by private companies and keeping certain types of aircraft in production when they had become obsolete. Up to 1917 most of the British aircraft that were deployed in combat had been designed on the drawing boards of the Royal Aircraft Factory.

Glasgow and Clydeside, with its many engineering firms producing ships and railways, was an obvious choice for establishing aircraft manufacturing to meet the needs of the Army

Beardmore's 'Seaplanes Sheds' at Dalmuir Naval Construction works are visible in the centre of this photograph which was taken in the 1920s. Completed seaplanes were wheeled out of the building and lowered into the River Clyde in the foreground. Most of the other small aircraft made by Beardmore in the First World War were also manufactured here and taken to the nearby Dalmuir Aerodrome for final assembly. The structure looming over the seaplane sheds is a giant gantry for the construction of large naval ships. (Glasgow University Archives)

and Navy. Many firms, however, already had full order books for their traditional products such as warships and armaments and were reluctant to branch out into new products. There was one major exception, namely Beardmore, which had in 1906 built the largest and best equipped shipyard on the River Clyde at Dalmuir, a few miles downstream from Glasgow. Its owner, William Beardmore, was interested in new ideas and technology. His company had offered the Admiralty a design for a seaplane carrier as early as 1912 and rather ironically had acquired the manufacturing rights for the German DFW biplane. A seaplane and landplane were transported from Germany and assembled by Beardmore in 1914 but work on the latter machine was never completed. The seaplane was commandeered by the RNAS.

Rather than have Beardmore design new aircraft, the Ministry of Munitions requested they manufacture already proven designs from the Royal Aircraft Factory. The first order was for B.E.2 (Bleriot Experimental) which had first flown in 1914. It was described as 'an extremely stable, single-engined two-seat biplane – a good platform for reconnaissance but a sitting duck for the enemy fighting scouts'.

To meet the order for the B.E.2cs, Beardmore had to assemble the first examples in their joiner's workshop. More suitable premises were erected inside the Dalmuir shipyard for aircraft production known as the 'Seaplane Sheds'. Located on the north bank of the River Clyde and under the shadow of a gantry and slipway for shipbuilding they were opened for use in late 1915. It eventually had a floor space of 63,000sq. ft with two galleries totalling 35,000sq. ft. These structures were typical of their era having gently arched corrugated iron roofs with grazed lights supported by timber Belfast roof trusses. Around the same time the Beardmore established a small aerodrome at Dalmuir, adjacent to their shipyard. It was known as Robertson Field after the name of the local farmer Peter Robertson. In 1916, two small hangars were built on the site. Aircraft built in the Seaplane Sheds were assembled at this aerodrome and test flown here. They included an initial order for sixty B.E.2cs. This was followed by orders for 140 Sopwith Camels and fifty Nieuport 12 fighters. Many of these were wheeled from the production line to the small hangars at Robertson Park where their wings were fitted. The Seaplane Sheds were not altogether inappropriately named as thirty-two Wight Seaplanes were also built here. With the River Clyde flowing just outside the doors of the assembly line they did not have to travel far for their first test flight. Many of the machines appear to have been lowered into the water from the quayside by a small crane. Further trials

This B.E.2c was the first to be completed at Beardmore's Dalmuir Works. At the controls is G.T. Richards, the company's aviation chief at Robertson Park, Dalmuir in 1915. (Glasgow University Archives)

Beardmore built Sopwith Pups at Robertson Field Aerodrome, Dalmuir. Aircraft were wheeled from the production line to this location where they had their wings fitted. They were then flown to Beardmore's other aerodrome at Inchinnan, near Renfrew, where they underwent flight tests. (Fleet Air Arm Museum – Bruce/Leslie Collection)

A general view of Dalmuir (Robertson Park) Aerodrome with Sopwith Camels for the RNAS built by Beardmore in the foreground. A partially completed machine is visible on the left-hand side of the hangar awaiting its wings to be fitted. The photograph was probably taken in early 1918. (Glasgow University Archives)

Wight Type 840 Seaplane under construction in Beardmore's Seaplane Sheds at Dalmuir. The date is 15 February, 1916. J. White & Co. based on the Isle of Wight were unable to expand their aircraft manufacturing activities due to their shipbuilding commitments. Beardmore was one of two companies subcontracted to build their Type 840 seaplane. The last example of this type in RNAS service could be found at Scapa Flow in 1917. (© The Trustees of the National Museums of Scotland)

Although there were no seaplane bases on the River Clyde in the First World War, Beardmore tested their newly completed machines on the river. They had their own shipway at Dumbarton where this activity was carried out. A Wight Type 840 Seaplane, 1400, is being lowered into the water by a crane. It was delivered to the RNAS in September 1915 and was based at Dundee Stannergate. Its career was relatively brief, as it was wrecked close to its base on 5 April 1916. (© The Trustees of the National Museums of Scotland)

A Sopwith 2F1 Camel built under licence by Beardmore. This version of the Camel was used on board Royal Navy vessels. It is probably pictured at their Inchinnan Aerodrome or Robertson Field Aerodromes. (Glasgow University Archives)

Beardmore W.B.V was designed as a single-seat fighter for the RNAS. Like several other aircraft designed by this company it never progressed beyond the prototype stage. Only two Beardmore W.B.Vs were built, the example in the photograph seen at Robertson Field in 1918. (Glasgow University Archives)

The Beardmore W.B.II was a development of the B.E.2, a design which this company was familiar with, as it had manufactured this aircraft under licence. Despite receiving favourable reports when tested by the military, only one example was built. (Glasgow University Archives)

of the seaplanes were carried out in the Firth of Clyde at Helensburgh where Beardmore had a seaplane slipway.

In 1915, Beardmore set up a department to design its own aircraft. The Royal Aircraft Factory had its own inspectors to ensure that the work they contracted out to private companies meet its rigid criteria. Lt George Richard carried out this task at Dalmuir until he resigned and took charge of the newly created design time at Beardmore. A number of prototypes were built and flown at Robertson Park. Despite favourable reports few orders followed. The company's most successful creation was the WB.III, based on the Sopwith Pup. They adapted it for use by the Royal Navy. It had folding wings, wingtip skids and some had undercarriage that could be jettisoned if they had to land on water. Around eighty examples were built with most being delivered to naval aerodromes such as Turnhouse and Donibristle near Rosyth Naval Base.

In 1916 Beardmore purchased stock in the British Cellulose & Chemical Manufacturing Company in an effort to secure supplies of acetate 'dope' for treating the fabric covering of their aircraft. As the war progressed, aircraft manufacturers throughout Britain faced an increasing shortage of raw materials to build their machines. Enormous quantities of linen were needed to cover the airframes and the government gave farmers free flax seed to encourage its growth. Many of the country's trees were felled during the war much of the wood going to supply the armaments industry. The manufacture of aircraft consumed large amounts of wood with ash being much sought after. In the closing years of the war there was concern about demand exceeding supply of this type of wood.

The building of large airships placed a particularly large strain on resources. Winston Churchill, who was the First Lord of the Admiralty in the early part of the war, placed little military value on large rigid airships and wished to concentrate on the building of aircraft. A.J. Balfour replaced Winston Churchill at the Admiralty in May 1915 which, with the backing of several senior naval officers, led to a renewed interest in producing a rival to the German Zeppelin. In October an order was placed with Beardmore for the R.24 rigid airship. Having no previous experience in this field Vickers were to provide technical advice.

For this project, an airship constructional station was established at Inchinnan on the opposite side of the River Clyde around 1½ miles to the south of the Dalmuir shipyard. A huge airship shed was built dominating the then open countryside. It was financed by the Admiralty and the Arrol Company received the contract to construct it. Work on the shed began in January 1916 and was completed at the end of September. When completed it was one of the biggest buildings in Scotland. It measured 720ft in length, 230ft in breadth and 122ft in height. There was enough room to accommodate two class 23 airships. The shed was steel framed and clad in galvanised steel sheet. There were massive sliding doors at each end counterbalanced with several hundred tons of concrete to prevent them blowing over when opened. The entrances were sheltered by two huge windbreaks built of steel and 700ft long and 60ft high. The windows were fitted with tinted glass and blinds could be drawn down across them for blackout purposes.

Numerous other buildings were erected around the airship shed to facilitate the construction of future airships. They included one for building airship cars and another for manufacturing the girders. There was also a gasbag testing facility. The site even had its own electric power station. Plans were drawn up to build a second airship shed parallel to the first but they never got further than the drawing board. Due to the rural setting of the site, the many workers initially had to be ferried there by car from Renfrew. To resolve this problem Beardmore built fifty-two houses for its key employees working on the construction of airships at Inchinnan. Work commenced on the R24 airship components in the 'Seaplane Sheds' at Dalmuir. Assembly began at Inchinnan in July 1916 despite the fact that the airship shed was not yet complete as the Admiralty were keen to establish a fleet of rigid airships as soon as possible. Between 1916 and 1917, the Dalmuir works also manufactured fifteen kite balloons for the Royal Navy.

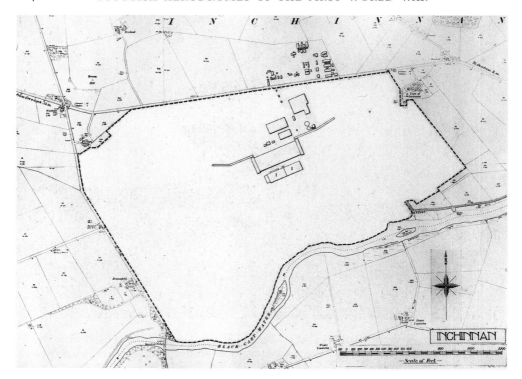

Inchinnan Airship Station and Aerodrome, 1918, near Renfrew, Glasgow. This site was where Beardmore for manufactured its rigid airships and large aircraft. Smaller machines were also brought here from its Dalmuir works for test-flying. In addition there were nearly 400 military personnel, based at the Aircraft Acceptance Park, involved in the delivery of the Handley Page V/1500. The site was dominated by the large shed for the construction of rigid airships. In its shadow stood numerous other buildings engaged their production. They included frame, girder and airship car workshops. Other structures included a gasbag testing shop, along with a silicol plant house and store. The complex had its own electric light and powerhouse. There were two large hangars for the newly assembled Handley Page bombers built by Beardmore directly in front of the airship shed on its south side. The military personnel working at Inchinnan Airship Station were housed in a camp on the opposite side of the road that ran along the northern perimeter of the station. It had its own telephone exchange and refuse destructor plant. A petrol gas plant provided lighting for the quarters. In 1921 Inchinnan Airship Station and Aerodrome closed for good. The site reverted back to open meadows on the northern bank of the Black Cart river. The area, however, has not altogether lost its association with aviation. On the opposite bank of the river is Glasgow (Abbotsinch) Airport. Jet airlines land and take-off only a few hundred yards from Inchinnan Airship Station. The flying machines of the early twenty-first century are only still a fraction of the size of the rigid airships that were once built here!

Not all the ground commandeered for military use at Inchinnan was intended for the airship shed and its associated facilities. Some of the land was set aside for an aerodrome to also be established here. It was intended that it would house an aircraft acceptance park. In the First World War there were twenty such facilities in Great Britain. Aircraft manufacturers delivered their machines to these aerodromes where they would be inspected and tested to ensure that they were suitable for military service. At some of these facilities, companies delivered wings, tails and fuselages for final assembly and test flights. Towards the end of the war Beardmore test-flew many of their new machines from Inchinnan. As the conflict continued, more and more aircraft were developed for specialist roles. There was particular interest in developing

Handley Page 1500 bomber, E8287, one of a small number completed by Beardmore, seen here at their Inchinnan Aerodrome. The original order was for twenty aircraft but the remainder were delivered in the form of spares. Behind the bomber in the photograph is a large camouflaged windbreak constructed for flying airships from this location. (Glasgow University Archives)

large long range bombers. In 1918 Beardmore received a contract to build twenty Handley Page V/1500 four-engined bombers which had a wingspan of 126ft compared to the Sopwith Camel's 27ft. They were the largest aircraft built in Britain during the conflict. A large hangar known as the Handley Page Shed was erected at Inchinnan to fulfil this order. The war came to an end before any of these huge machines were delivered. The initial order was for twenty machines but only nine ever flew with the remainder being completed as spares. A further ten of the second order were, however, also completed. The aircraft acceptance park at Inchinnan was staffed by RAF personnel who were geared up to handling this machine. Contemporary records states its role was acceptance and delivery work, testing, fitting of instruments, guns, etc and delivery of English 'V' type Handley-Page machines from Messrs William Bearmore, Dalmuir. The use of this station is allowed to the Air Ministry by the Admiralty. To carry out this work there were twenty-two officers, thirty-eight NCOs and corporals, and 269 'rank and file'. In addition, there were sixty-nine women employed for a variety of tasks. The aerodrome dimensions were 1,600 x 900 yards occupying some 290 acres. Of this area, station buildings occupied some forty acres. The most significant structures were the two aeroplane sheds, each 280ft by 150ft for housing completed Handley Page V/1500 bombers. There were plans to extend the aircraft acceptance park by building a large shed in which aircraft from other manufacturers in the Glasgow area would be processed. This function was then done at the near by Moor Park Aerodrome at Renfrew. The end of hostilities put paid to this plan.

In addition to the R.24 rigid airship, Beardmore's facility at Inchinnan also completed the R.27 and the famous R.34 which flew the Atlantic in 1919. The end of the First World War, however, lead to a drastic drop in the demand for new aircraft. By the end of 1921 both Robertson Park at Dalmuir and Inchinnan Aerodromes had closed, never to be re-opened. On 22 October of that year the land and buildings of Inchinnan Airship station were handed over to the Disposal and Liquidation Commission.

Rigid Airship R27 was constructed at Beardmore's Inchinnan Aerodrome. It is seen here in June 1918, shortly after its completion. Sheep can be seen grazing in front of the airship. (Glasgow University Archives)

After standing for only seven years, work began on the demolition of the huge airship shed. A contemporary article in the *Glasgow Herald* wrote the following about it:

> …it was created during the war under that veil of secrecy which enshrouded all the war work and although its great size and camouflaged appearance soon made it the most conspicuous object on the landscape for miles around, very little was known about the work for which it was intended. Only those associated with the work were allowed near it and its secrets were guarded with scrupulous care. At one time there were proposals for the building of airships so much larger than the R.34 that the shed would have extended for their construction but with the close of the war these proposals were departed from and it was found that the shed could not be used to advantage for any post-war purposes. For a time it was hoped that it would be adapted for the construction of commercial aeroplanes but the demand for aeroplanes of this kind was not sufficient for Messrs Beardmore or the Air Board in undertaking such work on the extensive scale that would been necessary if the undertaking were to meet with success.

Some of the other aerodrome buildings were more fortunate. In 1927 India Tyre & Rubber Company took over the remaining structures and adapted some of them for their use. They included the 'Handley Page Shed' which remained a local landmark until it was demolished in 1982.

Although Beardmore's venture into aircraft manufacturing was probably the best known example in Scotland, many other firms also contributed to the war effort in this field. As the First World War ground on ever more machines were required. Both the RFC and RNAS underwent a rapid expansion in operational squadrons. This was coupled with the fact that large numbers of machines were being lost through any action or infrequent crashes at training stations. In April 1918 Winston Churchill stated that: 'We are now making in a single week more aeroplanes than were made in the whole of 1914, in a single month more than were made in the whole of 1915, and in a single quarter more than were made in the whole of 1916'.

The engineering firm of G. & J. Weir based at Cathcart on the southern edge of Glasgow was enlisted to produce aircraft under licence. Like Beardmore, they were sub-contracted to produce the B.E.2c. There then followed orders for 450 F.E.2B and 600 D.H.9, of which 200 were later cancelled. Initially the aircraft were transported to the village of Carmunnock where there had a field for test flying. When the aircraft acceptance park at Moor Park Aerodrome, Renfrew, was opened G. & J. Weir transported their aircraft there for final assembly and test flying.

Parts for the F.E.2b being manufactured at G. & J. Weir's 'Albert' factory at Cathcart, Glasgow. The company assembled them into complete aircraft. (© The Trustees of the National Museums of Scotland)

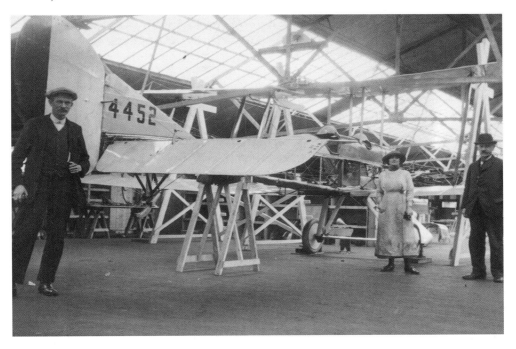

The Napier and Miller Aircraft Factory at Old Kilpatrick, situated a short distance to the west of Clydebank, Glasgow. The aircraft on the production line is a B.E.2c, No.4452. Women workers were widely employed in armaments factories including those building aircraft. (Glasgow University Archives)

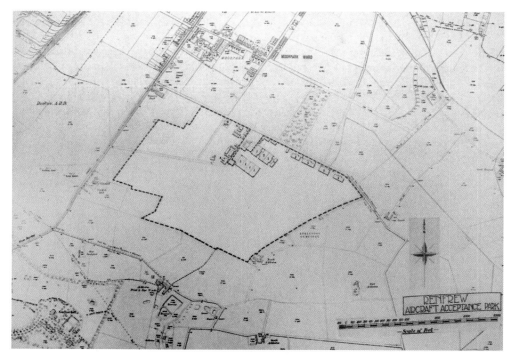

Renfrew (Moorpark) Aerodrome, 1918, was located about a mile south from Renfrew town centre. It extended across 120 acres with a length of 900 yards and breadth of 650 yards. The landing ground was described as undulating with a gentle slope towards the north. The eleven aeroplane sheds and technical buildings occupied twenty acres. There were seven sheds, each 170ft by 80ft, and a further four, of varying sizes. Some of them even had heating installed. Close by were offices, technical stores and a gunnery workshop. For carrying out tests on the newly delivered aircraft, the aerodrome had a compass platform and gun butts for checking the armaments. The motor transport fleet for the station included one Ford car, two light tenders, a heavy tender, a float lorry, a motor roller and a wing carrier. While the aerodrome's main role was an aircraft acceptance park, a large aircraft repair depot was established in 1918, immediately to the west of the main road shown running north-east to south-west on the plan. This new facility occupied thirty acres most of which was taken up by workshops for aircraft maintenance. They included two engine repair shops, each 210ft by 120ft, and a metal workshop of the same dimensions. In addition there was a vulcanising and cycle repair shop, a coach builders' shop and a motor transport repair shop. Transport allocated to the aircraft repair depot included three cars, ten light tenders, seven heavy tenders, five float lorries, eleven motorcycles, and five trailers for wings. These totals may not have actually been reached, as the First World War ended before this depot became fully operational. Buildings were erected to accommodate the large number of personnel expected to be based here, including twenty-eight huts, for the lower ranks, and a hostel for women. Renfrew Aerodrome continued to operate in the interwar years and eventually became Glasgow's main airport. It finally closed in 1966, as there was little room to expand. In the second half of the twentieth century, all traces of the site have disappeared. The M8 Motorway runs across the site of the old landing ground and houses have encircled the rest of the site. The road that separated the repair depot from the aerodrome is still there, and is the main route between Renfrew and Paisley. (The National Archives)

By the time the war ended this company had become the most prolific aircraft manufacturer in Scotland turning out some 1,427 machines (although some other companies also took on some of the work). Unlike Beardmore, G. & J. Weir did not attempt to design their own machines or aero engines. All the company's effort went on building complete aircraft, and not just airframes from established designs. They also had sufficient floor space in their factories to set up proper production lines for manufacturing large numbers of machines. At least eight other Clydeside engineering firms also became involved in aircraft production. They included several well-known shipbuilding firms, namely Fairfields at Govan who built 100 Sopwith Cuckoo Torpedo bombers and Denny & Bros. Ltd at Dumbarton who constructed 150 B.E.2cs. Barclay, Curle's & Co at Whiteinch built more B.E.2s along with F.E.2bs and Sopwith Snipes. It was one of the few firms in Scotland to build seaplanes in the form of the Fairey Campania. Alexander Stephens of Linthouse were contracted to make 100 F.E.2bs in conjunction with G. & J. Weir. Most of these firms sent their aircraft to Moorpark Aerodrome for test flying and 'acceptance' by the military. Beardmore was the only manufacturer in the west of Scotland to have its own aerodromes of any consequence. The 150 B.E.2c/e built by Denny & Bros Ltd were, however, tested at Cardross presumably flying from the large expanse of meadowland on the banks of the River Clyde.

The first steps to build an aerodrome at Moorpark took place early in 1916 when an order under the Defence of the Realm Regulations required that no ploughing should take place in certain portions of the lands of Newmains belonging to the Burgh, amounting to nineteen acres. On 13 March 1916, the town council agreed to insure the town hall, police buildings and gas works against damage by aircraft. It appears from negotiations with the farmers who owned the land that by the summer of 1917, construction of buildings on the site was well under way with aircraft sheds and a small camp for the personnel. The landing ground may well have been commissioned the previous year for the testing of Beardmore and Weir's machines.

When the aerodrome became fully established it was home to No.6 Aircraft Acceptance Depot, North-West Area. Contemporary records, written in the summer of 1918 reveal the following information about the function of this unit:

Acceptance and delivery work, including erection, testing and fitting of instruments, guns, etc. and delivery by air or storage (in accordance with allotments made by D.A.E. to meet requirements) of the following machines received from the contractors as shown–

Type of Machine	Contractor
Camel	British Caudron Co.
D.H.9	Weir
F.E.2b	Weir
Ship Aeroplanes	
Sopwith 2F.1	Beardmore
Fairey Type 3	Fairey
Torpedo Plane	Fairfield.

Average monthly output (for May and June 1918)– 50 machines.

The RAF Acceptance Park had a staff of eight officers, fifteen sergeants, nineteen corporals and 172 other ranks. There was also a Foreman and sixty-seven other women including twelve for household duties. Among the vehicles they had at their disposal were a Ford car, a motorcycle and sidecar, an ambulance, a motor roller and a float lorry.

The aerodrome's dimensions were 900 x 650 yards extending across 120 acres of which twenty were taken up by buildings. The aerodrome surface was described as undulating with a general slope to the north. A significant feature was the large number of hangars it possessed.

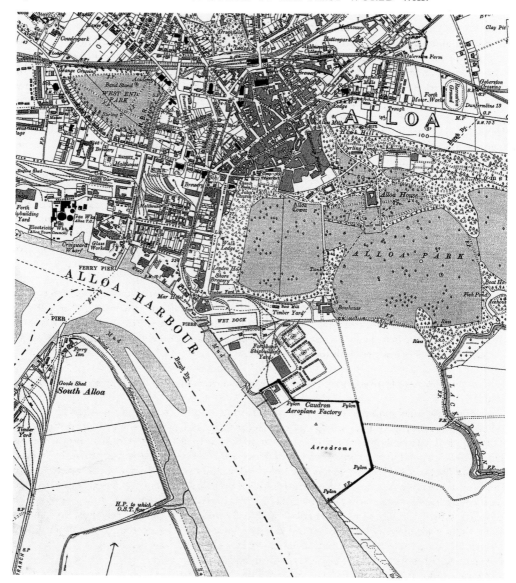

Alloa Aerodrome is shown on an Ordnance survey map dated 1924. It is located on the banks of the River Forth on the south-eastern edge of the town. The aerodrome was established during the First World War when the British Caudron Company opened an aircraft factory. This was situated immediately to the north. The aerodrome itself does not appear to have had any aircraft sheds or other buildings within its boundary. (Reproduced by permission of the Trustees of the National Library of Scotland)

A short distance to the west of the aerodrome a large complex of builders were being erected to house No.6 Scottish Aircraft Repair Depot due to come into commission at the end of 1918. Its facilities included engine repair workshops, a metal workshop, a salvage shed and a packing case store. Although the war had ended by the time the Aircraft Repair Depot opened in November 1918, it is unlikely that its projected strength of over 2,000 personnel would have been attained and if so it would have been only for a short period.

By 1920, both the RAF Aircraft Repair Depot and the acceptance park had closed and Moorpark Aerodrome was lying abandoned. Rather surprisingly it was Beardmore who was responsible for reviving its fortunes when they opened an RAF Reserve Flying School there. This company had already closed its two other aerodromes which had been located nearby. In time, Moorpark Aerodrome became Glasgow's main airport. It changed its name to Renfrew Airport and remained in operation until 1966 when all air services were transferred to nearby Abbotsinch Airport. A short time after its closure the former airfield had a motorway constructed across it and houses were built on the remainder of the site. Moorpark's RFC General Service Aeroplane Sheds which had survived up to that point all succumbed to the new development along with Renfrew passenger terminal built in 1954.

During the First World War there were some isolated pockets of aircraft construction outside Glasgow's hinterland. One such location was at Alloa, Clackmannanshire, not a place normally associated with any form of aviation. In 1913 a Caudron biplane took part in a gala day at Alloa Park, performing in front of a crowd of over 8,000. This was not the last time the town's inhabitants were to hear of Caudron. In 1914, a branch of this French company was established at Cricklewood, London, and traded under the name of the British Caudron Co. Ltd. The following summer a notice appeared in the *Alloa Advertiser*:

> It is understood that the Caudron Biplane Company are considering the establishment of the Aeroplane Factory on the river bound area of the town. The proposed site is a large flat field between Forthbank and the farm road leading from Bowhouse Farm towards the River Forth. Two acres have been ear-marked for buildings but some fifty acres are required for other purposes connected with the industry.

'Other purposes' more than likely refers to the aerodrome from which the aircraft would be tested.

A relatively small number of aircraft were turned out by the Caudron Aircraft Factory when it was established. Like so many other Scottish aircraft factories it produced the B.E.2 c/es. The B.E.2a was the first British aircraft to go to war in France. Progressive improvements led to the B.E.2c. Fifty examples of this stalwart, together with the more advanced B.E.2e, came out of the factory doors at the Alloa Factory. In addition Caudron built 100 of the more nimble Sopwith Camels here as well. Orders dried up once the fighting ceased leading to the inevitable closure of the complex. In 1922 a company called Kingwill & Jones bought the property which specialised in aerial advertising and photography. They also operated joyrides from the aerodrome The enterprise did not last long and in 1925, the Forth Shipbuilding Company chose the site to accommodate its works and built a 'wooden town' on the site. The hutments were replaced in the 1930s by a housing scheme.

At the southern end of Scotland, a small number of aircraft were manufactured in Dumfries. Arrol Johnston Ltd, who built cars before the war in their new Heathhall factory, received large orders from their parent company, Beardmore, to build aircraft engines and in the closing stages of the war complete aircraft. The initial order was for ten Sopwith Camel 2F.1. The first aircraft, N7140, was delivered by rail to No.6 Air Acceptance Park at Renfrew on 17 October 1918. A further order was received direct from the Air Department but only nineteen of these had been completed by the time the war ended. There was a landing ground at Tinwald Down Farm, around one mile north-east of Dumfries, for aeroplanes collecting spare parts from the Arrol-Johnson factory.

Far to the north, Aberdeen also played its part in supplying aircraft for the war. The Henderson Scottish Aviation Factory Ltd, who had a factory at Forbesfield Road and an assembly shop at Dafferish Place, are thought to have built around 250 Avro 504s. Rather surprisingly, there was no aerodrome or seaplane station of any significance in the vicinity of Aberdeen until the 1930s.

CHAPTER NINE

THE POST-WAR YEARS

The First World War came to an abrupt end in November 1918. On 23 August the Air Ministry had written to the Admiralty requesting information on the types and numbers of aircraft required on the assumption that the war continued into 1920. The recommendations included the provision of long range shore based air convoy escorts, merchant aircraft carriers and escort carriers for convoy work. Although the conflict ended before these measures could be put into practise, these ideas were adopted in the Second World War.

If the war had continued beyond 1918, it is interesting to speculate what its effect would have been on Scotland. Further aircraft carriers were on order. Both the Hermes and Eagle were already under construction when hostilities ceased. They probably would have both initially undergone trials in the Firth of Forth and possibly later launched attacks on the German High Seas Fleet from here followed. East Fortune Aerodrome would have been the main base for their torpedo carrying aircraft. The Naval aerodromes in the Firth of Forth would have seen a large build up in the numbers of aircraft. It is unlikely that any further sites would have been required as Donibristle and Leuchars had both been recently opened and could have contained any immediate expansion. A large aerodrome was under construction on the edge of Scapa Flow in late 1918 and this would probably have gone on to act as a shore base for some of the aircraft deployed on aircraft carriers:

> The superior Naval Power requires a superior Air Force to enable this Naval Power to be exerted to its maximum offensive strength and this can only be obtained by:
> 1. Greater numbers of equally fast and efficient air machines...
> or:
> 2. An equal number of more efficient machines.

Rear Admiral R. Phillimore, Admiral Commanding Aircraft, in September 1918 suggested that the following five types of aeroplanes should be developed for use with the Grand Fleet:

> 1. Single-seater aeroplane for use from light cruisers and turrets of large ships.
> 2. Two seater aeroplane for use from turrets of large ships and possibly later from light cruisers.
> 3. Reconnaissance aeroplane for use from Aircraft Carriers and intended to return and alight on deck of ship or in the sea.
> 4. Long distance reconnaissance or bombing aeroplane for use from Aircraft Carriers and intended to return to home territory after completing their work.
> 5. Torpedo carrying aeroplane for use from Aircraft Carriers.

> In conclusion, the forecast of aeroplanes for 1920 must, to a certain extent, be dependent upon Their Lordships' building policy as regards Large Carriers.

The tail of the large rigid airship, the R.34, at East Fortune dominates this photograph taken around 1919. In contrast, the non-rigid airship N.S.7 is floating above it in the background. It is less than half the length of the R.34. (© The Trustees of the National Museums of Scotland)

The submarine threat would have had a major influence on the deployment of RAF aircraft in Scotland if the war had not ceased. The twin-engined Vickers Vimy bomber would have been used to patrol the sea lanes around Britain replacing the stop-gap D.H.6. From November 1918 onwards it had been hoped to form one squadron a month, although initial deliveries of this aircraft were delayed. If these plans had gone ahead, the small aerodromes such as Cairncross and Seahouses would have most likely been abandoned and the anti-submarine aircraft concentrated at a few major locations. There were plans to use types such as the Vickers Vimy in conjunction with non-rigid airships for protecting convoys. In June 1919 there would be a total of 183 non-rigid airships in operation, mainly Sea Scout Twins and Sea Scout Zeros. It is probable that they would have continued to operate from the well established airship stations in Scotland such as East Fortune, Luce Bay and Longside. No further housing accommodation was envisaged for either rigid or non-rigid airships before 1 October 1919. There were no plans to expand the limited numbers of large rigid airships and East Fortune would have likely remained the only location in Scotland to have such craft based there on a permanent basis.

Despite the introduction of long-range land-based aircraft for maritime patrol, seaplanes would have continued to operate in this role as well. The smaller machines such as the Short 184 would have continued to be replaced by what contemporary sources refer to as 'Large America' flying boats. In 1918, the first seaplane station in the Shetland Islands commenced operation at Catfirth. There were, however, no aerodromes or seaplane stations on the Scottish west coast to the north of Glasgow in the First World War. Had the conflict dragged on it

Gravestones of First World War flyers in Comely Bank Cemetery, Edinburgh. Most of them perished in accidents at Turnhouse or Gullane Aerodromes. (Malcolm Fife)

is possible that aerodromes or seaplane stations may have been established on some of the western isles to protect the seaplanes. Rather surprisingly, the first visit by an aircraft to this location did not take place until 1928.

1918 saw several large new aerodromes built in Scotland in the form of Training Depot Stations. Some such as Crail and Edzell were little used before the war ended. Had it continued, it is likely that any further expansion would have been absorbed by them rather than the creation of further aerodromes. Zeppelin bombing raids had been replaced by Gotha bombers by 1917, but the latter machines only had a range that would take them as far as southern England. It is unlikely even if the war had lasted several more years that Scotland would have come within range of enemy bombers. The Germans had experimented with Zeppelins that could fly at high altitudes and out of reach of the British fighters. Had they persevered with this development it is possible they may have returned to the skies of Scotland attracted by the numerous Royal Navy facilities there. The enemy may also have mounted attacks with seaplanes carried on warships. The Germans, however, were far behind the Royal Navy when it came to shipborne aviation and did not possess any aircraft carriers.

When the Armistice took effect on 11 November it was followed by a rapid demobilisation. Patrols from many of the aerodromes and airship stations ceased a short time later. Within a matter of months many of them had closed for good. By the early 1920s the giant airships had vanished from the Scottish skies for good except for the occasional visiting craft. All the seaplane stations were also abandoned but flying boats returned in force to the northern waters of Great Britain in the Second World War.

Donibristle Aerodrome viewed from the air in the 1920s. It was one of the few military airfields in Scotland to remain in operation after hostilities had ceased. The aerodrome still looks much the same as it would at the end of 1918. The main hangars are at the top of the picture. Three or four biplanes are visible near the other hangar. (© The Trustees of the National Museums of Scotland)

At the beginning of the war Britain possessed around 150 military aircraft but by November 1918 there were over 22,000. Over the next few years the number rapidly contracted and again could be measured in hundreds and not thousands. Many of those were deployed policing far flung parts of the British Empire. Almost all the military aerodromes and seaplane stations had closed in Scotland by 1920. Only Donibristle and Leuchars survived. Both continued their association with naval aviation. With the outbreak of the Second World War, Scotland was again propelled into the forefront of naval aviation again. Scapa Flow, the Firth of Forth and Clyde all had Fleet Air Arm stations on their shores. Flying training also returned to Scotland, with East Fortune, Montrose and Turnberry re-opening for this task.

Aircraft were again manufactured in Scotland, including Sunderland flying boats at Dumbarton on the Firth of Clyde. When the First World War ended the orders had dried up for military aircraft. Many of the factories never built an aeroplane again. Even Beardmore, once in the forefront of Scottish aviation, closed their aviation department. With encouragement from the Government, it re-opened in 1924 and over the next few years produced a number of innovative designs. They included the Beardmore Inflexible, the largest aircraft built in Britain until the Bristol Brabazon in 1953. The company also set up a flying school at Moorpark Aerodrome, Renfrew. By the late 1920s it had become the main civil airport in Scotland. Unfortunately, few orders for Beardmore's products followed and they withdrew for good from the aircraft industry in 1929.

Although this aerial view of Turnhouse was taken in 1930, the aerodrome still retains its First World War layout. The railway features prominently on its eastern boundary and there are sidings to serve it. The main road from Edinburgh to Linlithgow and Stirling runs along the northern edge of the aerodrome. The route was closed in the 1970s when the airport was expanded to handle jet airliners. (© The Trustees of the National Museums of Scotland)

The legacy of First World War aviation lives on in the form of this replica of a S.E.5 fighter. It is appropriately pictured at RAF Leuchars Airshow, 2006. Nearly ninety years previously, original examples of this machine could be seen in the skies over Scotland. (Malcolm Fife)

Nearly 100 years later in the early years of the twenty-first century almost all physical evidence of the RFC and RNAS bases have vanished from the Scottish landscape. The legacy of the early fliers lives on in that they laid the foundations of modern aviation. Royal Navy aircraft carriers still visit the Firth of Forth and owe their origins to the experiments of launching aircraft from naval ships during the First World War. Edinburgh Airport was established as a training aerodrome as long ago as 1916. Two years later, Leuchars Airfield commenced operation and has remained in continuous use as a military airfield ever since. Floatplanes, although a rarity in Britain, can sometimes be seen operating on some Scottish lochs including Loch Earn in Perthshire. There was a plan in the 1980s to build airships again at Inchinnan, but this unfortunately came to nothing. The return of the large rigid airship for the moment remains nothing more than a dream.

RAF Tornadoes taking off from Leuchars Air Station. This is the only military airfield opened during the First World War that still functions in this role in Scotland in the early twenty-first century. (Malcolm Fife)

APPENDIX 1

AERODROME BUILDINGS

In the nineteenth century, the invention of the railway lead to the creation of a whole new genre of buildings. The same was true with the advent of the aeroplane in the following century.

The first purpose built structures were the aircraft hangars or sheds, as they were known then. Early aeroplanes could not be left exposed to the elements for long periods as they were constructed from wood and fabric which would soon deteriorate if left outside for any length of time. Aircraft sheds for military aircraft commenced construction in late 1913 at Montrose Broomfield to replace the canvas tents at Dysart Aerodrome. These buildings with the doors in their sides and a gabled front were laid out side-by-side in a crescent shape at Montrose. For the next two years this was the standard design used by the RFC, with further examples being put up at Turnhouse and Stirling aerodromes. Wood and galvanized iron were the main materials employed in their construction. The word hangar is derived from French and originally meant a covered space for a carriage. The early structures could probably have easily been mistaken as garages for carriages and motor cars rather than the home of early flying machines.

In 1916, a larger general service shed was adopted as the standard hangar for aircraft. They had their doors on the end of the building and they had a characteristic curved roof. Sometimes the roofs were covered in bituminous felt. At Montrose these structures were referred to as the black sheds by the pilots. Their walls were often built of brick a material not frequently used in Scotland in the early twentieth century. Often two general service sheds were coupled together. Despite an extensive building programme many of the aerodromes even in the latter part of the First World War, used the tent like Bessonneaux hangars. They were made out of wood and canvas and could be assembled by twenty skilled men in forty-eight hours. Also they were called hangars in contemporary language, and not sheds which was the usual terminology used to describe aircraft accommodation.

A wide range of technical buildings were also found on some of the larger aerodromes to service and repair the aircraft. They usually included a blacksmith's and carpenter's workshops. To repair the fabric covering on the aircraft there was a sail-maker's premises and a dope shop which applied the final touches to the machine once repaired. Sometimes there were also coppersmiths and engine repair facilities.

The Training Depot Stations such as Crail, Edzell, East Fortune and Leuchars were all designed to a similar plan unlike the earlier training aerodromes. Some variations were allowed for the peculiarities of each site. Each of them also had an almost identical range of buildings. All had six aircraft sheds and one aircraft repair shed. For training the cadet pilots, there was a general lecture hut, gunnery instruction hut, buzzing and picture target hut, and wireless and bombing hut. There was also a machine-gun range and ammunition store. Aerodromes also had their own oil and petrol stores. Often this fuel was delivered by rail and many had their own sidings including Donibristle, East Fortune and Leuchars. The RFC made extensive use of another new invention, namely motor transport. Most aerodromes had one or two sheds to house their vehicles. Usually there were two or three flight repair lorries equipped with tools and electric lightening equipment for carrying out work in the dark. Other lorries were used for transporting spare parts and camp equipment. The light tenders carried men and boxes of equipment with the heavy tenders transported spare parts and camp equipment. Finally there was usually one staff car attached to each aerodrome plus a number of motorbikes and sidecars for transporting personnel. Accommodation for the RFC and RNAS personnel was almost always in a hutted encampment. The structures were usually single storied and built of wood or brick. Sometimes they were supplemented by tents. Often the huts were located close to the aircraft sheds and technical buildings. At some aerodromes the camp was separated from them by a road such as the one at Crail, Inchinnan and Turnhouse.

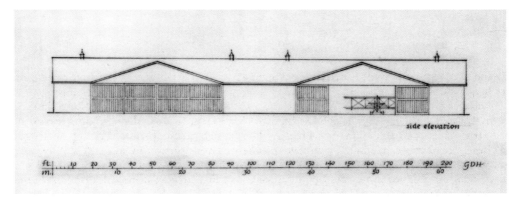

A side elevation view of the 1913 aeroplane shed at Montrose Broomfield. They were originally to be built at the original aerodrome site at Montrose Dysart before it was decided that this site was unsuitable for further development. (RCAHMS)

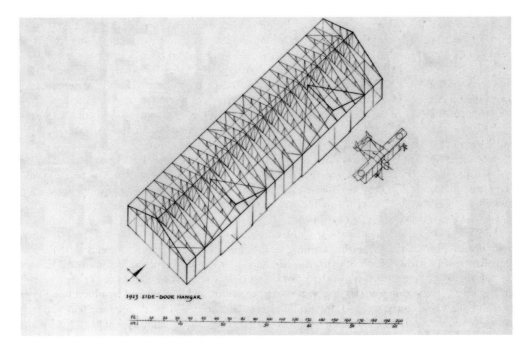

A vertical structural view of the 1913 side-door hangar at Montrose-Broomfield. (RCAHMS)

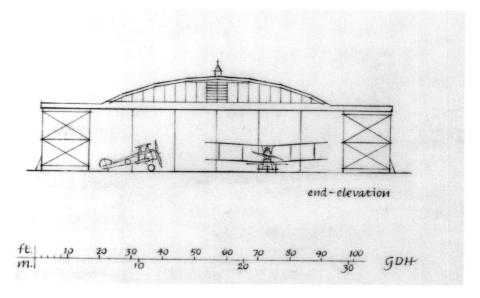

End elevation of 1917 aeroplane shed at Montrose-Broomfield Aerodrome. The arched shaped roof is typical of most of the types of hangars constructed to house RFC aircraft in the later part of the war. Six timber-framed doors clad with corrugated iron sheeting or vertical timber board were located at both ends of this type of hangar. Each door ran along steel guides in a concrete strip. (RCAHMS)

This photograph taken in 1980 shows the first permanent hangars to be erected at Montrose-Broomfield Aerodrome in 1913. The doors for the hangars were on the side of the building, rather than at the ends as used in most later designs. Resembling an oversized garage building for cars, similar sheds to those in the photograph were erected at other early military aerodromes in Britain, including Filton and Netheravon. The layout and position of these sheds were either side-by-side in a crescent shape with the technical buildings behind as at Montrose, or side-by-side in a straight line following a boundary. (RCAHMS)

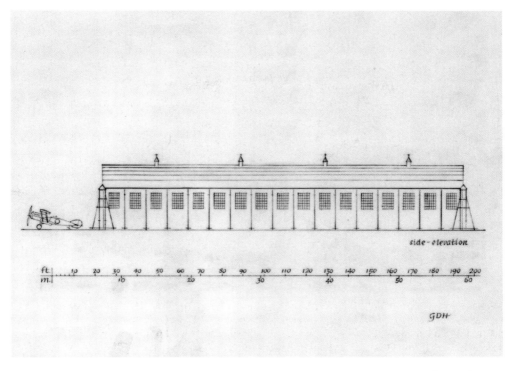

A side elevation view of the 1917 aeroplane shed at Montrose. To make maximum use of natural lighting, large windows have been fitted at short intervals along the entire length of the wall. (RCAHMS)

A view of one of 1917 aeroplane sheds at Montrose-Broomfield. The large wooden doors occupy the entire end length of the building. These structures still survive in 2007 and are the largest timber-clad buildings in Scotland. (RCAHMS)

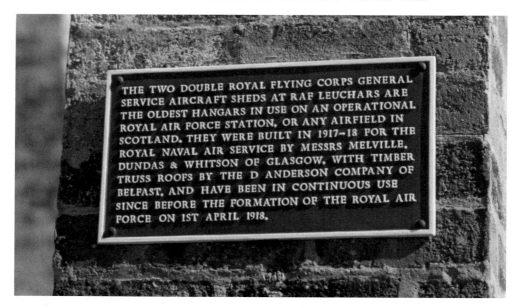

A memorial plaque on the external walls of the preserved First World War hangars at RAF Leuchars Air Station. The buildings are still in use in 2006, but the military aircraft based here are housed in more recent structures. (Malcolm Fife)

The petrol siding at Donibristle Aerodrome, December 1918. Nearly all the major aerodromes and airship stations on mainland Scotland were situated close to a railway line and many had their own sidings for handling goods and supplies. Petrol was a relatively new cargo to be transported by train, but vital for all the aerodromes at a time when the Royal Navy still primarily relied on coal. (Via Eric Simpson)

Brick huts under construction on the northern edge of East Fortune Airship Station and Aerodrome, February 1918. This type of structure was the standard type of accommodation for RFC and RNAS bases in Scotland. (Fleet Air Arm Museum)

Contemporary records refer to the accommodation blocks as the Regimental buildings. They were separate quarters for the officers who had their own mess and baths. The same often applied to the sergeants. Women personnel were housed in their own complex of huts. Other buildings found in the camp could include a reception station, drying room, coal yard, regimental institute and canteen store. Sometimes the officers were billeted in a near by country house or local hotel as at Turnberry. At Montrose, many of the personnel were housed in the Army barracks in the town, some distance away from their workplace. When there was no more room there, disused textile mills were enlisted to help.

The centrepiece of the aerodromes was the landing ground. During the First World War, these invariably consisted of a large grassed area. Surfaced runways were unheard of until the late 1930s and even in early part of the Second World War they were confined to a few major aerodromes. Despite the fact that in periods of wet weather grass landing grounds sometimes became unusable, they did have some advantages. Flying was not restricted by the direction of prevailing wind as the pilot could usually approach the rectangular landing grass area from most directions. When accidents occurred, a grassed area would absorb some of the impact, a factor lacking on a surface runway.

Another feature that was absent from early aerodromes was the control tower. This structure did not begin appearing at military stations until the 1930s. In the early days there was no aircraft control. A large windsock indicated the direction of the wind and in the 1920s the name of the aerodrome was often marked out in large white letters on the ground. If the personnel on the ground had to warn a pilot approaching the landing ground of an impending hazard, flares would usually be fired.

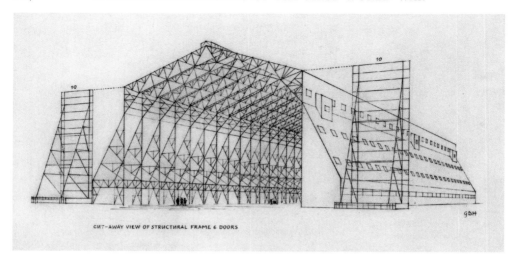

CUT-AWAY VIEW OF STRUCTURAL FRAME & DOORS

Cut away view of the large rigid airship shed at East Fortune. Note the very tall large sliding doors which extend to the roof. (RCAHMS)

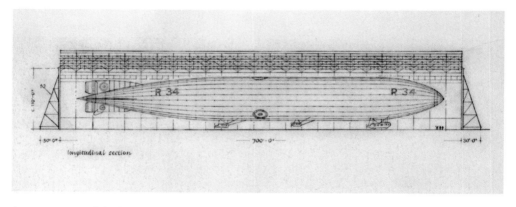

longitudinal section

A cross section of the large shed at East Fortune for dirigible airships. This type of airship required much larger accommodation than that used by the non-rigid types. This diagram shows the R.34 airship housed in the shed. When the war ended this airship was still under construction and was not delivered to East Fortune until May 1919. (RCAHMS)

Seaplane stations had their own distinctive aircraft sheds which usually differed greatly in appearance from those used by the RFC. They were corrugated asbestos or iron-framed structures capped with a sloping roof. Dundee had three different types of seaplane sheds. At the beginning of the First World War it was intended to have a landing grounds next to some of the seaplane stations but this proved impractical at Dundee and no other sites in Scotland adopted this combination.

The airship stations in many ways resembled the RFC aerodromes, there was a complex of sheds and technical buildings usually at the edge of a large expanse of grass. The main difference was the scale of building required to house even the small rigid airships. They dwarfed the aircraft sheds, both in height and length. The firm A. & J. Main & Co. Ltd built the airship shed at Luce Bay which was nearly 360ft long and made entirely out of steel. It was built with the assistance of two 10-ton travelling cranes running both sides of the structure.

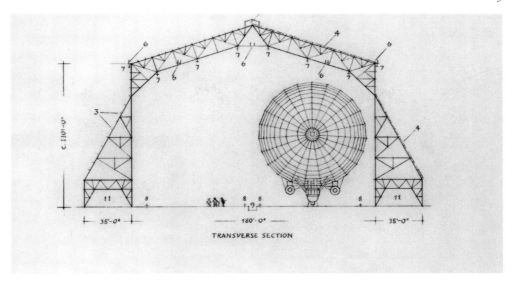

TRANSVERSE SECTION

A cross section of the large airship shed at East Fortune. This vast building could house two large dirigible airships side-by-side. Its entrance is around 180ft high and the interior of the structure is over 100ft tall. (RCAHMS)

Dominating the centre of the photograph is the rigid airship shed at East Fortune, c.1918. It measures 700ft in length and 180ft in breadth with a clearance height of 110ft. The coastal shed's dimensions were 320ft by 120ft with a clearance height of 80ft. A railway siding is visible on the left side of the picture. (Fleet Air Arm Museum)

The hydrogen gas production plant at Longside Airship Station. In the foreground is a large gas holder. There were a number of other structures associated with the manufacture of hydrogen including a water gas generating house, purifier house, cooling towers, silicol plant house, compressor house, filling shed and coke store. (Fleet Air Arm Museum)

Although most of the airship sheds were constructed by civilian contractors, the additional work such as providing the windbreaks, outbuildings, gas plants and storage sheds were the responsibilty of the Air Construction Corps of the RNAS. They also cleared and levelled airship and aeroplane landing grounds and removed obstacles such as trees and hedges. The Scottish Company, Sir William Arrol & Co. of Dumbarton erected some of the largest airship sheds. They had the required qualifications in this field of engineering having previously built the Forth Rail Bridge and Tower Bridge in London. The rigid airship shed at Inchinnan was built by them. It was 720ft long by 150ft wide inside with a clear height of 100ft. Over 2,300 tons of steel were incorporated in this structure. This company also built smaller Coastal Type airship sheds. All the main airship stations at their own gas plants by the latter stages of the war for producing hydrogen gas. It was usually produced using the Silicol Process which could yield gas within a hour of being initiated. Powdered ferrosilicon was stirred with water gradually fed into a chamber containing a hot strong solution of caustic soda. It produced a very pure form of hydrogen which was important, as if the content was as low as 80 per cent it could be dangerous to use in airships. Some minor stations did not have their own facilities to produce gas and inflated their airships with gas cylinders. Initially, Luce Bay used this source of supply until they had their own gas plant installed. To produce hydrogen gas, large quantities of water was required and there were often wells or large storage tanks to ensure an adequate supply.

Despite the huge sums of expense and work invested in constructing the airship stations, all had closed within a short time of the end of the First World War. In the early post-war years all the airship sheds, both large and small were dismantled. It is surprising that none of them were retained even for storage purposes. The only place where large rigid airships survive in Britain is at Cardington in Bedfordshire. One of them dates from 1917 and was built by A. & J. Main & Co. Ltd of Glasgow and London.

6·2·18

Above: The bomb store at East Fortune airship station, 6 February 1918. It is enclosed by a large earthwork. On the right of the picture is a gas holder. It probably feeds hydrogen into the nearby airship shed by an underground network of pipes. (Fleet Air Arm Museum)

Left: The wireless station at Longside airship station. The first air-to-ground wireless communication from a heavier-than-air aircraft was made in 1910. Despite being a recent invention, this form of communication was widely used by both airships and aircraft in the First World War. Along the east coast of Britain there were a series of wireless direction-finding stations which enabled airships to accurately pinpoint their position over the North Sea. (Fleet Air Arm Museum)

AIRCRAFT CARRIERS AND SEAPLANE SHIPS

When the cruiser HMS *Hermes* was converted to carry seaplanes in 1913 and subsequently took part in naval exercises, it was the beginning of a long Scottish association with shipborne aviation. A platform was built over the forecastle from which seaplanes could take off on trolleys. Two machines embarked on HMS *Hermes* for the manoeuvres, a French Caudron III amphibian plus a wireless-equipped Short S.64 twin float biplane. The latter had a novel feature, folding wings which eventually became an essential feature of aircraft deployed aboard ships. The Caudron III was flown off the deck of HMS *Hermes* on 3 September landing at Cromarty. The experiments using these two machines in the aerial reconnaissance role with the assistance of wireless communication had a significant development in naval aviation in the early years of the First World War.

Although HMS *Hermes* played no further role in this field having been withdrawn from service by the end of 1913, three cross-Channel ferries, *Engadine*, *Riviera* and *Empress* were converted to carry seaplanes. Canvas shelters were placed on their decks along with seaplane handling booms. It was intended originally to deploy them with the Grand Feet at Scapa Flow, but in the end they were attached to the naval force based at Harwich. A much larger vessel was eventually delivered to these north waters in the form of the aviation ship, HMS *Campania*. It was a former Cunard liner which in the late nineteenth century held the Atlantic Blue Ribbon. When it was purchase by the Royal Navy in November 1914 it was in fact on the verge of being scrapped. A forward hangar and a launching platform were added before HMS *Campania* was delivered to the Battle Fleet at Scapa Flow in the spring of 1915. Trials were carried out with Sopwith Schneiders flying off the platform on the bows of the ships. Trolleys were used to enable the seaplanes to take off.

Early in the war, ships equipped with seaplanes had to stop dead in the water to launch their seaplanes. This made them vulnerable to attack. Even then, seaplanes could only take off if the sea was not too rough. Admiral Jellicoe wrote to the Admiralty that:

> All experience throughout the war has shown that there are very few occasions on which seaplanes can be depended upon to rise from the water and there have been innumerable cases in which great preparations for air operations on an extensive scale have been neutralised by the inability of the seaplanes to rise from the water when the moment arrived. It has therefore long been evident to me that the only satisfactory type of seaplane carrier is one from which the machines can rise off the deck.

It was discovered that the platform on HMS *Campania* was not long enough to allow seaplanes equipped with a wireless set and a second crew member to become airborne. A solution to this problem was found by replacing the ship's forward funnel by two parallel ones and extending the launch platform between them. Equipment was also added for the operation of a kite balloon. HMS *Campania* returned to Scapa Flow in April 1916 after these modifications were carried out. It could now carry twelve seaplanes including the larger Short 184. Due to a breakdown in communication the ship failed to sail with the rest of the fleet, which a short time later became engaged with the German Navy at the Battle of Jutland.

This ship was also the first in history to have an aircraft designed specifically for it, in the form of the Fairey F.17 seaplane which became more commonly known as the Fairey Campania. It came into service in 1917 and operated from the forecastle platform with its floats placed on a trolley to enable it to take off without having to be placed in the water.

As well as performing reconnaissance for the Royal Navy, another function of the seaplane carriers was to launch attacks on Zeppelins. Throughout the war the Admirals of the Grand Fleet believed these craft gave the Germans a significant advantage. Although the Zeppelins are well-known for their bombing of British cities, most of their flights actually involved monitoring shipping movements in the North Sea. It was soon realised that seaplanes were far from satisfactory when it came to attempting to intercept them as there performance was greatly restricted by the drag created by their large floats. In 1915, Admiral Jellicoe wrote:

> ...our seaplanes are incapable of engaging the Zeppelins owing to their insufficient lifting power and our guns will not be able to reach them. I regret that I am unable to propose any means of meeting this menace, unless it be the use of aeroplanes, landplanes, rising from the deck of Campania, capable of climbing above the Zeppelins and able to land on the water and supported sufficiently long by air bags to rescue the pilots.

On 3 November, 1915 a Bristol Scout C took off from the launching platform on the bows of the seaplane carrier of HMS *Vindex*. This was the first time a landplane had taken off from a Royal Navy ship. From this date onwards this type of aircraft began to displace seaplanes onboard warships. New seaplane carriers such as HMS *Nairana* and *Pegasus* were constructed so they could carry a combination of seaplanes and landplanes. Both these vessels, sometimes

The seaplane carrier, HMS *Campania* at anchor. It was by far the largest merchant ship converted to carry aircraft in the First World War. On its bows is a downward sloping aircraft launching platform. HMS *Campania* was one of a very few carriers to have an aircraft designed specifically for her use in the form of the appropriately named Fairey Campania. It was launched by a trolley system from the forecastle ramp. (Imperial War Museum, FL7436)

The mixed-plane carrier, HMS *Pegasus* was launched in 1917 and spent the remainder of the war with the Grand Fleet. Its aircraft complement was two Sopwith Camels and five Fairey Campania Seaplanes. The ship is painted in a dazzle camouflage, invented by British marine artist Norman Wilkinson. The idea of the bewildering geometric shapes was to make it difficult for German submariners to calculate the precise distance and speed of its quarry. (Imperial War Museum, H76070)

The seaplane carrier HMS *Engadine* moored off Rosyth, 1916. Although this seaplane carrier sent most of its time in the southern part of the North Sea it visited Scottish waters on a number of occasions. In May 1917 the ship was stationed at Burntisland, Fife, with its seaplanes operating from there. Much of the rear part of its deck is taken up by accommodation for its seaplanes. Two cranes for lowering seaplanes into the water are also visible on the stern of the vessel. (Imperial War Museum, HU70101)

The early aircraft carrier, HMS *Furious*, at anchor in the sheltered waters of Scapa Flow. Unlike later aircraft carriers the ship's superstructure and funnels still occupy the centre of the deck representing a substantial hazard for pilots attempting to use the rear deck platform to land. (Imperial War Museum, HU71485)

referred to as mixed carriers were built on the River Clyde. In the latter stage of its life HMS *Campania* operated aircraft with wheeled undercarriages such as the Sopwith Pup and Sopwith 1½ Strutters. HMS *Nairana* was attached to the Battle Cruiser Force at Rosyth in August 1917 but saw little active service. Instead she was used for training pilots in deck take-offs and transporting aircraft to other warships equipped with launching platforms. It was joined by HMS *Pegasus* which performed a similar function. Both these ships at various stages in their careers operated Sopwith 184 and Fairey Campania seaplanes along with Beardmore W.B.111 and Sopwith 2F.1 Camel landplanes.

A significant milestone in naval aviation occurred on 4 July 1917 when HMS *Furious* joined the Battle Fleet. This ship was launched as a light battle cruiser but was altered to carry both seaplanes and landplanes. A large flight deck was built on the bows of the ship to launch these aircraft. Her initial complement of aircraft was five Sopwith Pups and three Short 184 Seaplanes. This vessel was the Royal Navy's first aircraft carrier (in those times they were sometimes known as aerodrome carriers). It was based at Scapa Flow where trials were carried out with its aircraft. On 2 August 1917 Sqn Cdr E.H. Dunning landed his Sopwith Pup on its flight deck. This was the first time an aircraft had successfully put down on a moving ship. Although landplanes had been carried on the mixed carriers, they could not return to the ship once launched and either had to put down in the sea and await rescue or fly to a nearby aerodrome. Sqn Cdr E.H. Dunning made his epic flight from Smoogroo Aerodrome to HMS *Furious* which was steaming inside the sheltered waters of Scapa Flow. Unfortunately he was killed a few days later when attempting to repeat this feat. His aircraft went over the side of the ship and he was drowned. In the autumn of 1917, HMS *Furious* took part in operations in the North Sea which lead to the decision to carry out modifications to the vessel. A landing deck was added on the stern. She was now taking on the appearance of an aircraft carrier in the true sense of the word. The main difference was that the flat top of the ship was pierced by the ship's bridge and funnel in its centre. HMS *Furious* could now carry sixteen aircraft instead of ten.

On 15 March 1918 the aircraft carrier was recommissioned at Rosyth as a flagship, Admiral Commanding Aircraft, Grand Fleet with Sopwith 1½ Strutters. While stationed in the Firth of Forth, Sopwith Pups fitted with skids in place of their conventional undercarriage participated in landing trials on it. The ship's superstructure created all kinds of eddies and turbulence

Sopwith Schneider Seaplanes No.1556 and No.1439 on the afterdeck of HMS *Engadine*, around April/May 1915. The seaplanes were used for anti-Zeppelin patrols over the North Sea. (Courtesy of Imperial War Museum, NU70085)

The aircraft carrier, HMS *Furious*, May 1918. It lead the Tondern Raid, two months later when seven Sopwith Camels, each armed with a pair of 50lb bombs, attacked the Zeppelin sheds there. The ship served throughout the Second World War, being finally sold for scrap in 1948. (Courtesy of Imperial War Museum, FL4895)

A dramatic reconstruction of the Tondern raid. Sopwith 2F.1 Ship's Camels are bombing airship sheds and destroying Zeppelins L54 and L60. (From a colour painting by Dugald Cameron)

A Sopwith Camel taking off from HMS *Pegasus* in the Firth of Forth. This aircraft is also recorded as flying from Donibristle Aerodrome in August, 1918. (Fleet Air Arm Museum – Bruce/Leslie Collection)

HMS *Argus* in the Firth of Forth in 1918. Naval aircraft are circling above the carrier. HMS *Argus* was built by Beardmore on the River Clyde and was the world's first flat top carrier. Note the lack of any superstructure above the level of the flight deck. (Fleet Air Arm Museum – Bruce/Leslie Collection)

After surviving over three years' war service with the Grand Fleet, the seaplane carrier HMS *Campania* was lost in the Firth of Forth when her anchor chain broke during a gale in November 1918. After colliding with the cruiser *Glorious* and the battleship *The Royal Oak*, the ship sunk off Burntisland in Fife. All the crew were saved. It was the largest ship ever to sink in the Firth of Forth, and much of its wreckage still remains on the sea bed. (Imperial War Museum, HU71490)

making landings very hazardous on the rear landing deck. Many of the Sopwith Pups were wrecked attempting this. It was eventually decided to abandon deck landings on HMS *Furious*. This, however, did not prevent it from mounting a raid on the Zeppelin base at Tondern in northern Germany in the summer of 1918. Earlier in the war, an attempt was made to attack it using eleven Sopwith Baby seaplanes launched from HMS *Vindex* and HMS *Engadine*. Only one reached Tondern but its bombs missed their target. Many of the other seaplanes failed to get airborne due to mechanical failure. When seven bomb-carrying Sopwith Camels took off from the flight deck of HMS *Furious* in July 1918 they achieved more success. Two Zeppelins, L.54 and L.60 were destroyed and the fear of a follow up attack resulted in Tondern being abandoned as an operational airship base. The seaborne attack launched from HMS *Furious* is regarded as the pinnacle of success of naval aviation in the First World War.

In September 1918, HMS *Furious* was joined by a second aircraft carrier HMS *Argus*. The latter ship had a completely flat top with no superstructure above it to impede flying operations. It spent the final months of the First World War in the Firth of Forth. The first landings and take-offs from her deck were made on 24 September by Sopwith 1½ Strutters. Had the conflict continued, torpedo carrying Sopwith Cuckoos would have embarked on it to mount an attack on the German naval bases. HMS *Argus*, however, returned to Scottish waters in the Second World War when it was used for training Fleet Air Arm pilots in deck landings.

This ship was appropriately built at Dalmuir by Beardmore, the same company that produced many of the aircraft for the RNAS. She started life as a cargo ship which was partially completed when war broke out in 1914. Orders were given to commence work on her conversion to an aircraft carrier in October 1916, but due to several changes in her design, her delivery was greatly delayed. William Beardmore & Company had drawn up a design for an aircraft carrier as early as 1912. It had a flat deck running the length of the ship for launching and landing aircraft. The ship's funnel and superstructure would have been placed either side of it with the deck running between them. The Admiralty rejected the idea as being ahead of its time and that not enough experience had yet been gained operating seaplanes to determine future naval requirements.

By the end of the the First World War, the Royal Navy lead the way in shipborne aviation. Much of the pioneering work was undertaken in the waters of the Firth of Forth and Scapa Flow. The Germans had no equivalent aircraft carriers to HMS *Furious* and HMS *Argus*. In the Second World War, aircraft carriers had become the most important surface ship in use by the major powers eclipsing the battleship which had a dominant role in the earlier conflict.

PRESENTATION AIRCRAFT

Although Scottish towns such as Crieff and Newport never possessed an aerodrome in the First World War they still had an affiliation to the RFC. Individual aircraft displayed these names on their fuselage. This had its origins in 1915 when the Overseas Club which represented British citizens in Commonweath lands had the idea of forming an Imperial Air Flotilla. In conjunction with the Patriotic League they would collect money from their members to fund the purchase of aircraft for the RFC. The scheme was soon extended to include contributions from cities, towns, companies and individuals in Britain. An official price list was drawn up for the purchase of various types of aircraft, a B.E.2c cost £1,500 and a Vickers Gunbus £3,500. In exchange the donor would receive a picture of the aircraft they had funded with their name painted on its side. If the original machine was destroyed or withdrawn from service, the name would be transferred to its replacement. The first examples of presentation began to be delivered in the summer of 1915. It was originally intended that such machines should only be delivered to front line squadrons but it time they found their way into home defence and training squadrons in Britain. Thus sometimes a machine bearing the name of a Commonwealth country or city would sometimes be seen flying from a Scottish air station. Aircraft supporting the names of Scottish contributors included:

Sopwith Camel C6778	*Alloa Scotland.*
F.E.2d B1877	*St Andrews No.1.*
Sopwith Camel E4376	*Sherriffmuir.*
Sopwith Camel E4375	*Wharrieolen, People of Dunblane.*
S.E.5 F8953	*Crieff No.2.*
D.H.9 D9807	*City of Glasgow.*
S.E.5A D6933	*Newport-Fife No.4.*
Sopwith Camel D9667	*Rossyln Castle.*
Unidentified aircraft	*City of Edinburgh (Tirisdeach.*

Sopwith Camel D3423, donated by the people of the Island of Tiree, crashed after an engagement with enemy aircraft on 11 August 1918. Its pilot 2nd-Lt J. Watt was slightly wounded. The aircraft which had come down in among the lines was salvaged but never flew again. By the end of the war, well over 600 aircraft had been purchased by funds donated by Britons living at home and abroad.

Tanks, guns and other armaments were funded by similar schemes. The public felt they were directly contributing to the war effort when they sponsored such purchases. In the Second World War large numbers of Spitfires were sponsored by cities, towns, companies and societies.

Edinburgh raised money for the purchase of no less than fourteen Spitfires which went to equip 603 Squadron staffed by many of its own citizens.

This de Havilland D.H.9 D3259 presentation aircraft was built by the Aircraft Manufacturing Co. Ltd whose works were at Hendon. On its nose it bears the inscription, *Biggar Parish No.4* in small white lettering. This machine was delivered to 211 Squadron in August 1918. At that time it was fighting in France and its D.H.9s were used in the reconnaissance and bombing roles. (© The Trustees of the National Museums of Scotland)

This S.E.5a D6940 presentation aircraft displays the inscription *Parish of Inch No.2* on its rear fuselage. The aircraft in the photograph is in immaculate condition and was delivered to 29 Squadron in July 1918. The following month it shot down three enemy aircraft and a further three in September. By October 1918, the machine was deemed unfit for further war flying and retired from service. (© The Trustees of the National Museums of Scotland)

APPENDIX 4

THE PHANTOM FLYERS

Scotland has a long legacy of ghosts and supernatural phenomena. Usually they were to be found lurking in the vicinity of castles or some other ancient ruin. In the twentieth century, however, a new domain was added to their list in the form of an aerodrome.

Shortly after the country's first military aerodrome was established at Upper Dysart near Montrose, two squadron took up occupation there. A few months later one of its pilots was killed in a flying accident. The local newspaper published an article on this tragic event:

> Lt Desmond L. Arthur of the 2nd Squadron of the RFC was killed near the aerodrome at Montrose about eight o'clock yesterday by falling in a biplane from a height of 2,000ft. Lt Arthur was flying in fair weather a mile from the aerodrome when one of the plane's wings was seen to collapse and the machine fell like a stone into a field. The pilot was found in an adjoining field 100ft away. Death was instant, his neck was broken. The aeroplane was the Government built machine, B.E.2, No.205, flown from Farnborough to Montrose by Maj. Burke last week.

The unfortunate pilot was the first military airman to die in a crash in Scotland. The wreckage was removed from the crash site near the sand dunes of Lunan Bay for examination. The Royal Aero Club was given the task of investigating the cause of the accident. They concluded that the B.E.2's right hand wing tip had been damaged in the past along with the main rear spar. The workmanship of the repair was of a very poor standard which almost certainly caused the structural failure of the upper starboard wing on the machine that was being flown by Lt Desmond Arthur. The person that carried out the repair was never traced. The accident report, however, recommended that future repairs at Montrose be checked by supervisors and that records be kept of all such work. Despite the report by the Royal Aero Club absolving the deceased pilot of any blame, in 1916 a committee of enquiry set up to investigate the spate of flying training accidents, stated that Lt Desmond Arthur had fallen out of his plane whilst stunt flying.

By this time No.2 Squadron had long since left Montrose and it had become the base of 18 (Reserve) Training Squadron. Late one August evening a staff officer, who some sources name as Maj. Cyril Foggin was walking up the path to the Old Mess, which had originally been used by No.2 Squadron ,when he became aware of a figure clad in flying gear walking ahead of him. As he was approaching the door of the old mansion which housed the mess his attention was distracted by an owl hooting on a nearby tree. When he looked around he found that the door was still shut and the pilot had disappeared. Two nights later, he came out of a hangar shortly after midnight when he caught sight of the same pilot again walking in the direction of the mess swinging his helmet in his hand. Over the next few weeks he saw the same figure on several more occasions, always at night and in a dim light. The staff officer became concerned about the state of his mind until in September the matter came out into the open in the mess and he discovered that he was not alone in experiencing these visitations. The Commanding Officer and several flying instructors who lived in the old mess had also seen this figure.

Some of these encounters had taken place inside the building itself. On one occasion another officer was asleep in bed after an arduous day when he was suddenly roused from his slumber with a feeling that he was not alone in the room. He raised himself and glanced towards the foot of his bed. There he saw by the light of a dying fire a man dressed in uniform at the foot of his bed. The startled officer tried to speak to the uninvited visitor but received no reply. Receiving no reply he moved towards the figure which suddenly vanished.

Further sightings continued in the closing months of 1916. In November, a visiting officer, who had served with Lt Desmond Arthur in the south of England several years earlier, believed that the apparition resembled his former colleague, a dark haired little Celt from County Limerick. While most encounters with the ghost were notable for their silence, several officers stated that they had heard it demanding a re-hearing of the verdict that blamed the pilot for the 1913 fatal crash. Just before Christmas 1916, the committee investigating flying crashes in the RFC published their final version of the report which reversed their earlier decision to put the blame on Lt Arthur for the accident that claimed his life. With the injustice having been rectified, sightings of the ghostly apparition became rare, with one final encounter at Panmure Barracks in January 1917.

Not everyone subscribed to the theory that the hauntings were linked to the spirit of the late Lt Arthur. Some stated it was a trainee pilot, often referred to in uncomplimentary terms as a 'Hun' due to the brutal way they treated their aircraft. They were contributing to the destruction of large numbers of machines and sometimes their instructors were doing the German's work for them.

One such individual had been sent up for his first flight alone and before going up had said that he did not like flying. Orders being orders, he took off and crashed a short time later killing himself. His ghost then came back to haunt his flying instructors. An article written in the *Aeroplane* magazine published in 1920 stated that 'eventually the story worked around the RFC where it was generally told either as a "creepy" story or as a joke against the Staff at Montrose and their nerves. Some few people perhaps took it seriously'. There was also mention of the War Office trying to hush up the matter. A clairvoyant who visited the site in the latter part of the twentieth century rather surprisingly said he thought the ghost may have been a prankster dressing up. He sensed it was somebody from a well-known local family, possibly suffering from insanity!

Montrose Aerodrome remained dormant for much of the inter war period re-opening in 1936, to resume its role of training pilots. Shortly after the outbreak of the Second World War the station's personnel were again witnesses to a number of supernatural events. During the winter of 1940, the ghostly figure first encountered a quarter of a century ago reappeared, being seen by many of the personnel. One night a Hurricane was scrambled to intercept a marauding Heinkel bomber. The pilot was unable to locate it and reported he was returning to base. As the Hurricane was about to land with a minimum of runway lights displayed the aircraft opened up its engine and went round again. The runway lights were switched on fully for the pilot's second landing attempt, as it was thought he may have had difficulty making out the runway in the darkness. After the Hurricane landed successfully on its second attempt, the pilot informed the ground crew that had gathered round him 'some madman in a biplane baulked me just as I was touching down – a thing like a Tiger Moth'. The Flt Cdr informed the angry pilot that there were no other aircraft flying in the area that night and that there were no Tiger Moths based at Montrose. Supernatural phenomena continued to be witnessed at this aerodrome long after the Second World War. They were no longer the sole preserve of this location as apparitions and hauntings were reported at numerous other stations the length and breadth of Britain. A First World War biplane reputedly appeared in the skies over Turnberry aerodrome shortly before an accident occurred there. Like Montrose, it had been returned to use as a training aerodrome in the conflict against Hitler.

Not all sightings of the First World War aeroplanes were as nebulous as those mentioned previously. It is alleged that personnel for RAF Ayr searching for the wreckage of a recently crashed aeroplane in the hills to the south of this station came across the wreckage of a near complete First World War biplane with the skeleton of the pilot still strapped in his seat. Over the next half century or so, this story has been recanted in newspaper and magazine articles. There is some doubt as to the authenticity of it, as there appears to be no documentary evidence of any discovery of this nature. The location of the gruesome discovery is attributed to other parts of Scotland as well. Another, perhaps more reliable source, stated that a First World War aircraft was found during the search for a 111 Squadron aeroplane which crashed ten miles north-west of Edzell in 1940. In many of the accounts the type is identified as a Sopwith Camel. The imprecise nature of the facts, however, casts doubt on the authenticity of this story.

The invention of the airship in the closing years of the 19th century did not always strike a positive response in the minds of the public. Sightings were reported of mystery craft in both Europe and North America. In some ways it resembled the UFO scare of the 1950s. When war broke out in Europe in 1914, it fuelled the state of paranoia that existed in the minds of some members of the British population. It was seriously believed that the Germans had a secret base in the English Lake District from which they operated a Zeppelin. This was only dispelled when an aircraft did a search of the area and no trace of a Zeppelin base was found. Scotland was also believed to harbour enemy flying machines. The Perth paper, *The People's Journal*, on 24 October 1914 ran the following article entitled 'Mysterious Aircraft Seen in the Highlands – is There a Secret Store?':

> The air is full of rumours regarding spies in the Highlands and if all the stories are true, the North is a regular hotbed of secret agents of the Kaiser. Hostile aircraft it is asserted, have been seen at many places in the North. They have passed over Aberdeenshire, scouted the Banff Coast, flew in the region of Ben Nevis and have been seen as far west as Gairloch. It has always been at dark that the mysterious aviators have come out from their hiding and many people in various localities have reported the appearance of strange lights in the heavens after nightfall. So well satisfied are people that they have reported the matter to the military and police authorities who have endeavoured – with what success is not known – to locate the supposed spies. The general impression is that spies are at work. Rumour has it that a petrol store has been discovered in a part of Darnaway Forest in the Uplands of Ardelash, Nairnshire. A Ferness resident supplies the statement and states there is great excitement about Glenferness. Fraserburgh gives a story of a find at the cliffs. There it is stated that two Germans were discovered in charge of an oil store. Elgin folks state that they have heard mysterious aircraft over the city.
>
> Moving lights seen at night at Banff indicate to the inhabitants there that aeroplanes are at work. Signalling too, has been seen in progress. If the reports are true, then it is clear that these aircraft must have been operating from a secret base in some remote and unfrequented part of the country where they are able to obtain supplies of oil, petrol and other stories. Such a base would probably consist of a concealed store of oil and petrol in charge of an armed caretaker. The only other store would be afloat. The Germans might have oil ships steaming around the coasts under some neutral country's flag and supply the aviators with petrol.

The following month, the same paper reported strange goings on around Blair Atholl in the heart of the Scottish Highlands:

> Since the outbreak of the war in August, Atholl has been the centre of a remarkable series of suspicious occurrences both in the air and on the earth which have been in the main associated with alleged machinations of the enemy. Possibly it is this very seclusion, say those who most firmly asseverate their belief in the actuality of the several manifestations, that adds value to any operations that might be carried on by representatives of either of the alien nations.
>
> But to come meanwhile to the occurrences themselves, it will be recalled that attention called 'airship' which for some three or four nights was said to have sailed in a northerly

direction toward the valley. This mysterious visitant showed vari-coloured lights – red, green and white – and as these were declared on reliable authority to flash in a regular sequence, the 'phantom' vessel was regarded with certainty as engaged in secret communications. The aircraft, strangely enough or perhaps most naturally during the evenings it was observed, invariably was sighted performing its nocturnal journey in the same northerly direction between 8.15 p.m. and 9.15 p.m. It was not only observed by private individuals but also attracted the attention of the authorities, who from what can be learned were convinced that there was good ground for entertaining active suspicion as to the 'phenomenon' but unfortunately the most searching investigation failed to adduce any satisfactory solution of an admittedly difficult problem. On one of the evenings the air vessel whose form could not be distinguished against the enveloping background of a murky sky was sighted by a number of young men who were in the vicinity of Moulin. They were convinced that no astronomical proposition could account for the presence of the unusual aerial visitant. Following its course with anxious and straining eyes they were amazed to note the unusual night voyager drop suddenly and so near at hand to appear to alight on Pitlochry golf course on the slopes of Craiglunie. But the finality of the descent had been only apparent on account of the imperfect perspective and no trace of the craft was to be found.

Further 'suspicious' activities were reported over the following weeks:

> The latest phase of nocturnal mysteries is concerned with the appearance of what is described as a 'searchlight', which the other night is stated to have swept Mid Atholl from the lower end of the Tummel Valley. The appearance of this new form of manifestation is vouched for on the unimpeachable authority of the observers of the light. It was noted shortly after eleven o'clock at night. The blinds of a room were being drawn up preparatory to retiring for the night when the bright shaft of light compelled attention.
>
> The conditions were very favourable for the use of a brilliant illuminant and its rays were followed with the keenest interest which developed into concern as the possibility of the searchlight being operated in the interests of the subtle enemy was considered. Houses clustered together in a populous centre were clearly revealed by the flitting illuminant as it swept along the northern slopes of the valley.
>
> Many are firmly convinced that the mysterious happenings alluded to are by no means to be treated with contempt and while the majority continue to sleep calmly o'nights, leaving the morrow in this respect to know that from the beginning the authorities have kept a firm grip on the situation and are fully cognisant of much that has not been allowed to be made public, but which is happily of a reassuring nature.

There were also reports of other spy plane scares from south-west Scotland. The residents of the isolated area of Glen Trool, near Newton Stewart, reported hearing aircraft engines and seeing flashing lights. The date was January, 1915 when such sightings were on the decline. The belief that the Germans may be operating clandestine seaplanes from the remote lochs in the area was strengthened when an abandoned tent was found 2,350ft up on a hillside. A group of soldiers were dispatched to Glen Trool with orders 'to watch for hydroplanes (seaplanes) which are thought to be landing on the lochs of Galloway and to look for signalling'. They even erected a line of ropes across the valley in the hope that the enemy seaplane would fly into them and slice off its wings. After spending a considerable time and effort searching the surrounding lochs and hills for a hidden base and associated fuel dump, the army detachment was withdrawn from Glen Trool. The Scottish Alpine Club later confessed to leaving one of their tents on the slope of Millfire Hill after a snowstorm.

Despite the numerous alleged sightings of enemy aircraft operating from secret bases in Britain in the early months of the First World War, no evidence for such activities was ever found.

First World War Aerodromes and Airship and Seaplane Stations

Listed below are all known sites in Scotland that saw service in the First World War. The map reference for them is given with the sheet number of the Ordnance Survey 1:50,000 Landranger Map. The areas are based on the council divisions of Scotland in operation in 2006. Several of them, including regions such as the Western Isles, Moray, North and South Lanarkshire never possessed any aerodromes or seaplane stations during the years 1914 to 1918 and therefore do not appear in the list below. Large areas of Scotland were devoid of any stations including most of the interior of the country. This was in part due to the hills and mountains that occupy most the area. Almost all of the the First World War areas were located close to the coast as this was where most of the low-lying land was found suitable for aerodrome construction. There were clusters of bases particularly around the Firth of Forth and in the Orkney Islands where the Royal Navy had their anchorages. A string of landing grounds ran down the East Lothian and Berwickshire coast in an attempt to thwart intrusions by Zeppelins. They extended into Northumberland and down the east coast of England. In the list below the word aerodrome has been used to signify a major base from where aircraft flew. Landing grounds, on the other hand, denote the fact that they only saw temporary deployments of aircraft and in some instances were only used very occasionally. Finally it should be noted that some of the map references for some of the little-used landing grounds may be inexact.

The Shetlands	Landranger Map No.
Catfirth Seaplane Station	03/HU 450530
Balta Sound Moorings	01/HP 635090
(planned for Catfirth Seaplanes)	
Lerwick Kite Balloon Station	04/HU 465433

The Orkney Islands	
Smoogroo Aerodrome	06/HY 3520046
Caldale Airship and Kite Balloon Station	06/HY 417105
Houton (Orphir) Kite Balloon Station	06/HY 330040
Kirkwall Bay Seaplane Station(1913)	06/HY 442115
Scapa Seaplane Station	06/HY 441090
Stenness Loch Seaplane Station	06/HY 300119
Houton Bay Seaplane Station	06/HY 319041
Pierowall (Westray) Seaplane Station	05/HY 440482

Highland Region

Delny House Landing Ground	21/NH 730720
Cromarty Seaplane Station	27/NH 785675
Fort George Seaplane Station	27/NH 761566
Nigg Seaplane Station (1913)	21/NH790690
Thurso Seaplane Station	12/NO 121689

Aberdeenshire

Longside (Lenabo/Peterhead) Airship Station	30/NK 030421
Strathbeg Seaplane Station	30/NK 082577
Peterhead Bay Seaplane Station	30/NK 130447

Perth and Kinross

South Kilduff (Kinross) Landing Ground	58/NO 083017

Angus

Edzell Aerodrome	45/NO 630705
Montrose (Broomfield) Aerodrome	54/NO 725598
Montrose (Upper Dysart) Aerodrome	54/NO 685545
Barry Landing Ground	54/NO 532334
Balhall Landing Ground	44/NO 510630
Aulbar (Albar) Airship Station	54/NO 570560

Dundee

Dundee (Stannergate) Seaplane Station and Depot	54/NO 433307
Broughty Ferry Landing Ground	54/NO 463303

Stirling Region.

Raploch (Stirling) Aerodrome	57/NS 785940
Kincairn (Gargunnock) Landing Ground	57/NS 71-95-?

Argyll and Bute

Machrihanish Airship Station and Aerodrome	68/NR 682201
Cardross Landing Ground	63/NS 33-77-?
Helensburgh Seaplane Slipways	56/NS 272834

West Dunbartonshire

Dalmuir (Robertsons Park) Aerodrome	64/NS 47-71-?

Renfrewshire

Renfrew (Moorpark) Aerodrome	64/NS 505665
Inchinnan Airship Construction Station and Aerodrome	64/NS 476684

Glasgow

Carmunnock(Cathcart) Landing Ground   64/NS 595578

Clackmannanshire

Alloa (Caudron) Aerodrome   58/NS 884920

Fife

Crail Aerodrome   59/NO 625085
Donibristle Aerodrome   66/NT 160840
Leuchars Aerodrome   59/NO 460208
Kilconquhar Landing Ground   59/NO 478020
Hawkcraig Point Seaplane Station   66/NT 198848
Port Laing (Carlingnose) Seaplane Station   66/NT 133814
Rosyth Seaplane Station and Depot   65/NT 099818
Leven Seaplane Station   59/NO 382003
Woodhaven Seaplane Station   59/NO 408271
Methil Kite Balloon Station   59/NO 377995
North Queensferry Kite Balloon Station   65/NT 125807

Edinburgh

Turnhouse Aerodrome   66/NT 155735
Colinton (Edinburgh) Landing Ground   66/NT 219689
Gilmerton (Edinburgh) Landing Ground   66/NT 297678
Myreside (Edinburgh) Landing Ground   66/NT 235715
Granton Harbour Seaplane Station   66/NT 240775

Midlothian

Tynehead Landing Ground   66/NT 380585

East Lothian

East Fortune Airship Station and Aerodrome   66/NT 550785
Gullane (West Fenton) Aerodrome   66/NT 510810
Penston Aerodrome   66/NT 453715
Belhaven Sands Landing Ground   67/NT 652792
Gifford Landing Ground   66/NT 545695
Hoprig Mains Landing Ground   66/NT 446736
Skateraw Landing Ground   67/NT 737753
South Belton (Dunbar) Landing Ground   67/NT 654775

South Ayrshire

Ayr (Ayr Racecourse) Aerodrome   70/NS 352221
Turnberry Aerodrome   66/NS 205072

East Ayrshire

Bogton Aerodrome	77/NS 472057
Loch Doon Aerodrome (not completed)	77/NS 485983
Loch Doon Seaplane Station	77/NS 490983

Scottish Borders

Cairncross Aerodrome	67/NT 892630
Whiteburn (Grantshouse) Aerodrome	67/NT 765639
Eccles Tofts Landing Ground	74/NT 759452
Horndean Landing Ground	67/NT 895505

Dumfries and Galloway

Luce Bay Airship Station and Aerodrome	82/NX 120550
Tinwald Downs Farm Landing Ground	84/NX 996792

(Loch Doon Seaplane Station and Gunnery Range-see East Ayrshire)

Northumberland

New Haggerston Aerodrome	75/NU 023429
Seahouses Aerodrome	75/NU 320189

(Only listed above are aerodromes near the Scottish Border, there were several others near Newcastle-upon-Tyne)

Compiled with the assistance of Mick Davis.

APPENDIX 6

CONFIDENTIAL BOOKS AND DOCUMENTS AT RAF LUCE BAY

The Commanding Officer of RAF Luce Bay compiled a list of confidential books and documents held at the air station in October 1918 at the request of Headquarters, 22 Group. The list gives an interesting insight into the information required to operate such a facility:

List of Secret and Confidential Books issued to small ships:

Instructions for the distribution of Naval Intelligence in the United Kingdom.
Notes on Naval Guns and Torpedoes, 1914.
Book of Range Tables for H.M. Fleet, 1910.
Book of Fuse Scales for H.M. Fleet, 1911.
Torpedo Manual, Vol.11, 1913.
Addenda to Handbook for RGF Torpedoes, 1913.
Prohibited areas and Examination Services.
Cover for Substitution Code.
Met. Officer Cypher, 1916.
Meteorological Cypher, No.2.
Handbook on the Handley-Page Biplane.
Handbook on Torpedo Control.
Code index (Short Service Edition).
Wireless Transmission Instructions, 1917.
Wireless Transmission Instructions for A.P. Vessels, 1917.
Gunnery, Vol.11.
General Signal Book, 1917.
Cover for Call Signs.
Allied Wireless Transmission Instructions.
State of the Development of the Airship Service on 1 January 1917.
Instructions for Handling Messages.
Cover for Aircraft Signal Books and Codes – Special Aircraft Edition.
Interallied Wireless Call Signs.
Aircraft Signal Book, 1917.
Instructions for Aircraft Signalling, 1917.
Standard Wireless Call Signs 1: Ships.

2. RAF

Substitution Code and Decode	No.5
	No.6
	No.7
	No.8

Service Wireless Call Signs (Home Waters)	No.7
	No.8
Cover for Vocabulary (Code)	
(Decode)	
Land Line Cipher Code	No.1.
Mercantile Secret Call Signs, January 1918.	
Allied Auxiliary Wireless Call Signs.	
Air Stations Wireless Code	No.9
Vocabulary (Code)	No.20
(Decode)	
Auxiliary Vessels Signal Book, 1918	
Cover for Mercantile Secret Call Signs	
General Auxiliary Code	
Vocabulary, (Code)	No.21
(Decode)	

Naval Magazine Regulations, 1918.

Notes on Submarine Hunting using Hydrophones.

Monthly Summary of War Orders, September, 1918.

General Instructions for the Entry of HM Ships into Defended Ports into the United Kingdom and Channel Islands, June, 1918.

Firework and Alarm Signals and Instructions for Local Signals (Home Waters).

State of Development of Airship Service on 1 January, 1918.

Commercial Call Signs Part 2, Alphabetical List of Ships.

Commercial Call Signs Part, Alphabetical List of Call Signs.

Enemy Submarine Report and Attack Table.

'Emergency' and 'Enemy Submarine Report and Attack' Tables.

HM Ships, etc, As Seen from the Air.

Instructions for Recording and Analysing Target Practise 1914.

Report of Exercises Carried Out with Whitehead Torpedoes in 1913.

Handbook of Aircraft Armament.

Key to Air Maps.

Annual Report: Airship Experimental Work, 1915.

German Navy. Destroyers and TBs.

   Gunnery Information.

   Torpedo and Mining Information.

   Submarines.

German Airship Raids over Great Britain, 1916.

Air Packet No.65 and Index.

German Rigid Airships.

German Rigid Airships (plates).

Wireless Shore and Ship Stations.

Prohibited Flying Areas D.A.R.387 A.

Intelligence Organization (Home).

Notes on aids to Submarine Hunting.

APPENDIX 7

SCOTTISH FIRST WORLD WAR ACES

Although no air battles with hostile aircraft took place over Scotland during the First World War, many Scottish airmen participated in air battles over France. Over fifty achieved the status of an ace, a pilot who has shot down five or more enemy aircraft. The term originated during this conflict when French newspapers described 'Adolphe Pegoud as L' as (French for ace, after he shot down five German aircraft). Among the top scoring aces of all nationalities were:

1. Manfred Von Richthofen	Germany	80 victories
2. Rene Fonck	France	75 victories
3. William Bishop	Canada	72 victories
4. Ernest Udet	German	62 victories
5. Edward Mannock	England	61 victories
6. Raymond Collishaw	Canada	60 victories
7. James McCudden	England	57 victories
8. Andrew Beauchamp Proctor	South Africa	54 victories

It should be noted that methods of compiling claims varied from air force to air force, so direct comparisons may not always give a true picture. Also some of the claims of individual pilots may be inaccurate and subject to dispute. Hence it may be found that totals may vary depending on which source is consulted. The figures used here include aircraft shot down, captured and out of control and compared with some other tables tend to err on the high side.

Scotland's top scoring ace was John Gilmour with thirty-nine victories. He was born in Helensburgh on the Firth of Clyde in 1896. Initially he served with the Argyll and Sutherland Highlanders, but he transferred to the RFC joining 27 Squadron in early 1916. This unit flew the ungainly Martinsyde G.100 Elephants on which John Gilmour scored three victories. The following year he became flight commander of 65 Squadron, equipped with a far more effective fighter, namely the Sopwith Camel. Between 18 December and 3 July 1918, a further thirty-six enemy aircraft fell to his guns. He was awarded the Military Cross in July 1918:

> ...for conspicuous gallantry and devotion to duty when engaging hostile aircraft, within a week he crashed to the ground four enemy machines and at all times when on patrol he never hesitated to attack any enemy in sight. His consistent dash and great fearlessness have been worthy of the highest praise. In all he has ten hostile machines to his credit.

Gerald Maxwell from Inverness was the country's second most successful ace. The nephew of Lord Lovat, he was commissioned at the beginning of the conflict seeing action at Gallipoli and in Egypt. In 1916 he joined the RFC and was posted to France in April 1917, flying S.E.5

with 56 Squadron. Gerald Maxwell notched up his first victory on his initial patrol over the trenches. When he returned to Great Britain in October 1917 he had claimed twenty victories. After serving a spell as an instructor at the School of Aerial Fighting at Turnberry, he returned to France in the summer of 1918, scoring a further six victories. His final total included ten enemy aircraft shot down and a further two shared with other pilots. A further ten were claimed as out of control, two of which were again shared. Gerald Maxwell served again in World War Two, commanding Ford Aerodrome. At the end of his career he had flown 167 different types of aircraft and had risen to the rank of Wing Commander.

A short distance behind comes William Campbell with twenty-three victories. He was actually born in Bordeaux to a Scottish father and French mother. In 1916 William Campbell joined the RFC and was posted to 1 Squadron in France in May of the following year, where he flew Nieuport Scouts. During the following three months he scored twenty-three victories, including the destruction of five enemy observation balloons. The latter achievement made William Campbell the first RFC balloon-busting ace. His operation career came to an abrupt end when he was wounded in action on 31 July 1917. He eventually returned to flying as an instructor. Campbell received the Military Cross in August 1917:

> For conspicuous gallantry and devotion to duty. He attacked an enemy balloon, bringing it down in flames and returned to our lines at about 20ft from the ground under heavy fire. On another occasion he attacked and dispersed a column of infantry from a very low altitude. He has shown great courage and initiative throughout.

Matthew Frew was born in Glasgow on 7 April 1895. In 1914 he joined the Highland Light Infantry. After serving in France, he transferred to the RFC in August 1916. His first posting was to 45 Squadron flying Sopwith 1½ Strutters and later Sopwith Camels. By February of 1918 he had claimed twenty-three enemy aircraft but then had to return to Great Britain as a result of an injury he sustained from anti-aircraft fire. He became an instructor and continued to serve with the RAF until he retired in 1948 at the rank of Air Vice Marshal.

George Thomson claimed a total of twenty-one victories, just two less than Matthew Frew. He came from Helensburgh, Dumbartonshire. After serving with the King's Own Scottish Borders he joined the RFC in September 1916. While he was learning to fly he was involved in a serious accident which left him with a scarred face. He succeeded in finishing his training and was posted to 46 Squadron in France in the summer of 1917. George Thomson scored no less than fifteen victories in March 1918 while flying Sopwith Camels. He was posted to an aerodrome in Great Britain but was killed two months later in a flying accident. In his short flying career he was awarded the Military Cross and Distinguished Flying Cross:

> …on 6 November the machine in which this officer was flying was hit by a shell and the left aileron control shot away. At once it began to fall completely out of control, At a height of 500ft, 2nd-Lt Thomson, with fine presence of mind and contempt of danger, climbed on to the right band lower plane enabling the pilot to bring the machine on an even keel and land safely in our own lines.

Unlike some of the other Scottish aces who continued to serve with the RAF after the conflict ceased, John Todd was so disillusioned with the slaughter during the war that he decided to become a doctor and left for Africa to become a pioneering medical missionary. His eighteen victories were all claimed while flying a Sopwith Camel with 70 Squadron in the first half of 1918. This was followed by a spell as an instructor in aerial combat at Montrose Aerodrome.

Charles Findlay joined the RFC in December 1916 and on completing his training initially served as an instructor. He was then posted to 88 Squadron flying Bristol F2b fighters. Thirteen of Charles Findlay's victories were Fokker D.VIIs. After the war he remained in the RAF until he retired in 1941.

While all the above flyers attained the status of an ace with the RFC; Maxwell Findlay's fourteen victories all took place while he flew Sopwith Camels with the RNAS. He was actually living in Canada when the war broke out but decided to return home to fight for his country.

Listed below are all Scottish aces who shot down five or more enemy aircraft and balloons:

1	John Gilmour	39 victories
2	Gerald Maxwell	26 victories
3	William Campbell	23 victories
4	Matthew Frew	23 victories
5	George Thomson	21 victories
6	John Todd	18 victories
7	Charles Findlay	14 victories
8	Maxwell Findlay	14 victories
9	James Fitz-Morris	14 victories
10	Thomas Purdom	13 victories
11	Ian Napier	12 victories
12	John Ralston	12 victories
13	Thomas Harries	11 victories
14	James Binnie	9 victories
15	Robert Gordon	9 victories
16	George Learmond	9 victories
17	Norman MacMillan	9 victories
18	George Reid	9 victories
19	Gordon Duncan	8 victories
20	James Grant	8 victories
21	James McDonald	8 victories
22	Phillip Prothero	8 victories
23	Charles Robson	8 victories
24	Walter Scott	8 victories
25	Herbert Hartley	7 victories
26	Ian Henderson	7 victories
27	F. Knowles	7 victories
28	William MacLanachan	7 victories
29	William Patrick	7 victories
30	James Robb	7 victories
31	James Tennant	7 victories
32	Alexander Tranter	7 victories
33	Robert Chalmers	6 victories
34	David Hall	6 victories
35	Andrew MacGregor	6 victories
36	Hugh Moore	6 victories
37	Thomas Rae	6 victories
38	David Smith	6 victories
39	John Smith-Grant	6 victories
40	William Winkler	6 victories
41	Lewis Collins	5 victories
42	Fergus Craig	5 victories
43	Gerard Crole	5 victories
44	Llewelyn Davies	5 victories
45	Ronald Graham	5 victories
46	William Grossart	5 victories

47	Kenneth Laing	5 victories
48	James Lennox	5 victories
49	John Lightbody	5 victories
50	Colin MacAndrew	5 victories
51	Harry MacKay	5 victories
52	Guy Reid	5 victories
53	John Robertson	5 victories

The above information was supplied by THE AERODROME/www.theaerodrome.com (Scott Hamilton)

R.N.Air Station
Dundee

9th February 1915

To the Commanding Officer

Sir,

I enrolled at Chatham on the 11th August last for service as Wireless Operator in the Royal Navy for the period of the War – having previously been a 1st Class Marconi Operator in charge on Merchant Liners – and I was signed on for that period under conditions for R.N.R. Wireless Operators. My pay has been five shillings per diem, which is I believe the minimum amount under the Conditions, and that paid to other Operators who enrolled but who had had no previous Sea experience.

After enrolling I was immediately drafted and since have served in the R.N.A.S. and acted as Wireless rating and Observer, remaining under the Conditions on which I was Enrolled. The Conditions however, I beg to submit, compare unfavourably with my rating and duties to other and lower ratings enlisted in the R.N.A.S.

I therefore respectfully Request that I may now be transferred to the R.N.A.S. either for the period of the War or for the minimum term of years and also that some adjustment maybe made in my pay to place it on a more equal footing with R.N.A.S. ratings.

I am, Sir
Yours respectfully

C.P.O. W/T

Application letter to be transferred to the RNAS. (The National Archives)

APPENDIX 8 - AIRCRAFT CRASHES TABLE

Sheet	Grid Ref	Aircraft Type	Serial No.	SQN	Location	Cause of crash	Date
66		Farman Longhorn	No. 71		Firth of Forth	Crashed in the sea – salvaged.	25–Aug–13
66		Farman F.22H	No. 139		Scapa Flow	Crashed and wrecked.	01–Aug–14
66		Farman F.22H	No. 142		Scapa Flow	Engine fire, force landed in sea and recovered.	24–Aug–14
54		Short type 74	No. 77		North Sea	Crashed on Ftr patrol from Dundee.	29–Sep–14
66		Sopwith Bat.	No. 38		Scapa Flow	Destroyed in gale.	21–Nov–14
59		Short Type 74	No. 79		2 miles North of Fifeness	Engine fire, force landed in the sea.	01–Jan–15
54		Short type 74	No. 76		Dundee	Crashed.	22–Feb–15
54		Short type 74	No. 75		Dundee	Side slipped turning and crashed.	24–Feb–15
27		Wright Navyplane	No. 155		Near Fort George	Wrecked and lost in rough sea during gale.	08–Apr–15
54		Spinning Jenny	No. 1067		Dundee	Collided with a tree.	14–Sep–15
66		Farman Pusher	1454	East Fort.	East Fortune	Crashed near hedge.	17–Mar–16
54		Wright type 840	No. 1400		Off Dundee	Wrecked.	05–Apr–16
54		BE.2c	A5499	18RES	Montrose	Crashed on Bents Road.	16–Nov–16
54		BE.2c	A8949	18RES	Montrose	Crashed on aerodrome.	12–Feb–17
76	19 – 07 –	Fe.2b	6975	2(Aux)AGS	300yds N of Turnberry L'house	Made a sharp turn, stalled & dived in from 30ft.	01–May–17
54		BE.2c	9974	18RES	Montrose	Crashed on aerodrome.	04–May–17
65		MFSH	A7029	26RS	Nr Turnhouse	Crashed. Pilot died in hospital.	04–May–17
54		MFSH	A2480	39Tr	Nr Dammure Barracks.	Crashed.	07–Jun–17
54		BE.2e	A1270	18Tr	Balkemback Farm	Crashed near Tealing.	14–Jun–17
76	21 – 06 –	Fe.2b	A817	2(Aux)AGS	West of Dalquat, 30yds from wood.	Stalled on turn at low altitude.	19–Jun–17
76	21 – 07 –	Fe.2b	4926	2(Aux)AGS	Field due East of Maidens, 200yds from Ayr Road.	Stalled on turn and crashed.	26–Jun–17
65		Sopwith Pup	9914	?	Turnhouse	Crashed on take-off.	03–Jul–17
54		Avro 504	B921	18Tr	North Sea	Crashed into sea.	30–Aug–17
76	20 – 06 –	Be.2c	5416	2(Aux)AGS	Turnberry Airfield	Stalled on turn and crashed.	04–Sep–17
54		BE.2e	B3983	52Tr	Montrose	Crashed on aerodrome.	13–Sep–17
59		Short Type 74	N1135		8 miles SE of May Island	Engine fire, force landed in the sea.	04–Oct–17
65		Camel	B2339	73TS	Nr Elphinstone.	Crashed. Pilot died in hospital.	04–Oct–17
76		Camel	?	73TS	Nr Turnberry	Lost control and dived in.	04–Oct–17
45	71–60–	DH4	A7438	52Tr	Wards Of Charleton	Crashed near airfield.	16–Oct–17
65	17–76–	Pup	B2247	73TS	East Craigie Farm	Crashed.	19–Oct–17
70	35–23–	Avro 504A	A9792	1ScAF	Nr South Sanquhar Farm	Crashed.	04–Nov–17
66		Be-2c	8724	EFNS	Nr Edinburgh	Crashed. Pilot DIH.	10–Nov–17
45	73–63–	Strutter	A6030	18Tr.	Nether Warburton Farm	Crashed St Cyrus.	11–Nov–17
65		Camel	B6262	73TS	Nr Turnhouse Railway Station	Crashed after colliding with Be 2 B4011.	14–Nov–17
65		BE-2e	B4011	77	Nr Turnhouse Railway Station	Crashed after colliding with Camel B6262.	14–Nov–17
54		Camel	B2502	18TS	Montrose	E/F on T/O. Spun in.	15–Nov–17
65		Camel	B6266	73TS	Turnhouse	Nose dived from 500ft.	18–Nov–17
65		Albatross	DUG56	73	Off Queensferry	Crashed in Firth of Forth.	23–Dec–17
54		Camel	B5614	6Tr	Montrose Bay	Spun into sea.	24–Dec–17
59		Short Type 184	N1638		12 miles SE of Fifeness	Force landed in the sea.	24–Dec–17
70		Camel	B5557	1ScAF	Ayr	Engine choked on T/O. Spun into trees.	27–Dec–17
54		Camel	B9164	18TS	Golf Links	Struck sandhill, Montrose	30–Dec–17
54		Camel	B5186	6TS	Montrose	Stalled during turn and dived in.	17–Jan–18

Sheet	Grid Ref	Aircraft Type	Serial No.	SQN	Location	Cause of crash	Date
65		Camel	B9228	73TS	Turnhouse	Spun in landing.	01-Feb-18
54		Camel	B7344	36Tr	Field next to Montrose	Spun in next to aerodrome.	03-Feb-18
54		Camel	B7342	6TS	Montrose	Dived in from 600ft.	05-Feb-18
65		Camel	B2548	73TS	Turnhouse	Choked engine at 50ft. Hit ground.	08-Feb-18
70		Camel	B5565	1AFS	Kincaidston Farm	Wing broke up in air.	08-Feb-18
45		Camel	B4037	18Tr.	Hospitalshields.	E/F. Dived in Marykirk.	21-Feb-18
70		Camel	B5562	1ScAF	Ayr	Stalled and spun in. Pilot DOI.	03-Mar-18
70		Camel	B7418	1SAF	Racecourse, Ayr	Spun in from 800ft.	07-Mar-18
70		Camel	B7469	1ScAF	Nr Ayr	Choked engine. Dived in from 150ft. Pilot DIH.	07-Mar-18
70		Camel	B7420	1ScAF	Ayr	Spun in.	07-Mar-18
70		Camel	?	1ScAF	Ayr	Spun in.	08-Mar-18
70	41-21-	Se-5a	D3436	AFS	Sundrum Estate	Crashed.	12-Mar-18
54		Camel	B7373	6TS	Montrose	Struck ground low flying.	14-Mar-18
70		Camel	B7472	1ScAF	Ayr	Failed to pull out of spin.	14-Mar-18
66		Be-2e	A1388	77	Penston Aerodrome	Crashed.	17-Mar-18
76	19 - 04 -	Camel	B9204	2(Aux)AGS	On shore 400yds South of Brest Rocks	Crashed into sea.	17-Mar-18
76	20 - 06 -	Camel	B9222	2(Aux)AGS	Turnberry Airfield	Crashed in flat spin from 70ft.	17-Mar-18
54		Camel	B7374	18Tr	Montrose Basin	Pilot fainted. Spun in.	28-Mar-18
54		Pup	B7529	36Tr	600yds N of Rossie Cottages	Collided with Camel B7338 & crashed in tidal basin.	04-Apr-18
54		Camel	B7338	36TS	600yds N of Rossie Cottages	Collided with Pup B7529 and crashed.	04-Apr-18
70		Camel	B7465	1AFS	Monkton Road , Monkton	Control lost in dive.	04-Apr-18
70		Se 5a	C1762	2SoAF	Turnberry	Banked too near ground. Spun in. DBF.	05-Apr-18
63		Camel	C8207	1AFS	Sunnyside Farm, Kilwinning	Collided with B5563 during AF practice.	08-Apr-18
63		Camel	B5563	1AFS	Sunnyside Farm, Kilwinning	Collided with C8207 during AF practice.	08-Apr-18
65		BE-2e	B4556	Turnh.	Donibristle Estate	Crashed.	08-Apr-18
76		Camel	B9210	2(Aux)AGS	Off Turnberry Light	Hit submerged rocks in sea.	11-Apr-18
54		Camel	C11	18TS	Montrose	Spun in from low height.	13-Apr-18
66		Camel	B4206	2TDS	Nr West Fenton	Crashed. Pilot DIH.	16-Apr-18
64		Camel	N6781	Turnberry	Nr Mgt. Hospital, Duntocher	Lost control and dived in.	17-Apr-18
54		Camel	C6	18Tr	Montrose	Spun in from 500ft. Aerodrome.	21-Apr-18
65		Strutter	A5986	Furious	Donibristle Estate	Crashed.	29-Apr-18
70		Camel	B9258	1ScAF	Ayr	Choked engine, stalled and crashed.	05-May-18
54		Camel	B4621	6Tr	Montrose	Spun in landing on aerodrome.	07-May-18
45		Avro 504	C652	18Tr.	Mains Of Logie	Crashed. NFD.	08-May-18
54		Camel	D6672	6Tr	Montrose	Crashed on aerodrome.	17-May-18
54		Sopwith Camel	N6766	?	Donibristle	Hit tree landing and spun in.	18-May-18
76	24 - 06 -	Camel	B9218	1AFGS	1000yds S of Kirkoswald	Stalled on turn at 100ft.	18-May-18
54		Avro 504	D6287	6Tr	Montrose	Crashed on aerodrome.	22-May-18
54		Camel	C111	6Tr	Montrose	Choked engine. Spun in to aerodrome.	22-May-18
54		Camel	D8131	18Tr	Montrose Bay	Spun off roll into sea.	26-May-18
76	23 - 06 -	Camel	B5560	1AFGS	1000yds SW of Kirkoswald	Dived in.	26-May-18
76	24 - 08 -	Camel	B7467	1AFGS	1000yds NE of Kirkoswald	Spun in.	27-May-18
76	20 - 06 -	Fe. 2b	B1178	1AFS	500yds W of airfield	Crashed.	28-May-18
54		Camel	D8135	36TS	Montrose	Choked engine on T/O. Hit tree.	31-May-18
76	20 - 06 -	Camel	B9262	1AFS	Turnberry Airfield	Stalled and spun in on turn.	02-Jun-18

Sheet	Grid Ref	Aircraft Type	Serial No.	SQN	Location	Cause of crash	Date
64		Camel	C6739	6AAP	Renfrew	Pancaked on landing. Overturned.	04-Jun-18
76		DH 9	C1231	1AFGS	2m S Turnberry Light	Broke up in air. Dived into sea, 20ft deep low tide.	05-Jun-18
54		Camel	B7345	18TS	Montrose	Crashed.	07-Jun-18
66		Camel	B5723	208TDS	East Fortune	Stalled on T/O. Written off.	17-Jun-18
66		Camel	D6670	2TD	North Berwick railway line	Crashed from 2,000ft onto railway.	18-Jun-18
54		Camel	C80	6TS	Montrose	Broke up in dive.	20-Jun-18
76	23 – 04 –	DH 9	D1080	1FS	Glenhead Farm, Kirkoswald	Crashed while testing Lewis gun.	21-Jun-18
67	75–76–	Airship	NS3	EFA	1m off Skateraw Harbour	Crashed in North Sea.	22-Jun-18
76	19 – 05 –	Dolphin	E4437	1FS	Nr Breast Rocks	Crashed.	25-Jun-18
54		Camel	E1446	36Tr	Montrose	Pulled out of dive too quickly and crashed on airfield.	02-Jul-18
66	49–86–	Camel	D6680	2TDS	Eyebrouchy Point	Landed in sea.	03-Jul-18
54		Camel	D8132	36TS	Montrose	Crashed.	05-Jul-18
65		Sopwith Strutter	A5257	Turn.AS	Turnhouse	Stalled on flat spin	06-Jul-18
45	71-60-	Pup	B7485	6Tr.	Charleton House	Crashed N of aerodrome. ? collision	08-Jul-18
45	71-60-	Pup	C381	6Tr.	Charleton House	Crashed N of aerodrome. ? collision	08-Jul-18
66		Bristol F.2b	B8037	I.T.	East Fortune	Spun in on T/O.	13-Jul-18
54		Camel	E1448	32TDS	Montrose	Hit telegraph wires low flying.	18-Jul-18
65		Camel	B5591	Turnh.	Turnhouse	Stalled at 200ft. Spun in.	18-Jul-18
65		Sopwith Camel	C6735	Fleet.PS	Four Mile Hall	Engine fire, spun into ground.	24-Jul-18
66	57 – 77 –	Sopwith Pup	9946	AFGS	Crow Wood nr Markle	Spun in from 2000ft.	24-Jul-18
67	57–77–	Sopwith Pup	9946	GFAFGS	Crow Wood, nr Markle	Spun in from 2,000t.	24-Jul-18
06	29 – 06 –	Sopwith Camel	N6636	Scapa AS	Clestrain, Orphin	Hit air pocket and dived in.	03-Aug-18
54		Camel	D6676	32TDS	Montrose Basin	Broke up in air.	12-Aug-18
66		Camel	C8329	2TDS	West Fenton	Struck ground in spin.	13-Aug-18
66		Avro 504	D4464	2TDS	Links Park	Crashed.	13-Aug-18
76		Camel	B9212	1FS	In sea 2 miles SW Brest Rocks.	E/F in dive. Spun into sea.	19-Aug-18
65		Sopwith Camel	E4414	4 AAP	Nr Turnhouse	Engine fire, force landed & crashed.	20-Aug-18
76	23 – 06 –	DH 9	C1334	1FS	Minnybae Farm	Mid-air collision with another aircraft.	23-Aug-18
44	58-74-	Pup	D4030	RAAF	Auchmull	Crashed.	25-Aug-18
54		Curtiss H. 16	N4891	RAAF	River Tay	Crashed.	27-Aug-18
45		Camel	C6761	26TDS	Nr Montrose	Pilot died in hospital.	03-Sep-18
66		Camel	C6750	2TDS	Gullane	E/F. Stalled in F/L.	03-Sep-18
65		Sopwith Pup	B8012	Fleet.PS	Firth of Forth, opp. Longrey Cottage	Collided with Strutter 9894.	04-Sep-18
65		Sopwith Strutter	9894	Fleet.AD	Firth of Forth, opp. Longrey Cottage	Collided with Pup B8012.	04-Sep-18
54		Camel	D9556	32TDS	Montrose	Wings broke up and spun in on aerodrome.	05-Sep-18
76		DH 9	C1333	1FS	Adjacent to public school, Maidens	Stalled after T/O. Spun in from 30ft. Burnt out.	05-Sep-18
45		Avro 504A	B4352	26TDS	Aerodrome	Crashed.	06-Sep-18
66		Avro 504	D5851	2TDS	West Fenton	Crashed.	06-Sep-18
59		Re 8	B6638	27TDS	Nr Crail	Crashed.	09-Sep-18
54		H. 16	N4070	249NAS	Eastern Wharf, Dundee	Hits ships mast. Crashed and burnt.	21-Sep-18
54		Avro 504	E1608	32TDS	Montrose	Crashed on aerodrome.	23-Sep-18
54		Camel	B5617	32TDS	Montrose Basin	Crashed.	23-Sep-18
45		Camel	E1583	26TDS	Edzell	Choked engine. F/L and hit hanger.	29-Sep-18
76	18 – 96 –	Camel	F1410	1FS	Field at Shalloch Park Farm.	Looped too near the ground and burnt out.	30-Sep-18
65		Sopwith Camel	D9525	Fleet.PS	Briggs Farm, Kirkliston	Nose dived and spun in.	01-Oct-18
66		Se-5 a	D3497	2TDS	Nr West Fenton	Crashed.	01-Oct-18
30	07 – 58 –	Short 184	N2794		Strathbeg	Crashed on T/O.	11-Oct-18

Sheet	Grid Ref	Aircraft Type	Serial No.	SQN	Location	Cause of crash	Date
45		Camel	C6752	26TDS	Aerodrome	Stalled on turn. Spun in.	14-Oct-18
68		Airco DH.6	C2121	272	Nr Machrihanish	Engine fire, force landed in sea.	17-Oct-18
76		DH 9	C1372	1FS	In sea N of Miltonburn	Stalled on climbing turn. Fell into sea.	20-Oct-18
68		Airco DH.6	C2111	272	Off Machrihanish	Force landed in sea	26-Oct-18
68		Airco DH.6	B2964	272	Off Machrihanish	Engine fire, force landed in sea.	27-Oct-18
68		Airco DH.6	C2120	272	Near Rathlin Island	Engine fire, force landed in sea.	27-Oct-18
66		Bristol F.2b	B8942	201TDS	East Fortune	Stalled in turn.	31-Oct-18
59		Camel	E7255	GFSoAFG	Leuchars	Hit hill in mist.	01-Nov-18
76		Camel	B7470	1FS	Turnberry	Hit slipstream. Spun into trees.	06-Nov-18
76		Camel	E7265	1FS	Turnberry	E/F on T/O. Overturned.	06-Nov-18
59		Bristol Fighter	?	27TDS	Crail	Lost speed and crashed.	20-Nov-18
59		Bristol Fighter	1793	27TDS	Crail	Spun in from low height.	23-Nov-18
76		DH 9	C1374	1FS	Turnberry	E/F crashed. 1 injured and 1 DOI.	25-Nov-18
54		Camel	F4207	32TDS	Gonshill Farm	Safety belt broke during stunting. Pilot fell out.	28-Nov-18
76		Se 5a	E3954	1FS	Park Farm, 0.5m E of airfield.	Stalled and spun in. Burnt out.	28-Nov-18
76		Camel	F1408	1FS	Turnberry	Stalled and spun in.	11-Dec-18
59	62-08-	Avro 504	H218	27TDS	Sauhope Farm	Stalled on turn and spun in.	28-Dec-18
76		DH 9	E679	1FS	Turnberry	Flat turn after T/O. Spun in.	31-Dec-18
59	60-09-	Avro 504	5918	27TDS	Grassmiston Farm	Crashed.	06-Jan-19
66		Avro 504k	E3037	201TDS	East Fortune	Engine fire, force landed and crashed.	13-Jan-19
59		Camel	D8234	GFSoAFG	Leuchars	Stalled and spun in.	18-Jan-19
59		Camel	N6824	SoAF+G	Leuchars	Stalled and crashed after flat turn.	04-Feb-19
59		Camel	F4987	GFSoAFG	Leuchars	Hit ground contour chasing.	06-Feb-19
66		Camel	D9535	2TDS	West Fenton	E/F on T/O. Stalled and spun in.	24-Feb-19
65		Avro 504	E3397	?	Turnhouse	Stalled soft from ground and crashed.	04-Mar-19
59		Camel	B5739	27TDS	Crail	Stalled and crashed into a building.	07-May-19
59		Camel	F8497	SoAF+G	Leuchars	Attempted slow roll too near to the ground.	09-May-19
65		Sopwith Camel	N7147	6 AAP	East of Forth Bridge	Spun into Forth from 200ft.	02-Jul-19
59		Camel	F5014	GFSoAFG	Leuchars	Stalled and spun in from 1500ft.	01-Aug-19
59		Camel	N6825	GFSoAFG	HMS *Vindictive*	Crashed.	13-Aug-19

(Alan Leishman)

APPENDIX 9 - BURIAL TABLE

NAME	RANK	FORCE	POSITION	TYPE	SERIAL	BURIAL DETAILS	DATE	FOUND	SHEET
JOHNSTON, C.	Flt-Lt	RNAF	PILOT	FARMAN PUSHER	1454	RAINHAM, KENT	17/03/1916		66
BALL, F.A.		RNAF	ENG.	FARMAN PUSHER	1454	HOLLYBROOK, SOUTHAMPTON	17/03/1916		66
FOWLER, W.	2nd-LT	RFC	PILOT	BE2	A5499	SLEEPYHILLOCK, MONTROSE	16/11/1916		54
MACMILLAN, T.	2nd-Lt	RFC	PILOT	BE2	A8049	EASTWOOD, GLASGOW	12/02/1917		54
BOWERS, C.W.H.	Sgt	RFC		FE 2B	6975	GIRVAN, AYRSHIRE	01/05/1917		76
STEVENSON, J.	Lt	RFC	PILOT	FE 2B	6975	EVIE, ORKNEY	01/05/1917		76
FOOT, D.V.	2nd-Lt	RFC		BE2	9974	BO'NESS	04/05/1917		54
TAYLOR-LOBAN, G.	Capt.	RFC		MFSH	A2480	SLEEPYHILLOCK, MONTROSE	07/06/1917		54
ALGER, G.C.	2nd-Lt	RFC		MFSH	A2480	SLEEPYHILLOCK, MONTROSE	07/06/1917		54
FINDLAY, L.	Capt.	RFC	PILOT	BE2	A1270	SLEEPYHILLOCK, MONTROSE	14/06/1917		54
APPLETON, S.C.	Sgt	RFC		FE 2B	A817	WARRINGTON	19/06/1917		76
BUNTINE, W.S.C.	Lt	RFC		FE 2B	A817	GIRVAN, AYRSHIRE	19/06/1917		76
COOPER, C.A.	Lt	RFC		FE 2B	4926	GIRVAN, AYRSHIRE	26/06/1917		76
TOWLSON, H.	Mech.	RFC		FE 2B	4926	NEW BASFORD, NOTTINGHAM	26/06/1917	29/6 DIH	76
MCLAREN, F.W.H.	2nd-Lt		PILOT	AVRO 504A	B921	BUSBRIDGE, SURREY	30/08/1917		54
DOWNING, G.G.B.	Lt	RFC	PILOT	BE2	5416	LLANISHEN, GLAMORGAN	04/09/1917		76
JARDINE, R.	2nd-Lt	RFC	PILOT	BE2	B3983	APPLEGARTH, DUMFRIES	13/09/1917		54
ANDERSON, P.A.	Lt	RFC	PILOT	PUP	B2247	COMELY BANK, EDINBURGH	19/10/1917		65
PRENTICE, J.	Lt	RFC	PILOT	AVRO 504	A9792	AYR	04/11/1917		70
MOORE, A.J.	2nd-Lt	RFC	PILOT	STRUTTER	A6030	SLEEPYHILLOCK, MONTROSE	11/11/1917		45
ARMSTRONG, H.M.	Lt	RFC	PILOT	CAMEL	B6262	COMELY BANK, EDINBURGH	14/11/1917		65
HUGHES, E.	Lt	RFC	PILOT	BE 2	B4011	COMELY BANK, EDINBURGH	14/11/1917		65
COLLETT, C.J.	Capt.	AFC	PILOT	ALBATROSS	DUG 56	SLEEPYHILLOCK, MONTROSE	23/12/1917		65
MOTT, A.E.P.	Lt	RFC	PILOT	CAMEL	B5614	COMELY BANK, EDINBURGH	24/12/1917		54
YOUNG, J.S.	2nd-Lt	RFC	PILOT	CAMEL	B7344	PARISH, NEW KILPATRICK	03/02/1918		54
BUSH, V.G.A.	Capt.	RFC	PILOT	CAMEL	B5565	NORTH MERCHISTON, EDINBURGH	08/02/1918		70
DEALY, T.S.O.	Lt	RFC	PILOT	CAMEL	B7418	STONEYHURST COLLEGE, LANCS.	07/03/1918		70
NATHAN, T.C.	Cdt		PILOT	SE5	D3436	AYR	12/03/1918		70
BALL, A.	Lt	RFC	PILOT	BE2	A1388	SEAFIELD, EDINBURGH	17/03/1918		66
MCNAIR, R.S.	Lt	RFC	PILOT	CAMEL	B9204	GIRVAN, AYRSHIRE	17/03/1918		76
HULL, E.C.	Lt	RFC	PILOT	CAMEL	B9222	BEDFORD	17/03/1918		76
LEWIS, F.A.	2nd-Lt	RFC	PILOT	CAMEL	B7374	SLEEPYHILLOCK, MONTROSE	28/03/1918		54
BURTON, E.W.	Lt	AFC	PILOT	PUP	B7529	SLEEPYHILLOCK, MONTROSE	04/04/1918		54
PAYNE, A.A.	2nd-Lt	RAF	PILOT	CAMEL	B7338	CASTLETON, DERBYSHIRE	04/04/1918		54
DIXON, H.	Flt-Lt	RNAF	PILOT	CAMEL	B7465	KENSAL GREEN, LONDON	04/04/1918		70
BRADER, G.A.	Cdt	RFC		SE5	C1762	?	05/04/1918		76
BALL, F	Lt	RAF	PILOT	CAMEL	C8207	AYR	08/04/1918		63
BROOKES, R.E.	Lt	RAF	PILOT	CAMEL	B5563	AYR	08/04/1918		63
DAVIS, N.P.	Flt-Lt	RNAF	PILOT	BE 2	B4556	SKETTY, GLAMORG.	08/04/1918		65

NAME	RANK	FORCE	POSITION	TYPE	SERIAL	BURIAL DETAILS	DATE	FOUND	SHEET
JONES, C.W.	Lt	RFC	PILOT	CAMEL	B9210	ABNEY PARK, LONDON	11/04/1918		76
GASTER, P.S.	2nd-Lt		PILOT	CAMEL	C6	CAMBERWELL, LONDON	21/04/1918		54
MEARS, H.F.	Lt	RNAF		STRUTTER	A5986	BROMPTON, SURREY	29/04/1918		65
MILLAR, G.H.	Capt.	RNAF		STRUTTER	A5986	DUNFERMLINE	29/04/1918		65
COHEN, B.	Lt	RAF	PILOT	CAMEL	B4621	GLASGOW WESTERN	07/05/1918		54
GRAHAM, W.J.K.	2nd-Lt	RAF	PILOT	CAMEL	D6672	SLEEPYHILLOCK, MONTROSE	17/05/1918		54
SQUIRES, G.	Lt	USAF	PILOT	CAMEL	B9218	?	18/05/1918		76
WALKER, R.P.	2nd-Lt		PILOT	CAMEL	C111	?	22/05/1918		54
ROACH, D.J	2nd-Lt	RAF	PILOT	AVRO 504	D6287	SLEEPYHILLOCK, MONTROSE	22/05/1918		54
PEACOCK, E.	2nd-Lt		PILOT	CAMEL	D8131	ST.JOHNS, NEWCASTLE	26/05/1918		54
TUCKETT, J.S.	Sgt	RFC	PILOT	CAMEL	B5560	BIRKENHEAD	26/05/1918		76
SMITH, H.R.	Lt	USAF	PILOT	CAMEL	B7467	?	27/05/1918		76
MAKEPEACE, R.M.	Lt	RFC		F2B	B1178	ANFIELD	28/05/1918		76
MCCLURE, T.A.	Lt	RFC		F2B	B1178	TOBERCLARE, EIRE	28/05/1918		76
BUTLER, H.R.H.	Lt	RAFC	PILOT	CAMEL	B9262	GIRVAN, AYRSHIRE	02/06/1918		76
ELLIOTT, H.W.	Lt	RFC		DH9	C1231	BOXWORTH, CAMBS.	05/06/1918		76
REID, R.B.	Lt	USAF		DH9	C1231	?	05/06/1918		76
WILKINSON, L.	Lt	RAF	PILOT	CAMEL	D6670	LUDDERDEN, YORKS.	18/06/1918		66
MALTBY, A.J.	2nd-Lt		PILOT	CAMEL	C80	ST.MARTIN, CHERITON, KENT	20/06/1918		54
HENDERSON, I.H.D.	Capt.	RFC		DH9	D1080	GIRVAN, AYRSHIRE	21/06/1918		76
REDLER, H.B.		RFC		DH9	D1080	WEST MONKTON, SOMERSET	21/06/1918	DIH	76
HOGESON, M.	Pet.-Off.	RNAF		AIRSHIP	NS 3	HOLLYBROOK, SOUTHAMPTON	22/06/1918		67
PRINTER, C.	Pet.-Off.	RNAF		AIRSHIP	NS 3	HOLLYBROOK, SOUTHAMPTON	22/06/1918		67
PAGE, A.H.	A.-Mec.	RNAF		AIRSHIP	NS 3	HOLLYBROOK, SOUTHAMPTON	22/06/1918		67
CRANMORE, J.	A.-Mec.	RNAF		AIRSHIP	NS 3	HOLLYBROOK, SOUTHAMPTON	22/06/1918		67
BISHOP, S.S.	A.-Mec.	RNAF		AIRSHIP	NS 3	HOLLYBROOK, SOUTHAMPTON	22/06/1918		67
CLARKSON, T.C.	2nd-Lt	RAF	PILOT	CAMEL	E1446	CHRIST CHURCH, DONCASTER	02/07/1918		54
HUNTER, W.A.	Lt	RAF	PILOT	CAMEL	D6680	PETTINAIN, LANARK	03/07/1918		66
DE VILLIERS, D.J.J.	Lt	RNAF		STRUTTER	A5257	SEAFIELD, EDINBURGH	06/07/1918		65
GARNER, W.M.	Pet.-Off.	RNAF		STRUTTER	A5257	SEAFIELD, EDINBURGH	06/07/1918		65
BARNETT, J.I.A.	Lt	RNAF	PILOT	CAMEL	C6735	SEAFIELD, EDINBURGH	24/07/1918		65
CASH, F.A.	Lt	RNAF	PILOT	SOPWITH PUP	9946	PRESTONKIRK, EAST LOTHIAN	24/07/1918		67
DUNBAR, J.D.	Lt	RFC	PILOT	DOLPHIN	E4437	GIRVAN, AYRSHIRE	25/07/1918		76
WALKER, J.P.	Lt			CAMEL	N6636	LOUGHTON, ESSEX	03/08/1918		6
CANGIAMILA, J.	2nd-Lt	RAF	PILOT	CAMEL	D6676	SLEEPYHILLOCK, MONTROSE	12/08/1918		54
MACALLISTER, G.W.	Lt	RAF	PILOT	CAMEL	C83290	COMELY BANK, EDINBURGH	12/08/1918		66
PARR, D.A.	Flt-Cdt	RAF	PILOT	AVRO 504	D4404	COMELY BANK, EDINBURGH	13/08/1918		66
GROVE, R.H.	Lt	RAFC	PILOT	CAMEL	B9212	GIRVAN, AYRSHIRE	19/08/1918		76
HEATH, G.	Lt	RNAF	PILOT	CAMEL	E4414	BRANDWOOD END, BIRMINGHAM	20/08/1918		65
MCFARLAN, A.	Lt	RFC		DH9	C1334	GIRVAN, AYRSHIRE	23/08/1918		76
HEPBURN, A.A.	Cdt	RFC		DH9	C1334	DUNFERMLINE ABBEY, FIFE	23/08/1918		76
HALL, J.H.	Pupil	RAF	PILOT	PUP	D4930	BURY	25/08/1918		44

NAME	RANK	FORCE	POSITION	TYPE	SERIAL	BURIAL DETAILS	DATE	FOUND	SHEET
SUTHERLAND, H.A.	Lt	RNAF	PILOT	PUP	B8012	DUNFERMLINE	04/09/1918		65
WRIGHT, A.	Flt-Sgt	RNAF	PILOT	STRUTTER	9894	HOLLYBROOK MEMORIAL	04/09/1918		65
REID, C.D.	Sgt	RAF	PILOT	CAMEL	D9556	CRAIGTON, GLASGOW	05/09/1918		54
RYMAL, W.A.	Lt	RFC		DH9	C1333	MOUNT PLEASANT, TORONTO	05/09/1918		76
MCLEAN, A.	Cdt	RFC		DH9	C1333	CRAIGTON	05/09/1918		76
HILL, H.B.	Lt	RAF	INSTR.	AVRO 504A	B4352	POLESWORTH, WARWICK	06/09/1918		45
MCKIEL, R.	Lt	RAF	PILOT	AVRO 504	D5851	COMELY BANK, EDINBURGH	06/09/1918		66
WINSTANLEY, A.	Flt-Cdt	RAF	PILOT	RE8	B6638	ANNFIELD, LANCS.	09/09/1918		59
HOLLAND, A.	Capt.	RNAS		CURTIS H.16	N4070	DUNDEE EASTERN	21/09/1918		54
MARRIOTT, E.	A.-Mec	RNAS		CURTIS H.16	N4070	HOLLYBROOK, SOUTHAMPTON	21/09/1918		54
WILSON, F.E.	A.-Mec	RNAS		CURTIS H.16	N4070	DUNDEE EASTERN	21/09/1918		54
PERCIVAL, H.K.	Flt-Cdt	RAF	PILOT	AVRO 504	E1608	SLEEPYHILLOCK, MONTROSE	23/09/1918		54
PRESTON, M.E.	2nd-Lt	RAF	PILOT	CAMEL	B5617	SLEEPYHILLOCK, MONTROSE	23/09/1918		54
LAMBURN, G.A.	Lt	RAF	PILOT	CAMEL	F1410	GIRVAN, AYRSHIRE	30/09/1918		76
MONK, H.I.M.	Lt	RNAF	PILOT	CAMEL	D9525	GOLDERS GREEN CREM., MIDDEX.	01/10/1918		65
WRIGHT, W.M.	Lt	RAF	PILOT	SE5	D3497	HELENSBURGH	01/10/1918		66
DERWIN, E.C.E.	2nd-Lt	RAF	PILOT	CAMEL	C6752	WESTON MILL, DEVON	14/10/1918		45
BROWN, J.S.	Lt	RFC		DH9	C1372	NELSON, LANCS.	20/10/1918		76
FLETCHER, C.A.	Lt	RFC		DH9	C1372	HADLEY, SALOP	20/10/1918		76
BISSELL, L.N.	Lt	RNAF		BRISTOL F2	B8942	ATHELSTANEFORD, EAST LOTHIAN	31/10/1918		66
BRAGG, E.W.	Lt	RNAF		BRISTOL F2	B8942	ATHELSTANEFORD, EAST LOTHIAN	31/10/1918		66
KETTLEWOOD, A.J	Flt-Cdt	RAF	PILOT	BRISTOL	?	WILBERFOSS, YORKS.	20/11/1918		59
MUNDY, C.R.	Lt	RAF	INSTR.	BRISTOL	1793	?	23/11/1918		59
GREEN, F	Fitter	RAF		BRISTOL	1793	CRAIL, FIFE	23/11/1918		59
HENDERSON, W.D.	Flt-Cdt		PILOT	CAMEL	F4207	GLOUCESTER OLD	28/11/1918		59
LILLEY, J.E.	Sgt		PILOT	SE5	E3954	SUNDERLAND MERE KNOLLS, DURHAM	28/11/1918		54
GODFREY, C.A.	Lt		PILOT	CAMEL	F1408	BANDON HILL, SURREY	11/12/1918		76
SCARRATT, J.A.	Flt-Cdt	RAF		AVRO 504	H218	CRAIL, FIFE	28/12/1918		59
MILLIKIN, J.	Lt			DH9	E679	BALLYLINNEY OLD, CO.ANTRIM	31/12/1918		76
BRUCE, J.A.		RAF	INSTR.	AVRO 504	5918	WEST KILBRIDE, AYRSHIRE	06/01/1919		59
COOPER, D.G.	Lt	RAF	PILOT	CAMEL	F8497	NORTHENDEN, ST.WILFRID, LANCS.	09/05/1919		59
UNDERWOOD, F.N.	Lt	RNAF	PILOT	CAMEL	N7147	COMELY BANK, EDINBURGH	02/07/1919		65

(Compiled by Alan Leishman. This is a list of some of the more serious accidents to occur. It is by no means an exhaustive compilation.)

BIBLIOGRAPHY

Where possible the text was based on original records in the Public Records Office, Kew, London (The National Archives).

Of particular importance was AIR 1/452/15/312/26 and AIR 1/453/15/312/26, a survey carried out of RAF air stations in the British Isles in 1918 published in six volumes. These volumes contain a plan of each station and brief notes on its function, personnel strength, weather record and accommodation.

BOOKS:

Allan, J., Wings over Scotland – *A History of the Scottish Aero Club, The First 75 Years, 1927-2002*, Scottish Aero Club Ltd, Perth, 2002.

Beedle, J., *43 Squadron – A History of the Fighting Cocks, 1916-66*, Beaumont Aviation Literature, London, 1966.

Berry, P., *Prestwick Airport and Scottish Aviation*, Tempus Publishing Ltd, Stroud, Gloucestershire, 2005.

Bruce, J.M., *The Aeroplanes of the Royal Flying Corps – Military Wing, Second Revised Edition*, Putnam & Co. Ltd, Aeronautical Books, London, 1992.

Bruce, J.M., *British Aeroplanes 1914-1918*, Putnam & Co. Ltd, London, 1957.

Bruce, J.M., Page, P. and Sturtivant, R., *The Sopwith Pup*, Air Britain (Historians) Ltd, Tunbridge Wells, Kent, 2002.

Buckton, H., *Birth of the Few*, Airlife Publishing Ltd, Shrewsbury, 1998.

Cameron, D., *Glasgow's Airport*, Holmes McDougall Ltd, Edinburgh, 1990.

Cameron, D., Galbraith, R. and Thompson, D., *From Pilcher to the Planets*, University of Glasgow, Glasgow, 2003.

Chant, C,. *The Zeppelin – The History of German Airships from 1900 to 1937*, Amber Books Ltd, London, 2000.

Chesneau, R., *Aircraft Carriers of the World, 1914 to the Present, An Illustrated Encyclopedia*, Arms and Armour Press, London, 1992.

Cole, C. and Cheesman, E.F., *The Air Defence of Britain*, Putnam & Co. Ltd, London, 1984.

Cooksley, P.G., *The RFC/RNAS Handbook 1914-1918*, Sutton Publishing Ltd, Stroud, Gloucestershire, 2000.

Connon, P., *An Aeronautical History of the Cumbria, Dumfries and Galloway Region. Part 2; 1915-1930*, St Patrick's Press, Penrith, Cumbria, 1984.

Christopher, J., *Balloons at War – Gasbags, Flying Bombs and Cold War Secrets*, Tempus Publishing Ltd, Stroud, Gloucestershire, 2004.

Cronin, D., *Royal Navy Shipboard Aircraft Developments 1912-1931*, Air Britain (Historians) Ltd, Tonbridge, Kent, 1990.

Fife, M., *Airfield Focus Special-Crail and Dunino*, GMS Enterprises, Peterborough, 2003.

Fife, M., *Airfield Focus – Donibristle*, GMS Enterprises, Peterborough, 2002.

Fife, M., *Airfield Focus Special – Drem*, GMS Enterprises, Peterborough, 2007.

Francis, P., *British Military Airfield Architecture – From Airships to the Jet Age*, Patrick Stephens Ltd, Sparkford, nr Yeovil, Somerset, 1996.

Gordon, T.C., *Early Flying in Orkney – Seaplanes in The First World War*, BBC Radio Orkney, 1985.

Goodhall, M.H. and Tagg, A.E., *British Aircraft Before The Great War*, Schiffer Publishing Ltd, Atglen, PA, USA., 2001.

Hughes, J., *Airfield Focus – RNAS Longside (Lenabo)*, GMS Enterprises, Peterborough, 2003.

Hughes, J., *A Steep Turn to the Stars – A History of Aviation in the Moray Firth*, GMS Enterprises, Peterborough, 1991.

Jefford, C.G., *RAF Squadrons*, 2nd edition, Airlife Publishing Ltd, Shrewsbury, 2001.

Jones, I., *Tiger Squadron*, White Lion Publishers Ltd, London, 1972.

Lamb, G., *Sky over Scapa*, Byrgisey, Orkney Islands, 1991.

Johnston, I., *Beardmore Built – The Rise and Fall of a Clydeside Shipyard*, Clydebank District Libraries and Museums Department, Clydebank, 1993.

King, B., *Royal Naval Air Service, 1912-1918*, Hikoki Publications, Aldershot, Hants., 1997.

Layman, R.D., *Before the Aircraft Carrier – The Development of Aviation Vessels 1849-1922*, Conway Maritime Press Ltd, London, 1989.

Layman, R.D., *Naval Aviation in the First World War-Its Impact and Influence*, Chatham Publishing, London, 1996.

Lynn, W. (compiler), *Montrose Airfield from 1913 – A History in Words and Pictures*, Montrose Air Station Museum Trust, Montrose.

MacMillan, N., *Sir Sefton Brancker*, William Heinemann Ltd, London, 1935.

McCloskey, K., *Edinburgh Airport – A History*, Tempus Publishing Ltd, Stroud, Gloucestershire, 2006.

McCudden, J.T.B., *Flying Fury – Five Years in the Royal Flying Corps*, Bailey Brothers and Swinfen Ltd, Folkestone, 1975.

Moore, W.G., *Early Bird*, Putnam & Co. Ltd, London, 1963.

Mowthorpe, C., *Battlebags – British Airships of the First World War*, Sutton Publishing Ltd, Stroud, Gloucestershire, 1995.

Munson, K., *Aircraft of the First World War*, Ian Allan, Shepperton, Surrey, 1967.

Murchie, A.T., The *RAF in Galloway 1910-2000*, G.C.Publishers Ltd, Wigtown, 2000.

Patrick, A., The *British Airship at War, 1914-1918*, Terence Dalton, Lavenham, Suffolk, 1989.

Roskill, S.W.(editor), *Documents Relating to the Naval Air Service, Volume 1. 1908-1918*, Navy Records Society, London, 1969.

Rimell, R.L., *Zeppelin! – A Battle for Air Supremacy in The First World War*, Conway Maritime Press Ltd, London, 1984.

Robertson, B., *British Military Aircraft Serials*, 1971, Fourth Revised Edition, Ian Allan Ltd, Shepperton, Surrey, 1971.

Shores, C., *British and Empire Aces of the First World War*, Osprey Publishing Ltd, Oxford, 2001.

Simpson, E. and Robertson, G., *Inverkeithing and Dalgety in Old Picture Postcards, Volume 2*, European Library, Zaltbommel, The Netherlands, 2000.

Smith, D.J., *Action Stations – 7. Military Airfields of Scotland, the North-East and Northern Ireland*, Patrick Stephens, Cambridge, 1983.

Smith, D.J., *Britain's Military Airfields 1939-45*, Patrick Stephens Ltd, Wellingborough, Northamptonshire, 1989.

Springs, E.W., *War Birds – The Diary of an Unknown Aviator*, Temple Press Books, London, 1966.

Smith, R., *British-Built Aircraft – -Northern England, Scotland, Wales and Northern Ireland*, Tempus Publishing Ltd, Stroud, Gloucestershire, 2005.

Sturtivant, R. and Page, P., *The Camel File*, Air Britain (Historians) Ltd, Tunbridge Wells, Kent, 1999.

Sturtivant, R. and Page, P., *The D.H.4/D.H.9 File*, Air Britain (Historians) Ltd, Tunbridge Wells, Kent, 1999.

Sturtivant, R. and Page, P., *The S.E.5 File*, Air Britain (Historians) Ltd, Tunbridge Wells, Kent, 1996.

Sturtivant, R, and Page, P., Royal *Navy Aircraft Serials and Units 1911-1919*, Air Britain (Historians) Ltd, Tonbridge, Kent, 1992.

Morrow Jr, J.H. and Rogers, E., (editors), *A Yankee Ace in the RAF – The The First World War Letters of Capt. Bogart Rogers*, University Press of Kansas, Kansas, USA, 1996.

Taylor, J.W.R., *Combat Aircraft of the World*, Elbury Press and Michael Joseph, London, 1969.

Thomson, J.U., *Edinburgh Curiosities 2 – A Capital Cornucopia*, John Donald Publishers Ltd, Edinburgh, 1997.

Thompson, R., *The Royal Flying Corps*, Leo Cooper, London, 1968.

Todd, R.M., *Sopwith Camel Fighter Ace*, AJAY Enterprises, Falls Church, VA, USA, 1978.

Treadwell, T.C., *The First Naval Air War*, Tempus Publishing Ltd, Stroud, Gloucestershire, 2002.

Webster, J., *The Flying Scots – A Century of Aviation in Scotland*, The Glasgow Royal Concert Hall, Glasgow, 1994.

Wragg, D., *Royal Navy Handbook, 1914-1918*, Sutton Publishing Ltd, Stroud, Gloucestershire, 2006.

Warner, G., *Airships Over The North Channel-Royal Naval Air Service Airships in Ulster During the First World War*, Ulster Aviation Society, 2005.

Williams, W.A., *Against the Odds – The Life of Group Capt. Lionel Rees*, V.C., Bridge Books, Wrexham, 1989.

Young, D., *Rutland of Jutland*, Cassell, London, 1963.

ARTICLES FROM JOURNALS AND INFORMATION SHEETS.

Berry, P., 'East Fortune Airfield', *Airfield Review*, No.77, December, 1997.

Burchmore, D., 'Airship Station Caldale, Orkney Islands', *Dirigible Magazine*, Autumn/Winter, 1999/2000.

Gunn, S., 'The Catfirth Boat Flying Station', *New Shetlander* No.139, 1982.

Newman, G., 'From Airships to Airshows – A Brief History of East Fortune Airfield' (information sheet).

Newman, G., 'Pioneering Torpedo Training at East Fortune', *East Lothian Life*, Issue 42, winter 2002.

Malcolm, E.H., 'Cromarty's Skies were Buzzing', *Scottish Local History*, Issue 62, winter 2004.

Smith, D.L., 'The Loch Doon Scandal and other Stories, Gently Flows the Doon', *A Guide to the Dalmellington, Patna and Loch Doon Area*, Dalmellington District Council, Dalmellington, 1972.

Ure, A., 'Flight from the Forth', Clackmannan District Libraries, 1986 (information sheet).

Cross and Cockade Magazine.

Daybell, P., 'The Aircrew Experience During the Great War, Part One', *Cross and Cockade International Journal*, Vol.33, No.4, 2002.

Davis, M., '6 Brigade RAF and its Predecessors – Some Further Aspects', *Cross and Cockade International Journal*, Vol.30, No.2, 1999.

Flanagan, B., (editor), 'Forgotten Fighters – History of the 41st Aero Squadron', *Cross and Cockade*, U.S. edition, Vol.12, No.1, spring 1971.

Flanagan, B., 'Memories of Montrose', *Cross and Cockade*, U.S. edition, Vol.16, No.1, spring 1975.

Ford, P.C, 'The Practical Training of Kite Balloon Observers', *Cross and Cockade International Journal*, Vol.35, No.1, 2004.

Goodhall, M., 'HMS *Hermes* and 1913 Manoeuvres', *Cross and Cockade Great Britain Journal*, Vol.7, No.1, 1976.

Hide, D., 'All at Sea – The Use of Kite Balloons in the Navy', *Cross and Cockade International Journal*, Vol.32, No.3, 2001.

Hide, D., 'The War Against the U-Boat', *Cross and Cockade International Journal*, Vol.33, No.3, 2002.

Layman, R., Skelton, M. and Wright, P., 'Capt. Melvin H. Rattray, RNAS/RAF, Part 2, Shipboard Service', *Cross and Cockade Great Britain Journal*, Vol.28, No.2, 1997.

Molson, K.M., 'War-Time Reminiscences by Flight Commander A.H. Sandwell', *Cross and Cockade Great Britain Journal*, Vol.13, No.1, 1982.

Mottram, G., 'Early Days of the RNAS', *Cross and Cockade Great Britain Journal*, Vol.10, No.3, 1979.

Newman, G., 'Pioneering Torpedo Training at East Fortune 1918', *Cross and Cockade Journal*, Vol.36, No.3, 2005.

Reynolds, P., 'Wireless and Corps Aircraft in the First World War', *Cross and Cockade International Journal*, Vol.33, No.4, 2002.

Skelton, M., 'Capt. Dawes and 2 Squadron RFC Prepare for War', *Cross and Cockade International Journal*, Vol.23, No.4, 1992.

Sturtivent, R., 'British Flying Training in the First World War', *Cross and Cockade International Journal*, Vol.25, No.1, 1994.

Turpin, B., 'Coastal Patrol Airships, 1915-1918, Part 2', *Cross and Cockade Great Britain Journal*, Vol.15, No.3, 1984.

Vann, R., and Waugh, C., 'Overseas Presentation Aircraft 1914-1918', *Cross and Cockade Great Britain Journal*, Vol.14, No.2, 1983.

Wright, P., 'The RNAS Airship Service and the Air Construction Corps, Part One', *Cross and Cockade International Journal*, Vol.32, No.4, 2001.

Wright, P., 'The RNAS Airship Service and the Air Construction Corps, Part Two', *Cross and Cockade International Journal*, Vol.33, No.1, 2002.

Wright, P., 'The RNAS Airship Service and the Air Construction Corps, Part Three', *Cross and Cockade International Journal*, Vol.33, No.2, 2002.

INTERNET SITES.

www.theaerodrome.com – Devoted to aviation in the First World War.

www.scran.ac.uk – Scottish-based online learning resource and picture library.

FURTHER INTEREST IN FIRST WORLD WAR AVIATION. SOME PLACES TO VISIT:

Montrose Broomfield, Angus – Montrose Air Station Heritage Centre has an exhibition on the history of Scotland's first military aerodrome housed in a new build Romney-style Hangar and Nissen hut. Also the original J. Burke's aircraft sheds or hangars have fortunately been preserved. Dating from late 1913, they are among the oldest surviving aerodrome buildings in Britain. Also, several metal T.2 hangars dating from the 1930s still stand although they have been adopted for commercial purposes.

East Fortune, East Lothian – The Museum of Flight is located on the site of the former First World War airship station and aerodrome. The museum itself is situated in the Second World War buildings on the south side of the aerodrome, whereas the earlier structures were on the north side, some of which still survive.

Loch Doon, Ayrshire – Some scant remains are visible of the seaplane station and the gunnery range on the banks of the loch. Few other First World War stations were situated in such an attractive setting as beside a large loch surrounded by high hills. The landscape has changed little since the time of the First World War.

Turnberry – Although few traces exist of the the First World War aerodrome, this attractive coastal location would have changed little since the time biplanes were landing and taking off on the golf courses. The Turnberry Hotel, which once housed the pilots, still dominates the site.

SOCIETIES:

The Airfield Research Group is dedicated to the study of both military and civil airfields in Britain. It publishes the journal *Airfield Review* three to four times a year.

The First World War Aviation Historical Society publishes the journal, *Cross and Cockade*, quarterly.

PHOTOGRAPHS:

Imperial War Museum, Lambeth Road, London, SE1 6HZ, has a large collection of photographs covering both world wars and other conflicts. Copies can be ordered for both private and commercial use.

CREDITS:

Bob O' Hara – Research in Public Records Office, Kew.
Stuart Leslie – for supplying many of the photos for this book from his collection and for checking my manuscript, The 10,000 plus pictures of the Bruce/Leslie Collection illustrating all aspects of the First World War aviation are now in the care of the Fleet Air Arm Museum, near Yeovil, Somerset.
Also: Ken Border, Aerodrome Buildings; Dugald Cameron, Paintings of First World War Aircraft; Mick Davies, Information on Scottish First World War Aerodromes; Richard Davies, Special Collections, Brotherton Library, University of Leeds; Marjorie Donald, The A.K. Bell Library, Perth; Neil Fraser, SCRAN; George Gardner, Glasgow University Archives; Scott Hamilton, Scottish First World War Aces; Elma Lindsay, Central Library, Stirling; Angus Johnson, Shetland Archives; Paul Johnson, The National Achives Image Library Manager; Alan Leishman, First World War Aircraft Crashes; Keith McCloskey, Turnhouse Aerodrome; Margaret Morrill, Turnberry Aerodrome; Susan Masson, Peterhead Library; David Mackie, Orkney Library and Archive; Louise Oliver, Imperial War Museum Photographic Collection; Laragh Quinney, Map Library, National Library of Scotland; Martin Rogers, Rosyth Seaplane Station; Mary Jane Millare–Adolfo, RAF Museum, Hendon; Catherine Rounsfell, Fleet Air Arm Museum; Fiona Scharlau, Angus Achives; Eric Simpson, Donibristle Aerodrome; Ray Sturtivant, Aircraft Accidents; Brian Turpin, Airships; Barbara Waibel, Zeppelin Museum; Kristina Watson, RCAHMS; Victoria Wylde, Printed Books, Imperial War Museum; Margaret Wilson, National Museums of Scotland.